WITHDRAWN

D1376725

Road Hunter in the Land between the Rivers

Crystal Clear Blue Skies Copyright © 2007 James E. Lewandowski

Cover design by James E. Lewandowski

Front cover humvee image by Lynn Nelson

Paperback ISBN 978-0-9821084-1-3
Hardcover ISBN 978-0-9821084-0-6
Paperback ISBN 978-1-4196706-2-6

Published by Prairie Hills Publishing
www.prairiehillspublishing.com

Road Hunter in the Land between the Rivers

Disillusioned Hearts and Minds

James E. Lewandowski

Prairie Hills Publishing

Road Hunter in the Land between the Rivers

Contents

Introduction
Crystal Clear Blue Skies

Chapters

For

Donna, my children, my family,

the courageous legion of convoy security escorts,

and the truck drivers they protect.

Introduction

During the early stages of the war in Iraq, the nation activated and deployed its National Guard and reserve forces to the region in support of Operation Iraqi Freedom. As part of this support, the military tasked many of these units with providing security for the thousands of trucks moving supplies within the war torn country.

Gaining no foothold initiating large direct confrontations with U.S. and coalition forces in the cities, the insurgents shifted their focus of the battle to the highways and attacked smaller segments of the military that traveled upon them. Units originally intended for support were now receiving a large number of casualties while engaged in direct fire and hidden roadside bomb attacks.

The humvee gun truck transitioned to the vehicle of choice in protecting the convoys of trucks and soldiers from the surprise insurgent attacks. Its various armaments provided the necessary tools in deterring many of the insurgents but its thin skin did not totally encase its occupants from harm.

The life of a gun truck crew became very demanding and extremely dangerous. Operating in exceedingly harsh conditions, the soldiers endured overwhelming stress as they searched the roadsides for bombs and snipers along the hazardous routes. Stretched to their limits, many performed countless missions in maintaining the important flow of the much needed supplies over the open road to the numerous camps throughout the country.

While deployed to Iraq, I served on a gun truck with a team providing security for convoys moving supplies daily over the hundreds of miles of treacherous highway. Each day presented something unique, something minutely or vastly diverse from the others. I pulled a handful of noteworthy occurrences from my journal, maintaining the timeline, and assembled them into a worthy story.

I commend all those with whom I served, indiscriminate of unit or branch. Everyone gave their absolute utmost in the role they performed. I would find it difficult to believe that anyone would participate in an event as serious as a war and not. Some may have faltered or fallen short of expectations but the point in being is that during this period of testing ones nature they presented their personal best.

As all would wholeheartedly agree, a special thanks to the families and friends who boosted our morale with a constant flow of love and concern with encouraging cards, letters, and goodies from home.

To the people of Iraq, God willing, may you one day receive peace.

Poem note. The title, *Crystal Clear Blue Skies* relates to the War on Terrorism. During the sobering days following 9/11, the sky revealed the brightest blue color I have ever seen. With air traffic grounded across the nation, the absence of contrails dissipating overhead reduced the continuous haze we all had become accustomed to. Admiring the brilliant contrasting color, I wondered if it resembled the sky my grandparents once knew.

Crystal Clear Blue Skies

Towers weep on peaceful shores.
Crystal clear blue skies.
Across the water, we answered the call,
Never questioning why.

Race over the berm and down the road,
Rebuilding ancient Babylon.
Smiles, waves, and shouts of joy.
Gratuities of hidden fire and roadside bombs.

Blistering sun and mouths full of sand,
White salt stains chalk the skin.
Handshake through a turret gun sight,
Peace attempted to win.

Pain, anxiety, disillusionment,
Seek comfort in each other.
Go back again, one more time,
Only for my sister or brother.

CHAPTER 1

Once upon a Time...

Ping! The radio sounded over the deafening roar of the lead gun truck's diesel engine. "Jaguar Two-Two, this is Two-One. Over."

A weary sergeant initiated quick adjustments to the truck's radio. "Come on. Come on. Work this time," he swore to himself. He keyed the radio handset and found his determined effort unavailing. The radio, unwilling to operate properly, refused to return contact with the convoy's command humvee.

After a long hesitation, the radio angrily sounded once more. Ping! "Jaguar Two-Two, this is Two-One. Answer the radio, damn it."

The radio speaker continued its dead silence. The convoy commander positioned in the command humvee had visual contact with the sergeant's gun truck. It traveled a half mile ahead of him, leading directly in front of the convoy of semi trucks. In frustration, he pitched the radio handset against the sand scarred windshield. It rebounded off the glass, nearly striking the driver, before falling below and dancing by its cord above the sandbag covered floor of the vehicle. His hand slightly trembled as he reached up to wipe the burning sweat from his eyes. "Why the hell won't they answer?"

A brownish orange sun slowly crept over the horizon. The light gradually filled the morning sky as its colorful rays squinted through a fine haze of dust and sand. The air temperature passed the 100-degree mark signifying a hot, torturous day lingered ahead.

As the sky's glow steadily brightened, sand began swirling over the top of the berm along the roadsides. A quick gust carried the minute grains over the paved highway and continued whirling as the granules landed on an assortment of scattered garbage strewn across the desert. Crushed plastic water bottles, empty soda cans, and other assorted waste lay half-buried in the sand.

An elderly woman labored underneath a long, black, silk abaya as she skillfully scavenged through the discarded refuse thrown by passing motor vehicles. She lifted a urine filled plastic water bottle into the air and closely examined its contents. Removing the cap, she poured the liquid onto the ground where it quickly absorbed into the loose, dry sand. She reached over her shoulder and placed the bottle into a dusty, brown woven sack she carried across her back. The trash supplied fuel to feed a fire.

A young mother patiently squatted on a berm a short distance from the busy highway. Dressed in black from head to foot, her olive face appeared through an opening in her abaya draped around her head. Dark eyes vacantly gazed through the passing traffic as she stared out into the emptiness of the lonely desert. Her right arm extended outward as she reached across her knee with a half-opened hand facing the endless sky. She occasionally glanced toward two young children begging next to the busy highway a short distance from her.

The sudden breeze caused by the passing motor vehicles pulled the loose sand and dust from the pavement and forced the fine mixture back into the air. The obscure cloud drifted above and slightly blurred the roadway. Many of the early morning drivers cruised along maintaining a constant speed while others accelerated, passing through and around the maze of traffic. The two small children continuously waved their arms in an effort to attract the attention of the drivers in hopes of food or water springing from one of the vehicle windows.

A rickety oil tanker slowly approached the young ones. The driver, a gray bearded man wearing a red and white cloth keffiyeh wrapped around his head, smiled nervously as he waved to his fellow roadway users. Other drivers became noticeably upset with his sluggish speed and in aggravation, sounded their horns while shaking tight fists. He reached down and adjusted the radio volume to mask the highway noise as he began humming along to the Arabic music.

Old and beaten under a fresh coat of bright blue paint, the tanker truck, detailed in tiny white, green, and orange stripes, rattled steadily down the roadway. Sparkling objects, decorating the cab's windshield, caught the early morning sunlight and emitted a brilliant spectrum of colors across the dash. Thick black smoke poured from the exhaust pipe filling the air with a dark shadow of noxious fumes.

As the truck neared the children, the driver sharply tapped the center of his steering column sounding the vehicle's musical horn. The children heard the whimsical tune and began waving their hands with excitement. For their efforts, a clear plastic bag soared from the tanker's window. The sack tore open as it bounced, tumbled, and rolled across the ground. Stale flatbread fell about, mixing with the sand and debris. It came to rest a quick sprint from the children who darted for their prize. They brushed the loose sand from the bread and placed it back into the tattered plastic bag. The driver watched the children through his side mirror and chuckled as they ran the dried bread to their mother.

As the morning continued, more children began appearing while lining the sides of the road. From toddlers to teens, all knew the routine as they stood evenly spaced and waved to the passing cars and trucks. For some, begging developed into a game, a simple process to pick up a quick snack. For others, the handouts provided much needed food for their families.

The old truck began to sputter and choke. Gauges on the instrument panel indicated a problem with the engine cooling system. The driver hastily scanned for an accessible location along the roadside to pull his truck over and stop. His eyes discovered a small dip next to the side of the road and he began applying the brake. He turned the steering wheel, sharply crossing two lanes of traffic. Screeching sounds abounded as cars darted left and right attempting to avoid the tanker.

Stopped on the highway's shoulder, the driver jumped down from his truck and unlatched the short blue hood. Lifting it, he felt the heat escaping from a buildup of steam and quickly pulled away allowing the hood to collapse back onto the truck.

He handily maneuvered the vehicle down a soft approach and began draining the oil into the ditch. A large stream of black liquid sprayed out onto the sand. The thick oil quickly pooled along the roadside. The man pulled an old rag from behind the seat in his cab. He wiped the oil from his hands and blotted the sweat on his forehead as he watched the traffic race by.

The convoy of semi trucks with a military escort approached in the distance. He became excited and quickly adjusted the valves, completely opening them trying to hurry the emptying of the large tanker's contents.

The convoy approached the two children motioning for food. The turret gunner of the lead gun truck reached down into the humvee and pulled out his half-eaten meal, ready to eat (MRE), a brown bag containing the assorted remnants of an unsatisfying breakfast. As they drew near the children, the gunner released a fast pitch imitating the form of a major league ballplayer.

"Eat that hajji," the gunner cursed and laughed as the bag left his hands with a quick snap. The loose contents emptied into midair and splattered the children with a mixture of gravy and Tabasco sauce.

"Knock that crap off!" the sergeant screamed as he angrily cracked the gunner across his shin with the radio handset. "This is the last time I am going to tell you. Leave these people alone."

The gunner grabbed his leg and urgently rubbed it in an attempt to reduce the sharp pain. He mumbled a few words of profanity under his breath and extended his middle finger in defiance.

The sergeant shook his head in disgust as he continued his effort to contact the command vehicle. The radio sounded again. Ping. "Jaguar Two-Two, this is Two-One. Over."

The radio had not worked properly since leaving camp earlier in the morning. Some of the data entered into the computerized system did not take. He worked quickly in an attempt to reset the information.

"I hope it works now," he said as he picked up the radio handset. "Jaguar Two-One, this is Two-Two. Radio check. Over."

Ping. "It's about time you answered the radio. Slow it down. We are spread out for miles and have big gaps in the convoy. Some of these hajji trucks can't keep up."

"This is Two-Two. You've got to be kidding me. Kick them hajjis in the rear. If we keep slowing down, we'll never make it back to camp before dark."

Ping. "We've been kicking and it's not getting us anywhere. These hajji trucks are maxed out and close to overheating. If we start losing trucks now, you can damn well bet we won't make it back until well after dark."

The radio sat quietly, bearing a long uncomfortable hesi-

tation. All felt the great weight of frustration. They previously suffered numerous problems with the convoy including flat tires, loose
loads, and leaving a truck along the roadside with a bad engine. Now,
they will need to slow down and risk driving in the dark. The convoy
soldiers hoped to avoid that most of all. Bad things happen in the
dark.

"Roger. Slowing down. Two-Two. Out."

The lead gun truck reluctantly reduced speed and continued
with the mission—a line of twenty-five semi trucks hauling loads
containing fuel and various supplies to military camps throughout the
country. The mission represented one leg pieced to a long journey for
most of the drivers.

A convoy security escort team consisting of two gun trucks
and a command humvee provided protection for the semis. With
every mile they traveled, the day grew hotter and their patience
weaker.

The sergeant of the lead gun truck spotted the tanker parked
in the ditch draining the load of oil onto the ground. "What in blazes
is going on here?"

"Wait until the Environmental Protection Agency finds out
about this one," the driver joked as he pulled out his camera and
handed it over the top of the radio to the sergeant. Click. An image
appeared on the camera's display screen portraying another example
of the bizarre sights witnessed since their arrival. Both shook their
heads in disbelief while the trucks continued moving forward with
the convoy mission.

Waiting anxiously by the fresh pool of oil, the tanker driver
smiled and waved as the convoy trucks passed. With his load spread
throughout the ditch, he made a dash for the cab of his truck and
pulled the empty tanker back onto the busy highway. Within a short
period of time, he caught up with the long line of trucks.

The gunner on the rear humvee waved the tanker back to a
safe distance, keeping him away from the convoy. He leaned down
and informed the truck commander of the tagalong.

The commander sized him up through his side mirror and
grabbed his radio handset. "Jaguar Two-One, this is Jaguar Two-
Three. Over."

Ping. "This is Two-One. Over."

"The hajji oil tanker parked along the side of the road a few miles back has caught up with us. It looks like he is going to be trailing us for a while. Over."

Ping. "He's probably worried about getting hijacked by the Ali Baba. Keep an eye on him. Make sure he doesn't get too close to us. Over."

"Roger. Out."

The convoy continued with the mission. Exhaust fumes, dust, and sand saturated the hot, dry air as the morning passed.

The lead gun truck's sergeant noticed a small, white pickup traveling toward the convoy one hundred meters off the right-hand side of the road. The short pickup matched the description of a suspect vehicle reported over the radio earlier in the morning. He slapped the turret gunner's leg.

"Yeah, I see him," the gunner yelled as he swung his .50 caliber machine gun around and placed its sights on the target.

The white pickup slowed down and came to a dusty stop next to a young boy herding sheep in the field along the road. A tall, bearded man, dressed in a long, white thawb and wearing a red and white keffiyeh around his head, stepped out of the vehicle. He talked sternly to the boy as he pointed at the sheep. Visibly upset, the boy instructed his dog to move the herd farther down a narrow, worn, sandy path.

The sergeant picked up his radio handset. "Jaguar Two-One, this is Two-Two. Over."

Ping. "This is Two-One. Over."

"We've spotted a small white pickup stopped one hundred meters off the road to our right. Looks to be friendly. Over."

Ping. "Roger. Out."

The shepherd boy stopped and waved at the convoy as he and the bearded man watched the trucks scream past. The trail gun truck finally brought up the end of the convoy with the oil tanker following close behind spewing its signature cloud of black smoke from its exhaust.

The tall, bearded man turned away from the highway and reached his hand deep inside his robe. He pulled out a small cellular telephone and carefully pressed a series of numbers.

Boom!! A thundering explosion disrupted the calm serenity of the desert. A mangled and burning humvee catapulted across the paved highway. Trucks quickly switched lanes as they squealed to a halt trying to avoid a collision with the burning wreckage as well as one another. Painful screams abounded as frantic attempts hastened to extinguish the fire.

The radio sounded. Ping. "Lion's Den, this is Jaguar Two-Three. Request MEDEVAC. Over."

More than nine months had passed since President George W. Bush declared an end to major combat operations in Iraq but the number of casualties continued to climb. American soldiers captured Saddam Hussein as he hid in an underground spider hole in the small village of ad-Dawr near his hometown of Tikrit. Released reports stated no weapons of mass destruction found and prewar intelligence relating to them proved "almost all wrong".

Insurgent attacks on convoys became more and more prevalent throughout the country. Roadside bombs, or improvised explosive devices (IEDs), detonated daily near American and coalition forces.

We arrived in theater beginning our yearlong tour in Iraq. For some of us, convoy security would become our mission for the next twelve months. Long days, sweltering heat, roadside bombs, and snipers, we would soon find these harsh characteristics a familiar part of a vicious, unforgiving job.

CHAPTER 2

The Land between the Rivers

My eyes ripped open from a sudden jolt on my body as the air force C-130 cargo plane banked hard left. An abrupt awareness followed as the rear of the aircraft promptly elevated above the nose. Sitting knee to knee, buckled onto parallel rows of nylon mesh benches, we anxiously glanced across the lines at one another in reassurance the plane ride would soon end. Eyes widened and bodies tensed as a sensation of weightlessness engulfed us. Some quickly pulled small plastic bags to their faces to expel the churned contents of a preflight meal. The large airplane dropped lower and rapidly leveled off as we flew in at a slight angle over the runway.

Less than an hour ago, we departed Ali Al Salem Air Base in Kuwait and now circled in contemplating our final approach into Tallil Air Base in southern Iraq. After completing three weeks of preparations in theater, seventy of us out of the battalion arrived into the country by airplane while the bulk of the unit convoyed the vehicles through the desert for the previous two days. Those of us traveling by air may have had the quicker trip but we surely paid for it now.

The huge plane shook as its wheels bounced on the paved runway. Worried faces gradually smoothed to expressions of relief as the plane's wheels slowed and eventually rolled to a stop. We made it. A hydraulic pump whined as the large ramp at the rear of the plane slowly lowered onto the pavement.

"Welcome to Iraq!" a deep voice announced.

We grabbed our equipment and walked toward the plane's rear opening. Feelings of excitement overcame me as I stepped down the short ramp and onto the tarmac. My first step on Iraqi soil, a place the ancient Greeks referred to as Mesopotamia, the land between the rivers. A location in the world, until then, I only recognized through television newscasts.

The forceful stream of hot air propelled from the C-130 engines pushed me along as I moved away from the aircraft. A foul smell suddenly overpowered my senses, the same fetid odor noticeable upon arrival in Kuwait.

"There's that wonderful smell again," one of the guys confirmed.

I laughed. "It doesn't seem to be as strong here. Maybe it's the cooler temperature but it's definitely different."

"Yeah," he said as he wrinkled his nose, "it's that third world shit smell. We might as well get used to it. We'll be smelling it every day for the next year."

We arrived in the middle of February, which harbored a seasonable light touch of coolness in the air. A golden tint, created by fine sand particles suspended in the atmosphere, slightly darkened the midday sky. I inquisitively scanned the surrounding landscape and found the terrain to be completely flush with miles and miles of sand in every direction.

Guided toward a small, white shuttle bus idling on the tarmac, we ambled along weighted down by our equipment and overstuffed duffel bags. The bus waited silently to transport us to a holding area where we would remain until a ride turned up to escort us to our final destination—Camp Cedar II. An air force sergeant rested comfortably in the driver's seat folding his hands across the steering wheel.

"How was the flight?" he asked with a smile.

I looked at him and shook my head.

"It was the worst landing I have ever seen," he began explaining. "I thought the pilot was going to have to take it up and try landing again."

We waited patiently in the holding area, which consisted of an air-conditioned tent with a few rows of chairs and a television propped in the corner. I thought of how we finally arrived and speculated as to what lay ahead for us during the next year. We left our homes and our families two months ago and now began the long journey back to them.

As I observed the others quietly settle in, I thought back to the early morning we departed from home station, late December, Donna's birthday. I did not offer a pleasant gift to my fiancé, leaving her for a year and a half to serve in Iraq. A strong person, one in a million, she would not let anything come between us, not even a war. I felt fortunate having someone such as her care so much for me.

I left her and my family in tears on the sidewalk in front of the guard armory. It gave me a deep, empty, sick feeling, one I hoped I would never have to experience again. I remembered the bus passing by my two children on our way out of town. Both stood bravely next to the highway, knee deep in snow, waving at the buses in hopes they would see me and I them just one last time.

I had difficulties thinking of that cold December day. I looked around the holding tent hoping no one noticed as I choked up. Thinking of how the ones I loved so much could possibly never see me again crushed my heart. My mind raced to think of something else, anything other than that.

My thoughts traveled back twenty years ago to basic training. The Cold War and the U.S. involvement in Central America prevailed as the hot topics.

"I can guarantee you this!" the drill sergeant yelled. "Before your enlistment is through, you will either be fighting a controlled nuclear war with the Soviets or sweating your asses off in the jungles of El Salvador."

"Yes, sergeant!" we replied at the top of our lungs.

After completing my initial enlistment of seven years, the time arrived as it does in every person's life to concentrate on a family and a career. Ten years later, I walked back into the guard armory and reenlisted a few years before 9/11. Not many men my age, those in their mid-thirties, were physically or medically capable of handling the demands of a state call-up for a local disaster such as a flood, tornado, forest fire, or blizzard. I felt that if I could still do it, I had the responsibility to step up and help.

A call-up for federal active duty always lingered in the back of my mind. If called, the time away from home would be comparable to those activated for the Gulf War, six months. A half year seemed like an enormous amount of time to be away from family but doable.

The call-up for Operation Iraqi Freedom (OIF) became the largest since World War II. My family felt just as proud as I did of my impending service to the country. My unit became part of the first rotation with future rotations learning from our experiences.

When we received the activation orders, I could not believe the ominous words printed on the paper. Many others exhibited the same sorrowful feelings. During the activation ceremonies, as the staff officer read the orders through the microphone, gasps echoed throughout the auditorium.

"…for a period of activation not to exceed 535 days."

Numerous heads dropped and hung low. The amount of time proved greater than anyone would have ever expected.

One weekend of duty per month, two weeks guard camp per year, helping in a disaster, and maybe, just maybe, in twenty years of service, you would see a deployment of six months. This became the guard to us. We experienced it this way and sold it to our families.

Many spouses would not make it through this deployment, after all, 535 days seemed like a lifetime to some. One of the guys had already suffered this painful experience. In the first eight short weeks away from home, his wife left him. Married only a few years and with one small son, he and his family had already paid a heavy toll for this deployment.

How long would we actually be there? Most stuck to "one year boots on ground" as stated by the army, meaning, we would be there for at least twelve months beginning at the time of arrival in theater.

I spoke with those soldiers already there and approaching the end of their tour in Iraq. Some received extensions. They would be there for a longer period of time than their original orders declared. The other branches of the service selected different lengths of tour. The Marine Corps established seven months as their tour of duty and the air force less time than that. The truth being, we did not actually know how long we would be there. We would remain there for as long as they needed us and we would not leave until told to do so.

I made a decision before I left home that in spite of the length of time there, I would live each day to its fullest. This would not be a wasted year of my life. I would experience everything I possibly could and remember every moment, no matter how terrible it became. Looking at it from the standpoint of encountering a rare opportunity, I would not bargain away even one minute of this deployment. I resolved to journal my experiences so in the years that followed, I would never forget the events we would undertake during this tour.

"They're here," a yell came from outside the tent. Two olive drab colored, five-ton trucks rolled to a dusty halt next to the pile of duffel bags and equipment. The vehicles and soldiers driving them belonged to the Third Battalion of the 18th Field Artillery Brigade. Excitement covered their faces upon seeing us, after all, we were their replacements.

Assembling us around the gear, they gave a quick briefing on what to expect during the short trip to Camp Cedar II located roughly six miles north of the air base.

"OK, everybody load up!" the driver yelled.

The elevated rear of the truck quickly filled and packed tight. A mountain of green duffel bags stood high in the center of the vehicle with soldiers compressed around them. While some of us continued to load into the vehicle, it became evident the truck would not accommodate the entire group.

With safety a concern, I informed the driver, "It looks pretty tight. We'll wait for the next one."

"This is it," he said with a grin. "There ain't gonna be a next one. We're a truck short today so everyone and everything will fit."

Tossing the duffels onto the truck, we climbed up to the top of the pile in its center and nestled in. "Wow, what a view," I thought. I could see quite a distance from up there.

Once an important Iraqi air base, Tallil provided air security throughout the southern region of Iraq from its location several miles southwest of the city of An Nasiriyah. During the Gulf War in 1991, the base received extensive damage from bombs dropped by U.S. forces. Situated in the country's Southern No Fly Zone, sanctions prohibited the Iraqis from using the site for air support. Over the years, attacks continued for various reasons by U.S. forces carrying out authorized operations that destroyed many of the buildings and roads. Some of the lesser insignificant structures remained intact.

The name Tallil, an Arabic word interpreted as "ruins", referred to the historical site of the city of Ur located adjacent to the air base. Many considered Ur, one of the earliest known cities of the world, as the location of the beginning of civilization and maintained its religious significance as the birthplace of the biblical patriarch Abraham.

The two five-ton trucks, following an escort gun truck, rumbled out of the front gates of Tallil in route to Cedar II. The partially paved road we traveled held many potholes, which the trucks cautiously weaved through to avoid. Small reed and stick huts staggered the roadside with local vendors selling various goods. Alcohol, Iraqi army uniforms, and hand-sewn flags lined their make-shift stands.

Iraqis of all ages stood in the bare fields and along the road's edge with some waving and shouting as we passed.

"What are they yelling?" the soldier seated next to me asked.

I smiled. "They're yelling America, America."

He listened as we passed by another group. "Wow, that's cool, I never expected that."

A short distance away from the road stood the Temple of Ur, a massive mud brick pyramid lying quietly upon the desert sand. Our presence added to the long list of foreign armies the ancient structure has endured in its four thousand years of existence. How appropriate, I thought, the onset of our tour in Iraq originated at the location considered the beginning of civilization.

Loose gravel covered the final stretch of road leading into Camp Cedar II. A fine, white powder clouded the air as the trucks pounded against the many ruts. Through the dust, I had difficulty identifying the vehicles traveling directly in front of us. The inability to see did not deter the drivers. They maintained their hurried, steady pace until we arrived at the front gate.

The military designated Camp Cedar II a convoy support center (CSC), a rest stop along the highway for the continuous flow of military and civilian truck convoys moving north and south. The camp offered little but refueling, a meal, and maybe a quick night's sleep to those passing through.

Kellogg, Brown, and Root (KBR) built and maintained the infrastructure of the camp. A subsidiary of Halliburton, the KBR filled the contracts providing housing and logistics for many of the camps throughout the country. According to the battalion's orders, this would be our base camp, our new home away from home. We would remain there until those orders changed.

The KBR constructed the camp on an ancient river bottom where the Euphrates River once flowed. The water gradually shifted during the past four millennia moving a few miles to the north. The perimeter of the camp, a series of dozer-constructed sand berm ac-companied by miles and miles of razor wire, provided a semi-secure boundary requiring reinforcement by continuous security patrols.

We were members of a National Guard field artillery unit originating out of northeastern South Dakota, the Second Battalion of the 147th Field Artillery Brigade. With many awards, the battalion displayed a long history of excellence in unit readiness and field artil-lery operations. We came from an exceedingly rural portion of the country with strong work ethics and religious convictions rooted as staples of our lives. Fathers, sons, brothers, uncles, and cousins stood side by side within the ranks, your typical small town guard unit.

Our advanced skill in field artillery operations did not apply during this deployment. The army replaced our rocket launchers and computers with gun trucks and guard towers. Convoy security oper-ations and ammo site security instantly became our new jobs.

The battalion's convoys began arriving at the camp as we entered the front gates. They moved in smaller serials with each consisting of one of four batteries—Alpha, Bravo, Charlie, and Headquarters and Headquarters Support (HHS). I located the HHS convoy and assisted in unpacking the personal and unit equipment from the trucks.

We found vacant tents quietly awaiting us to occupy with our personal gear. Each tent housed a work group or convoy escort team. The eight-man tents consisted of a fez design woven from cotton cloth, which looked well worn, as they stood assembled on plywood-constructed floors. Brightly colored tarps covered the flimsy tents preventing the seasonal rains from saturating its occupants. Over-sized rock scattered between the neatly lined tent rows made for a difficult walk but provided a barrier during the rains against the tacky sand and clay mixture below.

We filled the following five days with various duties per-forming position improvement and repetitive training for convoy operations. It did not take long to settle in. We located lumber in the supply area and used it to construct wooden entryways onto the tents. Plywood doors provided an easy access for moving in and out of the tent as opposed to continuously stitching the cloth flap with its attached rope ties. With the remaining scrap wood, some built crude nightstands and storage bins for their personal items.

Convoy operations training involved refresher courses of the convoy drills we previously learned and performed at Fort Sill, Oklahoma, and Camp Virginia, Kuwait. Some of us accompanied the security escort teams of the 3/18th gaining experience on the road before we would ultimately assume control of the escort missions.

The radio call signs of the convoy escort teams identified them with their commanding unit. The battalion designated the name "Road Hunter" for our escort teams. After numerous changes, a final listing of team members provided light on many unanswered questions. I, along with eight others, formed Road Hunter One-Six. The day following the 3/18th ride-along, the battalion would take control of the convoy security escort missions.

After a late gathering of team members, I walked to the morale, welfare, and recreation (MWR) center to use the Internet access before calling it a night. Specialist Mark Reif and I placed our names on the computer list earlier in the day for a late time slot. He and the others felt worn-out and turned in for the night. I craved a little contact with home, something to soothe my mind before going to bed. With my name previously added to the list, I went alone, not wanting to waste the opportunity.

The computers and telephones were set up in an enclosed room at the MWR. Two soldiers manned a folding table at its entrance and managed the time schedule for its use. Anyone desiring to utilize the computers or telephones placed their name on a designated thirty-minute time slot.

"The phones are full. You'll never get on tonight. Come back tomorrow," the specialist shouted over the noise of the game room as I approached the table.

"No, I'm here for the computers." I picked up the clipboard.

"Computers? There's at least a three hour wait."

"I came in earlier and reserved an 11 P.M. time slot. I'm just double-checking my time." I located my name and returned the clipboard to the specialist.

"You're lucky you signed up when you did, it's a busy place tonight." He placed the list back onto the table.

"The phones are full. You'll never get on tonight. Come back tomorrow," he shouted around me at another soldier walking up to the table.

The MWR overflowed with transient soldiers, airmen, and marines. The sounds of three tables playing dominos, four televisions of X-Box video games, and a group watching CNN on the big screen filled the large, plywood-walled tent.

I found an open seat on a wooden bench next to the wall and sat down placing my M-16 rifle lengthwise between my knees with the muzzle pointed toward the floor. A short ten-minute wait separated me from the beginning of the computer time. Resting my hands on the butt of my weapon, I watched the news on the big screen TV. The day's activities in Iraq dominated the newscast.

"Are you waiting for the computers?" I asked a soldier as he sat down next to me.

"Yeah, I've got another half-hour to wait. I was on for two hours and now I have to wait an hour to get back on again." He rubbed his eyes. "I'll be on most of the night."

"Most of the night? I thought you could only sign up for one thirty-minute block at a time."

He placed his weapon on the floor and stretched out his legs. "You can get around that. Just write your buddy's name down on a different time slot. When your turn is up, take your buddy's. They don't question it."

"My buddy wasn't able to make it. If you want, I'm sure you can take his time slot."

"Really? Thanks man." He smiled and watched the big screen.

The noise level increased as two soldiers began cussing over a domino move at one of the game tables.

"What do you do on the computers that you would need to be on all night?" I continued the conversation.

He shrugged his shoulders. "Play games."

"Play games? Don't you need to get some sleep?"

"No, I'm fine. I slept all day. I'm tired of sitting around that tent. I need to get out and do something."

The domino argument continued and started drawing a small crowd.

"You don't have a job? They don't have you doing anything?" I asked.

"No, there's nothing to do. I haven't done anything in weeks and neither has anyone else. We're just waiting, waiting to go home."

He glanced down at my uniform, which looked bright and new in comparison to his faded and worn-out camouflage. "You must be one of the guys replacing us. We were excited to see you arrive and take over. What do they have you doing here?"

"Convoy escort," I answered.

He shook his head.

"Not a good job to have?" I curiously asked.

"It's dangerous. Not a job anyone really wants to have. We rotated through the missions where we each only had to do about two convoy days a week."

"Wow, twice a week?" I sat up a little straighter taking interest in his comments. "That would be nice. They have us scheduled to do convoys every day."

He glanced at me with a serious expression. "You're kidding me. Every day? It's too demanding to do every day."

"Every day," I repeated.

"Don't let them do that to you." He pointed his finger at me. "That's bullshit. That's just plain bullshit."

"Time's up!" the specialist manning the table shouted to the computer and phone users.

The spirited domino game ended and we walked to the doorway waiting for those who finished using the computers and phones to vacate the cramped, congested, little room.

"Have a safe trip home," I wished the 3/18th soldier.

"Yeah, good luck with your tour and thanks for getting here to replace us."

Watching the 3/18th prepare to leave brought about bittersweet feelings. Knowing we were at the beginning of our tour and would be away from our families for at least a year but understanding, one day we would be in their shoes, training a group of replacements and preparing to leave for home.

My e-mail inbox contained letters from Donna. She sent e-mail daily but my time did not allow me to check it as often as I would have liked. I read and reread her letters hearing the pleasant sound of her voice with every written word. It felt comforting to know my family held things together back home with an enormous amount of support.

I returned in the darkness to the tent and went to bed trying to clear the numerous thoughts racing through my mind. Continuously checking my watch, I observed midnight come and go. I desperately needed the sleep to stay alert on the road so I lay quietly in the dark and concentrated on the sound of the camp generators humming in the background, 5 A.M. would arrive all too soon.

CHAPTER 3

Lessons in Road Hunting

Click! The fluorescent lights softly flickered, casting gray shadows against the light green walls of the tent. The guys appeared tired as they quietly moaned and slowly stirred into motion. They, as I, did not sleep well. Lying awake in the darkness, I heard them tossing and turning throughout most of the night.

Shave, dress, and leave for the mission seemed the priorities of the moment. Pulling my personal equipment from under my bed, I made a quick inspection of each piece—body armor, Kevlar helmet, protective mask, some of the more important items required for the road. I rummaged through an extra bag that I packed to take along in the humvee. It contained two MREs, toilet paper, and a change of clothes. The unit suggested we carry the extras along. With an unexpected change in plans, we could possibly be away for a few days. No guarantee existed of returning to Cedar at the end of each mission.

Specialist Lynn Nelson silently left the tent earlier in the morning and drew our gun truck from the humvee line in the motor pool. He parked the woodland green camouflaged vehicle next to the tent, which made it convenient for pre-convoy preparations. Camp security frowned on driving the humvees within the tent area, only allowing time to load and unload.

I lifted the latch handle on the passenger-side fiberglass door and watched as it slowly glided open and bumped into the hood.

"Where's the armor?" I asked.

"Armor?" Nelson laughed. "What do you mean armor?"

I wobbled the door back and forth rattling the window glass within its frame. "If we're working convoy security we should have one of the gun trucks with the homemade, 3/8th inch steel plates bolted to the doors. These doors wouldn't stop a pellet gun."

Nelson threw his bag into the rear of the gun truck and slammed the hatch shut. "You have to remember who we are, Lew. It's just you, me, and Leptien. Do you think we rank an armored humvee? We should consider ourselves lucky to have a gun truck with all four doors attached."

I shook my head as we loaded the humvee with the remainder of our personal equipment, a case of MREs, and a cooler for the bottled water.

Specialist Tony Leptien fastened his squad automatic weapon (SAW) to the pintle in the turret ring located on top of the gun truck. He considered himself fortunate to have found the pin. The unit ran short on SAW pintle so some of the other gunners were not as privileged. They would support their weapons in hand, as they traveled down the highway. It can be enormously fatiguing after an hour, not to mention all day.

We were one of the few Road Hunter teams performing convoy security operations. Some commented about the Road Hunter name, which they related to a popular sport they experienced back home. They felt their knowledge in road hunting game birds and wild animals from a moving vehicle prepared them for convoy operations—drive and shoot.

I climbed into the gun truck, slid across the green canvas seat, and grabbed the radio handset. "I'll make a radio check with the TOC (tactical operations center) to see if we have contact with them."

"I'm way ahead of you, Lew," Nelson said as he laid his M-16 horizontally behind the steering wheel just below the windshield. "I got it covered."

"Yeah, Lew, he's way ahead of you. He's got it covered," Leptien broke in from his seat in the turret. "Don't you know? Nelson's the man. He's ahead of everyone. No one can catch him."

"Wow, you're good, Lynn. Good job." I placed the handset on top of the radio.

"Now, if those other jokers would get to it and finish filling their radios," Nelson continued, "we would be good to go."

"Yeah, now that's what I'm talkin' about," Leptien stood up in the turret and yelled at the others. "Did you hear that? We would be good to go if it weren't for you jokers."

Leptien continued trash-talking with the others while we waited for the team to complete their preparations.

Ping. The radio sounded. "Road Hunter One-Six, this is One-Six Alpha. Radio check. Over."

The call sign of One-Six Alpha referred to the crew of the lead gun truck commanded by Staff Sergeant Bryce Hanson. Sergeant Todd Moss stepped in at the last minute to fill as their driver while Specialist Chad McMillan, their original appointed driver, remained in camp to assist his section with radio maintenance for a few days. Their armament consisted of a .50 caliber heavy machine gun mounted on the turret manned by Specialist Danny Bloom. The lead truck regulated the speed and direction of the convoy while providing security.

Ping. "One-Six Alpha, this is One-Six. Roger. Out."

One-Six, commanded by our team leader, whom we referred to by his rank as lieutenant or LT, held overall responsibility for the convoy team by operating as the command and control (C2) vehicle. Equipped with an unmistakable long, green, fiberglass roof looking much like an inverted duck boat, it did not support a gun turret. Specialists Gary Scotting and Mike Boswell rotated through its driver's position.

I picked up the handset and established radio contact with the C2 vehicle. "Road Hunter One-Six, this is One-Six Bravo. Radio check. Over."

Ping. "One-Six Bravo, this is One-Six. Roger. Out." With team radio contact established, we anxiously waited, ready to roll.

The team included an odd assembly of military vocations consisting of a mechanic, cook, legal clerk, radio/communication specialist, surveyor, three field artillery computer operators, and one field artillery officer. Before deploying, we mostly knew one another through attending monthly guard drills. As the year progressed, we would eventually come to know one another more than anyone should comfortably know another person.

Two months ago, we were completely unapprised of the tactics and risks involving convoy security operations. With a few days of convoy training at Fort Sill, a few more in Kuwait, and a little hands-on familiarity with the 3/18th, we now opened for business. The teams stood short on experience and training but we had no other choice. With convoys needing protection, we would soon escort a group of trucks down the dangerous highways of Iraq.

Following the established convoy operations handoff procedures, two riders from the 3/18th accompanied each team during our first day on the road. They made sure we knew at least the basics of convoy security operations. One of the soldiers rode with the lead gun truck and the other with the command vehicle. After today, they were completely through with convoys. In a few weeks, they would be on their way home.

The lot stood unusually empty. The small number of convoys presently leaving the camp had previously received their assigned security. We were one of the teams without a convoy. Instead, we patrolled the highway in route to Camp Navistar, located roughly fifty miles southeast of Basra on the Iraqi-Kuwaiti border, a journey of approximately 130 miles. Once there, we would acquire a convoy and return to Cedar II. As explained by our seasoned riders, the trip to Navistar goes much quicker without a convoy. Barring any unforeseen incidents, we could possibly arrive there in under two and a half hours.

The LT gathered us around the C2 vehicle for a quick convoy briefing to discuss current Intel for the journey.

"OK, the intelligence shows that in the past two days the convoys have had contact around the hajji markets, which are located about halfway to the border."

The markets consisted of an assembly of mud and stick huts positioned next to the highway where the local Iraqis sold and traded goods to travelers passing by.

"During contact, a small, white pickup pulled beside the convoys and started firing AK-47s at the trucks. There are quite a few small, white pickups on the road. Chances are you won't spot them until after they begin firing."

As we left the front gates, each of us inserted a thirty-round magazine into our weapons and chambered a round. This action followed the standard operating procedure when leaving the camp.

While in camp, we normally did not carry a round in the chamber of our weapons, ready to fire. Inside the perimeter, a degree of safety existed. The status of the weapons depended on our location and the tasks we performed. If conditions suddenly turned hostile, we could easily insert a magazine and place a round into the chamber.

To establish a "show of force", we traveled down the highway with the barrels of our weapons protruding from the open windows of the gun trucks. The weapons display intimidated anyone seeking to engage us in some type of unfriendly activity.

The intense journey created a continuous sense of immediate contact, an extreme awareness that at any moment something could happen. A sniper, a roadside bomb, or a passing motor vehicle carrying rocket propelled grenades (RPGs) or AK-47 machine guns could appear at any time and unexpectedly engage us.

As we drove along, we attentively scanned the sides of the highway and the sand berm in the distance, looking for anything out of the ordinary, anything possibly considered a threat. The insurgents became very skilled at making and adapting roadside bombs or improvised explosive devices (IEDs). They concealed explosives in a variety of objects—soda cans, garbage bags, and dead animals, anything that blended into the surroundings.

While at Fort Sill, the military trainers instructed us to travel down a highway and look for an object considered a possible IED. We came upon a lone box sitting next to the side of a desolate road and reacted to it. We passed the roadside bomb test. Without the presence of another object anywhere on the highway, the road looked completely bare except for the test box.

The conditions in Iraq proved to be much worse. A massive amount of garbage littered the roadways. It seemed almost impossible to determine if an object actually contained an IED or trash thrown from a passing motor vehicle. We searched for other signs that might signal a concern, it's placement, where and how, or if wire lay next to it, anything that would cause the object to stand out from the surrounding waste. With the enormous amount of debris and the high speed at which we traveled, we spent most of the journey tightly clenching our teeth and praying we would not hear the deafening roar of a well-hidden explosive.

We reluctantly shared the highway with sporadic civilian traffic. It varied from almost nonexistent to completely congested. The civilian cars and trucks cautiously crept around us. We caught first glimpse of the vehicles through the side mirrors as they approached the rear of the humvee. Nelson watched through the mirror attached on his side of the vehicle as he drove and I angled the mirror next to me for my use. Between the two of us, we could see completely around the humvee when scanning the traffic.

Leptien occupied the best advantage point from the turret of the gun truck. At his elevated position, he searched down into the passing motor vehicles. If its occupants proved suspicious, he refused their attempt to pass and quickly reported them. Some drivers appeared apprehensive in passing. They held their position behind us and seemed content with follow the convoy. At times, traffic congested to the point where Leptien waved the vehicles forward and around the gun truck to keep the road clear behind us. In the event of a breakdown, we did not want a large number of vehicles passing around us all at once. We could not control a dangerous situation such as that.

A variety of civilian vehicles passed by, cars, pickups, trucks, buses. Most seemed like older models with faded paint and multiple dings, dents, and scratches. Some suspended old curtains in their windows to cool the interior by restricting the sunlight from entering. With their cars packed tightly with as many passengers as could possibly fit, we rarely saw a vehicle with an open seat.

As they passed, some graciously waved, while others stared intently ahead as if deliberately choosing not to make eye contact. They did not want to be mistaken for trouble. I did not blame them. I remembered reading a story in the newspaper a few months prior regarding an Iraqi family motioned to pass around a moving convoy. When they reached a gun truck traveling in the center of the column, the gunner became alarmed and opened fire on them.

More and more young children began standing along the sides of the road as the morning passed.

"Where do all these kids come from?" Nelson yelled over the engine noise.

"I'm not sure. They must live somewhere out there." I pointed to a scattering of mud shacks in the distance.

"This is crazy. Why would anyone let their kids beg along the road like this?"

"When you're starving, I imagine most would do just about anything to get food, especially the kids."

The children stood barefoot wearing soiled, ragged clothes. Smiling through dirty faces, they waved to catch our attention in hopes of receiving food. With sleep filled eyes and tattered hair they searched for their first meal of the day.

Nelson shook his head. "These kids could get killed out here begging along the road. Who in their right mind would let their kids do that? Their parents should be whipped."

I understood his frustration. He had two small boys back home and could never imagine himself doing anything like this to his children. I waved to the kids in acknowledgement as we passed—an indication of nothing to give them at the moment.

"They're probably lucky to still have parents alive," I said as I waved my arm out the window. "I wonder how many were orphaned by the war."

We arrived at Navistar and pressed by the 3/18th to continue moving, quickly acquired a convoy mission for the return trip to Cedar. You could certainly tell they were experienced with retrieving convoys from Navistar. They seemed to know of every hidden short-cut into the movement control team (MCT) lot. Instead of traveling through the main gate, we managed to squeeze between two concrete barricades and found a convoy waiting, a line of supply trucks with a destination north into Iraq.

Third country nationals (TCNs) drove the semi trucks in the convoy. The TCNs originated from countries other than Iraq such as Pakistan, Egypt, and the Philippines. Hearing a sudden sharp bark as a signal to prepare to depart, the drivers rushed to their vehicles and climbed into the driver's seats. Multiple puffs of black smoke shot into the air as the diesel engines roared to life. One by one, after sitting silently in an organized row for many hours, the trucks began lurching into motion.

One of the 3/18th soldiers jumped into the backseat of our gun truck for the return trip. He provided us a few quick pointers on convoy control as we readied to pull into position trailing the convoy vehicles.

The soldier became upset with one of the TCNs who had difficulty starting his truck.

"Come on you fuckin' hajji! Get moving!" he screamed and swore out of the humvee window.

The driver tried feverishly to place his truck in motion. He looked very concerned as his starter continuously whined in an attempt to start the stalled truck engine.

The soldier threw open the humvee door and stepped out. He reached back inside the gun truck grabbing a long, wooden pickax handle from the rear and pointed it at the driver. "You fuckin' hajji! I said get moving!" he screamed. "Don't make me come after you! You don't want me to come after you!"

The truck suddenly started. A look of relief came over the driver as his vehicle quickly leaped forward after the other trucks that had passed through the MCT lot gate.

The military leadership permitted the use of two names in describing the enemy—Ali Baba and hajji. Ali Baba, taken from *Ali Baba and the Forty Thieves* of the *Arabian Nights* stories, related to thieves, murderers, and thugs. The Iraqis commonly used this name. With it, they associated those caught stealing or those they knew of as members of crime mobs or gangs.

Hajji became the name used to identify those we fought against in this war. Psychologically, the term conveniently separated them into a class other than human. We were not actually killing people. We were killing hajjis. The use of the name expanded to include the people along the road begging for food, the people selling from their market stands, and the people driving in their cars down the highway. All were hajjis.

It did not end with just the Iraqis. A hajji became anyone of Middle Eastern appearance and not part of the coalition forces. The drivers of the trucks, the servers in the chow hall, and the workers around the camp, all were hajjis. They came from a variety of countries throughout the Middle East and around the world but in our eyes, their origin did not make a difference. If they looked like a hajji, they were a hajji. This made our jobs easier in treating them the harsh way that we did.

The convoy moved swiftly along in route to our destination at Cedar. The segment of highway we traveled contributed to a main supply route (MSR) called Tampa. Tampa meandered through Iraq connecting many smaller supply routes. The military determined each route's name. With many of the highways and roads labeled with numbers or Arabic names, combining frequently traveled roads into one named route aided in easier directions. Instead of referencing a dozen roads between two points on a map, it simplified the process by naming the whole route.

The segment of Tampa we traveled spread into a wide six-lane highway separated by a sand-filled median strip. We used the three southbound lanes during the trip down to Navistar and now occupied the three northbound lanes for the return to Cedar. The standard operating procedure specified the main convoy travel in the left lane next to the median. We positioned the gun truck in the middle lane leaving the right lane available for passing traffic.

The convoy moved at a steady speed of sixty miles per hour with the trucks traveling bumper to bumper. The close interval made even minor braking very dangerous for the drivers. If the distance between the trucks increased, the convoy could double or even triple in length making it much more difficult to provide security.

The humvee tires growled loudly as we drove over a rough patch of the paved highway. The blackened section indicated a previous fire had burned the road to a coarse texture.

"That's ours." The soldier pointed with excitement to the charred pavement. "It happened a few months ago when we escorted a convoy of fuel tankers. One of the tankers rolled over and some of the others crashed into it. It was one hell of a fire. The burning fuel killed some of the hajjis, roasted them to death. It might not have happened if the fuckers would have paid attention to what they were doing."

We continued with the mission as we scanned the sides of the road, berm, and passing traffic. Numerous knee high steel posts lined both sides of the median strip with the hundreds of miles of guardrail once attached to them now missing, plundered for its scrap metal value. Many of the steel posts themselves gone, pulled from the ground leaving an abundance of deep, narrow, open holes, just the right size to hide an artillery round for use as an IED.

Seasonal rains and wind eroded the approaches to the graffiti covered, concrete bridges crossing over Tampa leaving large crevices draping down their sides. The roads leading away from the bridges amounted to little more than sandy paths. Intel warned of cables suspended from bridges by the insurgents attempting to decapitate unsuspecting turret gunners.

"We're starting to get a gap in the convoy." The 3/18th soldier nodded to a large space between the trucks moving ahead of us. "Kick it down. Let's get up there and close it up."

The open space measured roughly one hundred meters from the rear of one truck to the cab of another following directly behind it. Our rider explained once again how the trucks should move practically bumper to bumper.

Nelson stomped on the accelerator and drove up next to the cab of the slower moving truck matching its speed. The driver blankly stared at the back of the white trailer in front of him, unaware of his mistake. The soldier shook his head as he leaned out the backseat window and angrily motioned to the driver.

"Close it up! Close it up!" the soldier yelled and cursed as he pointed to the opening between the trucks.

The startled driver quickly glanced over at the soldier. He looked down at his instrument panel and back up again. He turned his palms up indicating he could do nothing about it.

"He's not fuckin' with me today. I'll speed him up." The soldier reached inside the humvee and grabbed his M-16. He shoved it out the window and pointed it at the driver in the truck.

"Close it up hajji or I'll fuckin' shoot you!" he yelled.

The driver looked frightened as he attempted to increase his speed but the gap continued to widen.

The soldier pulled back inside the humvee and yelled up the turret to Leptien, "Aim your SAW at him. Tell the motherfucker to close up the gap or you'll shoot his ass."

Leptien quickly swung his SAW around and pointed it through the truck's passenger side window aiming it at the driver. He yelled and motioned with his hands. The driver tried frantically to make adjustments. A puff of black smoke shot from his exhaust pipe. With a look of relief on the driver's face, his truck began gradually picking up speed. Within a few minutes, his truck moved closer to the trailer in front of him, slowly closing the gap.

The soldier sat back in his seat and shook his head. Threatening the driver did not bother him one bit. The routine became part of his job, all in a day's work, the common process of doing business here.

"You've got to keep them hajjis tight," he explained. "Once

they start to form gaps in the convoy, you'll end up with a big mess. The trucks in the rear will suddenly slow to a crawl and then the next minute they are cruising at eighty miles per hour trying to catch up. They end up yo-yoing. You know, like an accordion. If the convoy becomes too long then it is tough to provide security and you become an easy target."

As he talked, one of the trucks suddenly pulled out of the convoy and over to the right-hand side of the road. The others did not break from the steady course and continued moving on at their present speed in the left lane.

"A hajji pulled over," he yelled as he pointed. "Stop right next to him and we'll see what he's trying to pull."

We gradually slowed as the humvee neared the truck. The door swung open as the truck rolled to a stop. The driver jumped from his cab directly onto the pavement without touching a step. He ran back to an outer compartment mounted underneath his vehicle. Opening it, he pulled out a towel and sprinted back to the cab. As he slammed his door, the truck darted forward and rejoined the convoy.

The soldier shook his head once again. "Those crazy fuckin' hajjis. Now that could have waited until we got back to Cedar. Why would you pull a truck over for that, a towel? It's dangerous out here. Every time a truck or the convoy pulls over only increases your chance of being shot at or hit with an IED."

We certainly received an eye opening education on handling the drivers. Deep down it did not feel right. Should we be treating these people this way? I did not possess the experience to question the procedures with this only being our first convoy mission. The 3/18th had performed security escorts for some time now. We quietly listened and learned as they filled our heads with their knowledge of the road.

Convoy operations seemed similar to herding cattle. Keep them moving in the right direction and try not to let them spread out. Every once in awhile you would need to persuade one of them to do what you wanted him to do. At that point, I saw only one major difference in the treatment of the drivers as opposed to the treatment of cattle—we would have treated cattle much better.

Over the next few weeks, we excelled in our abilities at performing convoy operations. The teams quickly honed their skills keeping the trucks tight and moving at a steady high tempo.

The stress remained high but we quickly adapted to the experience of the road. The constant threat of IEDs, drive by shootings, and snipers, combined with excessive speed and an overabundance of adrenaline produced a rush so great no existing narcotic could ever compare.

Each separate mission provided its own unique run of problems. Many trucks broke down with troubles ranging from bad tires to overheated engines. Dealing with the breakdowns is how we learned to become very good at being very bad. When a truck pulled over with a flat tire or engine problems, an M-16 rifle muzzle motivated the driver to make the twenty-minute deadline or deal with the consequences.

The Iraqis living along the road also felt this wrath, as the convoys waited for repairs, the locals darted for the trucks to beg from the drivers. It remained our job to keep them away from the vehicles. Many on the teams yelled and swore at the people, most of them young children, to move back and away from the vehicles.

In the evenings, some of the Road Hunter team members gathered around the smoke area laughing and sharing hajji stories of their convoy missions. Those who worked in the camp during the day listened attentively to the wild vivid details. The convoy stories fueled an already raging fire of abuse. As other team members listened, they began believing the stories as acceptable behavior on the road. The presence of the unit leadership, who sat and joined in with the teams' enthusiasm, provided reinforcement for the extreme behavior.

"Let the bodies hit the floor, let the bodies hit the floor, let the bodies hit the floor…," Leptien sang along to music playing from his MP3 player as we charged down the highway. The sound of a sixty mile per hour wind blowing by his ears became tiresome. Music helped him to remain focused.

"Tony," I yelled, "what kind of music are you listening to today?"

He pulled a bud from his ear. "What?"

"What kind of music are you listening to today?"

"It's my hate music. It motivates me and keeps me awake," he explained.

I laughed. "Yeah, I didn't think you were listening to the hits of the eighties."

He smiled as he continued singing and nodding his head to the beat of the music.

Missing its roof liner, the gun truck's interior echoed with the engine's loud roar. Yelling became our means of communication, which also added to the intense fervor.

Unable to hear the radio traffic over the humvee engine, I solved the problem by wearing foam earplugs during the convoys. After inserting the earplugs, I adjusted the radio volume to its maximum level and propped the handset against my ear, lodging it between my Kevlar chinstrap and cheekbone. The earplugs filtered out much of the engine noise. With the speaker blasting against my ear, I never missed a call.

We traveled on the main roads when escorting convoys but after releasing the trucks at the border, we took the shortest route at high speeds over and around anything in our path. It felt like the American Wild West, we drove anywhere we wanted and nobody questioned it.

The presence of a gun truck created both respect and fear. As we traveled, it attracted numerous stares from civilians as well as coalition forces moving along the highway. When we stopped for various reasons, either people moved toward us to talk and look or they cautiously stayed away. This immediate recognition proved not always advantageous. It elevated the gun truck into the unpopular status as a preferred target for roadside bomb attacks by the insurgents.

Performing convoy operations did not always involve excessive intimidation. Occasionally, we did something helpful for the Iraqi people. The young kids begging along the road became a major problem for the convoys since before our arrival. Not wanting to miss a chance at receiving handouts, many of the kids took great chances and stood directly on the pavement next to the passing trucks while begging for food. The truck traffic produced a dangerous setting near the road. An unfortunate slip could result in a deadly accident.

The leadership provided a solution for this. They handed us leaflets to pass out to the kids along the road. The half sheets of paper displayed a colorful picture of children along with Arabic writing explaining to the parents the great dangers involved with their children begging near the roadside.

Sitting patiently on the berm behind their kids, many of the parents encouraged the children to beg. Begging provided food for their families. By the depressing expressions on the kids' faces, some appeared somewhat distraught as they stood next to the highway. Others, being too young to understand the extreme danger involved, stood bravely as sand and dust filled their eyes.

Each gun truck received a handful of the leaflets. I folded most of ours into small paper airplanes, something special, a little different from what the other gun trucks handed out. Moving down the road, we threw a few of the leaflets through the windows of the humvee. At the excessive speed we traveled, most of the paper swirled in the humvee's air currents and gently landed on the road directly behind us. Curious as to the nature of the paper churning in the breeze, the kids sprinted out onto the highway to retrieve them. Throwing the leaflets from the moving vehicle seemed to contribute to the problem we attempted to suppress.

As we pulled into the outskirts of Safwan, a city located on the Iraqi side of the border, we found the kids lining both sides of the street as they typically did. They waved with hands clutched full of paper leaflets thrown by those in the gun trucks who preceded us. Thinking it money, many of the kids ran up to the humvee asking for more of the small, colorful sheets.

Experiencing heavy congestion at the border crossing, the convoy slowed to a crawl. This presented a perfect opportunity to throw the paper airplanes. Leptien and I launched our squadron of paper out through the windows and down from the turret of the gun truck.

"Tah-e-rah, tah-e-rah," (airplane, airplane) I explained as we drove by the children.

We laughed as we watched the kids retrieve the folded paper from the ground and attempt to make them soar through the air.

The traffic decelerated to the point where the convoy stopped completely. A young girl quietly stood alone next to the road. I pulled the latch handle, opening the door of the humvee and stepped out holding a paper airplane for her to see.

"Tah-e-rah, tah-e-rah," I explained as she closely examined it.

With a quick flick of the wrist, the airplane shot high into the sky and drifted on a slight breeze. Her eyes widened as she watched it silently float through the air and land a short distance away. She ran over, picked it off the ground, and closely inspected it again. She sprinted back to the humvee and placed the folded paper into the palm of my hand. Not understanding her Arabic, I capably interpreted her request by the look on her face.

I laughed and gave the airplane another toss. She seemed very excited in my ability to make the paper fly through the air.

"Lew, the convoy's moving. Let's go." the guys yelled from the gun truck.

With the convoys beginning to advance, we needed to follow and protect the trucks. The young girl pulled on my arm wanting me to remain there and play with her as I tried my best explaining we must leave. Smiling, she carefully cradled the paper airplane in her small hands and ran toward a mud brick house standing at the end of a narrow path.

The leaflets would offer little if any assistance in keeping the kids away from the trucks. The abundance of vehicles providing food proved too great a temptation. Our efforts were not in vain. In working to move the kids away from the roadsides, we easily made many small friends.

CHAPTER 4

Team Leader's Guidance

"Hey! Hey! Hey!" an infuriated, raspy voice shouted.

After releasing the convoy at the border, we began leaving the fuel point destined for Navistar when we heard the loud bark of an angry bystander.

"Hey you, Stop! Stop!" he continued yelling.

Glancing around, I spotted an older man, bearing the stripes of a master sergeant on the collar of a new desert camouflage uniform (DCU), wildly waving his arms through the air in an attempt to stop us.

"We better stop the humvee," I casually leaned over and instructed Nelson. "He's upset about something. I'll find out what he wants."

Nelson wrinkled his face and slowly shook his head indicating his preference to continue ignoring him and proceed on to Navistar. The thought briefly crossed my mind as well. As usual, we advanced quickly to join the team and retrieve the next mission. Even a small delay could bump us down a position on the security escort list at Trade Center South. I knew these things, no matter how trivial they looked to us, seemed important to others. If we declined to stop now, the possibility existed that the problem, whatever it may be, could come back and blindside us when we least expected it.

"Stop the humvee," I firmly repeated.

Nelson reluctantly slammed the brake pedal to the floor. The forward momentum of the vehicle pulled the door open and I stepped out of the gun truck as it plowed through the rocks and sand to a stop. Walking toward the man as he slowly moved from his nylon folding chair in the shade, I did not recognize him as someone familiar to the fuel point. His sunburned light skin indicated he had not been in theater very long.

"Is there something I can help you with?" I asked.

"Look at that humvee," he growled. "Just look at that hum-vee."

I spun around expecting to find something terribly out of order with the gun truck but saw nothing. Turning back toward him with a puzzled expression, I slowly shook my head.

"You take a good look at that humvee," he continued. "You tell me exactly what is wrong with that picture."

I examined the gun truck once again. All four tires present and inflated properly, nothing important dragging from the vehicle, Leptien in the turret, Nelson driving, I could not understand why this man became upset to the point of demanding we stop.

"I'm sorry, but you're going to have to point it out," I explained. "I really don't see anything out of the ordinary."

He thrust a bony finger into the air aiming it at Leptien. "Your gunner. Your gunner. You don't see that? This ain't no hay-ride. Your gunner can't sit out of the turret on top of the humvee like that."

It finally made sense. The sergeant served as a safety officer with a job to locate and correct problems that could result in an injury. A busy day lay in store for him. All of the gunners sat out of the turret when we ended a convoy mission. It provided a chance to stretch their legs after many long hours of squatting motionless below the roofline in the sling.

I pointed at Leptien. "You need to get off the roof and sit down inside the turret."

Leptien muttered a few brief comments under his breath and grudgingly dropped himself through the turret ring.

"You can't let those guys ride up there like that. This ain't no hayride."

"That's a good idea. I'll keep an eye on him. This is all new to us," I continued explaining. "We're with a field artillery unit and not normally issued a humvee with a gun turret. Our specialty involves larger pieces of equipment that can blow things up with excessive firepower." I gave a quick laugh in hopes of easing the moment.

He glared at me, lacking any hint of amusement. "That don't make no difference," he growled. "You can't ride on the roof."

With the problem corrected to the sergeant's liking, we had

no need to remain there any further. I reassured him we would share the safety information with the others in the unit. He seemed satisfied for the time being as he strolled back to his chair resting under a small piece of green camouflage netting.

Breaking into laughter at the unusual meeting with the master sergeant, we joked about the reprimand but realized it as only the beginning in a recent tightening of the rules. Finding the truck lot empty, we entered into Navistar and met up with the team at an agreed upon location in the Post Exchange (PX) area. Leptien informed the others about the strange run in with the agitated sergeant. Some of them shared similar encounters as well.

We sat patiently in the shade of the humvees and talked as we monitored the radio traffic for a call informing us of our next push north. The time eventually approached the cutoff deadline of 2 P.M.. If we did not receive a mission by then, we would leave Navistar and patrol the highway back to Cedar without a convoy. The specified cutoff time provided a safety guideline for those performing convoy security. If held longer than 2 P.M., a breakdown on the road could delay us further requiring the team to travel in the dark. We tried avoiding that as much as possible.

Nelson started the humvee's engine as the LT informed Trade Center South of our planned departure from Navistar. The trip back would be quick without a convoy, a fast pace and no truck breakdowns to contend with.

The radio sounded. Ping. "One-Six Alpha, One-Six Bravo, this is One-Six. Over."

"Now what?" Leptien groaned.

Ping. "This is Alpha. Over."

I picked the handset off the radio. "This is Bravo. Over."

Ping. "Road Hunter One-One missed their push so we need to head over to the MCT lot and take it to Cedar. Over."

Ping. "One-Six Alpha. Roger. Out."

"One-Six Bravo. Roger. Out."

After a few choice words by the guys in the gun truck, we followed the team over to the MCT lot to escort Road Hunter One-One's push. The time dropped past 2 P.M.. We were cutting it close and taking a chance. If the convoy proceeded smoothly, the team would make it back to Cedar just before dark. If plagued with truck breakdowns, we could be in for a risky convoy mission.

Nelson pulled the gun truck into position at the yard and began counting off twenty-five semi trucks as they left the lot following behind alpha and the command vehicle. The trucks represented an assortment of ragtag vehicles compiled of whatever remained from the previous convoys—food, water, equipment, and trailer houses. The movement control team held these trucks from previous convoys because of various problems we hoped the drivers corrected by now.

As we counted, two trucks collided into each other directly in front of us. This reduced the numbers to escort but caused another delay as the convoy stopped for the MCT people to examine the trucks and clear the scattered debris from the path. Forty-five minutes later, we finally arrived on the six-lane and began increasing speed north on MSR Tampa.

The last three trucks in the convoy carried small buildings and trailer houses designed for use as offices, living quarters, and dining facilities. Although tightly secured to the trailers with ropes and chains, they received a powerful beating during the long trip. Constructed of wooden frames, tin siding, and tin roofing materials, the cumbersome structures easily fell apart from the tremendous force produced by the high convoy velocities as they moved down the highway.

The main convoy approached speeds close to sixty miles per hour but the three trailer house drivers refused to travel faster than forty-five. In an attempt to close the large gap now forming, Leptien tried intimidating the lead driver with the threat of using his SAW. The driver ignored us and maintained his slow pace gradually pulling us farther and farther behind the convoy.

I contacted the LT about the situation. "One-Six, this is One-Six Bravo. Over."

Ping. "This is One-Six. Over."

"We have been trying to motivate this hajji back here but he doesn't seem to be able to drive faster than forty-five. You will need to slow the convoy down or you'll lose us. Over."

Ping. "Roger. We'll slow the convoy down. Keep on trying to motivate him. Let me know when you get him to speed up. Over."

"Roger. Out."

Leptien screamed and cussed from the turret while Nelson yelled out his side window but the driver continued falling behind.

"Leptien," I yelled, "tell the two hajjis following him to pass around and catch up with the convoy."

Confused with my request, he hesitated. "But the hajjis aren't supposed to pass each other."

"I would rather deal with one slow truck than three. Tell them to pass."

Leptien waved the two trucks forward. They shot around the lead truck and hurried on their way to join the convoy. This upset the lead trailer house driver who finally began to increase his speed. The three continued leapfrogging around one another until all eventually reached the main convoy.

"One of the hajjis just pulled over," Nelson yelled as he hit the brakes.

I quickly informed the LT and the convoy slowly came to a stop up the road to wait for us. We pulled the humvee in behind the stopped truck and I stepped out to find the reason for the delay.

As I approached the truck, I located the driver standing at the front of his vehicle and curiously examining both tires. He nervously looked at me as if expecting a sudden scolding for the breakdown. His situation appeared somewhat strange. Both tires looked low in air pressure, not completely flat, just extremely low and in need of replacing before we could continue on.

"You've got twenty minutes, get moving." I motioned to the driver to begin his work. If not repaired in the twenty-minute time period, we would take the driver with us and abandon his truck along the road as directed by the unit's standard operating procedure. With two tires in need of replacement, they could not afford to waste one second. The driver began the difficult task with assistance from two others who searched the remaining trucks for additional, matching spare tires.

I yelled to Leptien, who observed from the turret as he monitored the traffic, "call the LT and let him know both the front tires are flat and they are working on the problem."

A few minutes later, the LT arrived at the breakdown. He seemed somewhat concerned with a small, white pickup continuously circling the area, most likely local scavengers waiting for us to leave the truck so they could steal it. With the alpha gun truck positioned a little ways up the road securing the main convoy, the LT informed them to stay alert for the suspicious vehicle.

Ringing sounds of metal wrenches bouncing off the pavement, followed by a series of agonizing grunts, echoed down the highway as the drivers worked steadily changing the tires. The convoy safety rules forbid us in assisting with repairs during the breakdowns. The drivers needed to perform the work themselves. Too many chances existed of something going terribly wrong with someone getting hurt, besides, our main duty involved providing protection for the drivers and securing the convoy as we waited.

The hot sun beat down upon us as we stood guard on the highway and scanned the immediate area for possible threats. Cars passed slowly with their occupants cautiously acknowledging us with a slight wave of the hand or nod of the head. A herder in the distance, curious as to the roadside activity, gradually moved his sheep in our direction. On the horizon, four small, white trucks pulled highway dust from the road as they raced toward our location.

"Here come the IP," Leptien yelled down from the turret.

The IP, Iraqi police, they patrolled the highways searching for accidents, controlling the flow of traffic, and providing a semblance of law enforcement.

"I suppose they all have AK-47s too." Nelson abhorrently shook his head.

I laughed. "What's wrong, Lynn, don't you trust them?"

"I don't trust any of them. I sure wouldn't trust them enough to give them AK-47s."

"Someone thought they should be armed." I reassured him. "We'll keep an eye on them just in case."

The white pickups pulled up in a cloud of dust, parking in the opposite, southbound lanes. As their vehicles rolled to a stop, two dozen men stepped out dressed in dark blue pants with light blue shirts. All wore dark blue body armor and carried AK-47s in their hands. Every one of them displayed a big smile from ear to ear.

With the LT occupied in the command humvee conveying a text message to the battalion back at Cedar regarding the breakdown, I introduced myself to the group leader. He spoke only a few words of English. Through a series of hand gestures and word fragments, he gradually indicated they arrived to assist and they wanted to provide security for us.

After shaking my hand, he quickly set his men into motion. In less than a minute, they established a protective perimeter around the vehicles. Some lay on the hot pavement positioned in prone, some kneeling, and others standing. They placed the butt of their weapons against their shoulders aiming out into the open desert as if readying to fire. The unforgiving afternoon sun scorched us but the Iraqi policemen held steady in their positions. Scotting, in an effort to offer relief, walked around with a case of water and handed each one a bottle.

Concerned the breakdown put us well past the twenty-minute time limit, I moved toward the command vehicle to discuss the delay with the LT when the head police officer stopped me. He spoke in Arabic as he pointed to his men. I did not quite understand at first what he desired but quickly realized he wanted to show me how well he arranged his men on the perimeter. He seemed very proud of their placement.

I smiled. "Very good. Very nice." I gave him the thumbs up.

He gleamed with pride as he placed his hands on his chest and looked around inspecting them.

"Come with me." I motioned him to follow as I walked over to the C2 vehicle. I opened the humvee door, reached into the backseat, and pulled out an open case of Boz's Coke that he retrieved from the MCT lot in Navistar. The Coke, along with a variety of other soft drinks, sat on pallets within a refrigerated truck, free to those wanting to take it.

"Boz, can I borrow your Coke? I'll get you a new case tomorrow."

Boz glanced at the box leaving the backseat. "No, not my Coke." He began to chuckle. "Yeah, OK, pick me up a case tomorrow."

I handed the open case to the leader. "Coca-Cola. Coca-Cola." I pointed at the shiny, red, aluminum cans sparkling in the sunlight.

He smiled and laughed. "Yes, Coca-Cola."

He turned around and yelled to his men, "Coca-Cola!"

Coca-Cola must have been their code word for all clear. The

Iraqi policemen stood up and left their positions practically running to the humvee. Many hands reached into the open case and each pulled out at least one can of soda. They quickly emptied the case so I found a few extra Cokes and passed them out to those who had not received one.

They popped the tops and guzzled the caramel colored liquid down. The Coke felt warm but they enjoyed it all the same. They chattered away filling the air with sounds of burps and laughter. Soon, the metallic resonance of empty cans bouncing along the highway echoed as a slight breeze sent the cans rolling into the ditch.

"Let's go! They're done," Nelson shouted.

With the drivers finished making repairs, we needed to leave immediately. I thanked the Iraqi policemen for their assistance. They shook our hands and loaded into the white pickups parting in the direction in which they arrived.

"I don't know why you even bother, Lew." Nelson shook his head.

The low tires cost us an hour of precious daylight. To avoid a further delay caused by slow speed, we positioned the troublesome trailer houses at the head of the convoy and started on our way. With any luck, we would arrive at the camp just after sunset. I questioned the sudden decision to wait longer than the normal twenty-minute period but the LT insisted we would return to Cedar with all the trucks.

As we traveled along, we stared directly into the bright orange sun as it slowly lowered in the western sky and rested just above the horizon. The day proved to be miserably hot and long. We were eager to return to camp and end the mission.

Suddenly, one of the trucks, positioned a few vehicles up from the rear of the convoy, quickly darted into the center lane and turned hard to the left. The tall semitrailer swayed deeply to the right, rolling over onto its side and spraying the highway with a brilliant shower of white sparks and sand as the truck ground against the concrete pavement directly in front of us.

"Stop! Stop! That truck rolled over!" I yelled as I pointed through the windshield.

Nelson hit the brakes along with the two remaining semis that followed closely behind the rolled truck. The trucks managed to maneuver skillfully around the accident as the humvee tires screeched to an abrupt stop behind it.

I grabbed the radio handset. "One-Six, this is One-Six Bravo. Stop the convoy. One of the hajjis rolled his truck. Over."

Ping. "Roger. Stopping the convoy."

The tractor-trailer lay motionless upon its side covering the middle and inside lanes of the highway. I jumped out of the humvee and ran to the truck to see if the driver survived the accident. Cupping my hands against the shattered windshield, I located the driver attempting to stand lengthwise through the center of the cab.

"Are you all right?" I yelled through the glass. It seemed as though he did not notice my presence in front of him. "Are you all right?" I yelled once more.

He gradually crawled up through the cab, pulling his way to the passenger side window at the top of the wreck. He did not seem injured but looked slightly dazed as he climbed through the open window and sat on the top of the vehicle. After briefly catching his breath, he steadily slid his way down to the concrete.

I firmly grasped his arm and spoke directly into his face. "Are you all right, buddy?"

He slightly nodded but said nothing. His trembling limbs seemed to work fine so I sat him down by the side of the road allowing him time to acquire his bearing. A few final, faint sounds emanated from the truck's still engine as the burning smell of hot oil and rubber hung over the scene.

The command vehicle raced back to the accident. In examining the truck, Boz noticed various liquids beginning to seep from the shipping container and pool around the wreckage.

"Was this truck carrying chemicals?" Boz asked.

"I'm not sure what's in there," I replied. "You better ask the driver. If it is carrying chemicals, then we may have a problem. Some do not mix very well."

Boz questioned the driver about the contents of the trailer. The driver spoke very little English, which made it difficult to determine what the trailer actually contained.

"Manifest, papers, where is your manifest?" Boz continued questioning him.

The driver eventually understood and reluctantly crawled

back inside the cab to retrieve his papers.

"Looks like it goes to a DFAC (dining facility) in one of the camps up north," Boz explained as he read. "Pop, this truck is carrying pop, cases and cases of soft drinks."

The alpha gun truck pulled in next to our humvee to assist. Something about the accident felt unsettling. It looked as though the driver may have intentionally laid the truck onto its side. Did the driver organize the rollover to leave the truck here? He may have prearranged the accident with others who would scavenge through its contents once we left. With no time allowed for an in-depth investigation while on the road, we would never know the specifics involved. We needed to continue with the mission as soon as possible.

The convoy sat idling in the middle of nowhere and sun slowly set. Civilian traffic began driving carefully around us as the guys gathered by the gun trucks and discussed the accident. An immense excitement surrounded the wreckage as we observed the massive truck on its side but priorities dictated the need to maintain convoy security.

We secured the perimeter of the truck as the darkness gradually hid the desert from our sight. The moonless sky revealed countless, bright stars. Faint shadows occasionally danced in the pitch-blackness when passing motor vehicle headlights moved along the highway. We positioned the gun truck with its headlights aimed at the oncoming traffic to slow movement around the turned trailer. The wreckage blocked all but one lane. The recovery team out of Cedar would need to remove it before the highway returned to normal.

The civilian traffic soon became agitated with the obstruction and crossed the median strip of the highway into the southbound lanes to move around us. We monitored a few of the vehicles exhibiting suspicious activity.

"Lew, that same set of headlights just turned around again," Leptien informed me. "He's been circling us for quite some time now."

"Keep an eye on him, Tony. He may just be a thief waiting for us to leave but be ready in case he has other plans."

In the darkness, we could not see the occupants or their

movements inside the vehicles. Each time a set of headlights passed, we braced for a possible engagement.

The LT approached us from the shadows. "OK, let's move out. Secure anything coalition and leave the truck. Let's get out of here."

"Do we have anything to place down as a warning signal?" I asked. "In the dark, someone could easily collide with the wreckage and kill themselves, if not Iraqi, possibly coalition forces."

"That's not our problem," he informed me. "Our orders are to leave now."

The convoy produced a signature of colored lights as we traveled down the highway. Hundreds of red and amber, cab and trailer lights glowed brightly through the night. The last portion of the trip moved along smoothly and without further incident. After a few minor delays in the truck release area, we finally entered Camp Cedar at 10:30 P.M., which set a longstanding convoy record for late arrival.

An hour later, the lieutenant convened a quick after action review (AAR) in the tent to discuss the events during the mission. The guys felt tired from the long day and not up to contributing very much. I voiced my concerns on the separation time from the yard in Navistar, the amount of time to repair the tires, and the speed at which we set up security around the accident. The LT disagreed with my thoughts and felt all went well with no major problems.

The next morning, I sat in the gun truck at the Cedar MCT lot while we waited for a push to Navistar. With a sense of excitement, the guys described the previous day's events to the other teams' members who eagerly listened, as the incidents were unfolded in detail.

"Hey, Lew, did you know we were involved in an attempted hijacking yesterday?" Nelson laughed.

"Oh, is that right?"

"Yeah, according to today's Intel reports, Road Hunter One-Six had an attempted hijacking on MSR Tampa yesterday. Two flat front tires on one vehicle with a small, white pickup spotted in the area."

I shook my head at the news. "That would have been nice to know at the time it was happening. I wonder whose idea that was."

I did not know who labeled the incident an attempted hijacking. It may have been the LT but most likely, someone higher up the chain of command. They could brand it what they wanted. It did not matter. We would have additional breakdowns to contend with that day.

That evening, I walked into the tent and discovered the lieutenant holding another AAR with half of the team absent. The topic relating to the events from the previous day's mission remained on the table. Apparently, the lieutenant had his rear end chewed by the commander on his handling of the escort mission.

"I don't care what they say," the LT spoke, "I still think we did the right thing. We will continue to run things with business as usual using our standards. If I had it to do all over again, I would not change a thing."

I became a little confused. No one in their right mind would interpret the previous day's events as business as usual by any means.

"Our standards?" I questioned him. "Which standards are those, sir?"

He stood silently looking at me without attempting an answer.

"We have only been on convoys for a little over two weeks," I explained. "We really don't have the experience to deviate from the standard operating procedure set by the battalion. As you are aware, those procedures were taken from the 3/18th who pulled convoy security for quite a few months before we arrived."

The others nodded quietly in agreement but I sensed by the expression on the LT's face that he did not want to hear what I had to say.

"We should be looking at what went wrong and correcting it," I continued. "At this point, I feel we need to stick with the standards. Once we have been out there for a while, we will gain a better perspective of the road and can then improvise. If we start making our own rules now, we may end up with serious problems."

The LT rolled up a few sheets of paper he gripped tightly in his hand. "I see it differently. We will stick to our standards. If any problems develop then I will stand up and take what's coming to me."

The others remained silent.

"That's very honorable of you to accept responsibility for your actions, sir," I responded, "but the fact of the matter is, if Leptien gets killed as a result of our straying from the unit standards, it's not going to make a bit of difference to him or his family how honorable you are. He will be dead and there will be no changing that."

In discussing the matter, I sensed the lieutenant did not intend to change his mind. He led the team and wanted to do things his way, even if it conflicted with the battalion's procedures.

The LT looked visibly upset and was through listening to my suggestions. "Lew, this is the way the team is going to be run. If you have any problems with that, then let me know. I will make some changes."

I did not respond to his ultimatum. He turned and walked out of the tent without saying another word. At that point, I knew I must do what I could to remain a member of Road Hunter One-Six. I had nothing against the lieutenant's enthusiasm but to ensure that all of us continued to return to camp after each mission, he would need some help. He would need a little guidance when the conditions became overly stressful.

The LT's remarks indicated his disapproval with my comments but my concerns stood with doing the right thing for the safety of the team.

CHAPTER 5

Dangerous Highway

A month slowly passed since the battalion became partial heir to the convoy missions of the 3/18th. As with all inheritance, we could not return it to the former holder. As the new proprietors, we quickly adopted the harsh ways of the previous caretakers in dealing with the extreme uneasiness of the road, not by choice but by pure necessity. Day after day, we held the trucks tight while staying alert for those seeking to disrupt the convoy or possibly take our lives.

Each of us changed, if only a little, from whom we were back in the real world. When in the camps, many were friendly and quick to laugh at one another's slight jokes and amusing comments. When out on the road, thoughts distorted to a completely different mindset. Anger, disgust, and frustration gushed from our souls. Resembling crazed demons, we yelled and cussed at each driver's every wrong move.

The powerful emotions stemmed from the fear we faced every day on the road, the treatment we received from the leadership, and the thoughts of leaving our families. For some, it developed into a detestation of the hajjis. They blamed the hajjis for their dreadful misery. From the drivers in the trucks, to the people along the roadside, they hated them all.

Some did not know how to handle the overwhelming stress of the convoys. Their mind's defense mechanism freed them from the harsh reality they faced. They disregarded the danger, although very real, and acted as though the escort missions were a casual drive through the countryside. Complaining that convoy security seemed boring, they slept as we traveled down the highway. Others fell asleep because of extreme fatigue. For them, the job became almost impossible to keep up with.

Pointing a weapon in anger at the hajjis became too easy.

The difficult to cross barriers of language and culture divided us. It took time and patience, which many had little of.

Upon discovering a problem, the initial response involved explaining the expectations in correcting it. When this failed, yelling and screaming quickly followed. Finally, in anger, a rifle barrel shoved into the hajjis' faces made the point clear. Those with less patience went straight to the barrel in the face.

This became the accepted method of problem solving. On occasion, when tempers flared between soldiers, I felt troubled as to where actions may soon lead. It would only be a matter of time before some would employ weapons to establish a point with one another or the coalition allies.

Our gun truck performed no differently than the others. During convoy missions, we yelled and screamed at the drivers when their trucks developed problems. As we traveled, Nelson pulled up next to the problem trucks and I tapped on Leptien's leg. He swung his SAW around in the turret and threatened the drivers to correct the difficulties. Over the course of time, Nelson became very good at waving the pickax handle out of the window with one hand and steering the humvee with the other.

After watching the 3/18th perform during the ride-along convoy mission, I immediately decided I would not threaten the drivers with the barrel of my weapon. It felt uncomfortable even to think of doing it. They were not the enemy. They were truck drivers. People attempting to earn money to send back home to their families.

One day, I decided that the abuse would stop. We were not going to shove the barrels of our weapons at the drivers any longer, at least not in our gun truck.

I yelled up at Leptien as we approached a problem truck, "Leptien, don't point the SAW at him. Don't point the SAW at the hajjis anymore."

Leptien stopped the rotation of the turret in mid-cycle and looked down under his arm at me. "Why?" he yelled back.

For the past month, we screamed and threatened the drivers with an uncontrollable rage. In following the rules set by our predecessors, we used the SAW as our main tool of persuasion. The leadership has never questioned it considering the practice an acceptable standard operating procedure. Now, I began changing the process, a method that had worked quite well for us. I fully understood why Leptien needed to know the reason behind this change.

I hesitated for a moment. I could have warned against an accidental discharge that would have killed the driver but as per the unit's standard operating procedure, we traveled with the SAW in Amber status, meaning a round never entered the chamber. The chance of a discharge did not exist.

I looked up at Leptien. "It scares the hajjis," I explained. "It scares the hell out of them. We can motivate them without it."

Nelson looked over the radio at me. Both stared as though I lost my mind.

I looked back up at Leptien. "I'm asking you not to point the SAW at the hajjis. It's wrong. We can talk about it when we hit the border."

Leptien smacked the butt of the SAW to the side and began waving and yelling at the drivers. They listened just as well without the intimidating threat of automatic fire.

When the trucks broke down on the road, I continued my soft approach. A smile and a nod went further than a yell and definitely further than a rifle barrel in the face. The drivers disliked the breakdowns along the road as much as we did. They usually worked quickly to fix their problems.

We waited in the MCT lot at Cedar for a push to Navistar. There were very few scheduled for the morning. If we did not receive a convoy in the lot, we would drive down to the holding area on the highway and locate a column of trucks to escort south.

"Keep your eyes open today, Lew," Boz nervously said as he read the Intel reports. "It says here, there was an IED and a sniper on MSR Tampa yesterday."

"Oh yeah, where were they located?"

"Does it matter?" Boz closed the report binder and placed it back inside the command humvee. "They could be anywhere today."

I nodded in agreement. "You know, you probably shouldn't be reading those reports. It will only upset you. It's best not to know those things, if it happens, it happens. That way you can concentrate on what you are doing and not worry yourself sick about being killed."

"Oh, if it is going to happen, believe me, Lew. I want to know. Yes, I want to know."

The LT broke up our early morning conversation informing us that no pushes remained in the MCT lot at Cedar. New orders requested we stop by the tactical operations center (TOC) and pick up a few riders before departing to the ROM to find a convoy with a destination of Kuwait.

The letters in the acronym ROM referred to refuel on the move, a location where convoys obtained fuel for their vehicles while continuing on their journey. Located four miles south of Camp Cedar, the ROM stood directly on MSR Tampa. The military blocked off a five-mile stretch of the main highway to utilize as a refueling point for convoys and routed the civilian traffic around.

The ROM highway consisted of six traffic lanes with three designated for northbound convoys and three for southbound. A median strip of sand and knee high steel posts separated the two sides. In the ROM, trucks lined both sides of each northbound and southbound lane. Military checkpoints on the north and south ends provided protection for the numerous supply trucks awaiting security escorts to accompany them to their next destination.

Garbage and human waste filled the ditches. A dozen plastic portable toilets staggered the median but most lay upon their sides, half wrecked with their doors torn off. When the drivers relieved themselves, they urinated next to the trucks or walked a few hundred feet off the highway and squatted in the ditch. Driving through the ROM, we commonly saw people defecating along the sides of the road. The drivers had no privacy but they did not seem to care.

The truck drivers originated from many foreign countries such as Pakistan, India, Nepal, Egypt, and the Philippines. When stopping in the ROM for the night, most of the drivers placed old blankets or cardboard upon the ground to cover the urine stained pavement so they could lie down. Some became good friends during their travels and sought one another's company when their convoys stopped for the night. They unpacked small cook stoves from the compartments mounted underneath their trucks and prepared hot meals for one another.

In the dark of night, the ROM took on a completely different life than during the daylight hours. The local Iraqis crept into its confines and sold cigarettes, alcohol, and drugs to the drivers. Many openly practiced their homosexuality. Fights broke out with those wanting to settle old scores from the road. Drivers lined their bobtails in a row and raced them on small, open stretches of the roadway. The drivers who did not partake in the wild events of the nightlife, climbed into the cabs of their trucks and hid from the iniquitous activity.

The two riders we retrieved from the TOC were part of the First Battalion of the 201st Field Artillery Brigade, a National Guard unit out of West Virginia. The 1/201st, one of our sister battalions of the brigade, recently arrived in Iraq. Also tasked with convoy security missions, they established escort teams with the radio call sign of Bulldog. Today, we provided the Bulldog members their first taste of the road.

We traveled down MSR Tampa in route to Navistar with a convoy of assorted third country national (TCN) trucks that we collected from the ROM. Talkative and friendly, both riders shared stories of their pre-deployment, which sounded very familiar to our own experiences. One of them served some time on active duty with the regular army and before deployment entered the National Guard to complete his enlistment on a split program. Not expecting to return to active duty or deploy to Iraq, he told of how he probably would have fared much better had he stayed with the regular army. They might not have sent him there.

I began picking up radio traffic from the two Road Hunter teams following directly behind us. They discussed whether they were capable of passing our convoy or if they should stay in position. We traveled at a good speed but their conversation indicated they might be moving slightly faster.

Before making a decision to pass another convoy, the convoy commander customarily contacted the forward convoy and received permission before making an attempt. A courtesy not always followed. Egos tended to get in the way of common sense. I glanced at my side mirror and spotted Road Hunter Two within one hundred meters of our tail putting our gun truck in a dangerous position. I signaled to Nelson to plan an escape route and be ready to move.

The trucks in the convoy traveled a close bumper to bumper

at speeds in excess of sixty miles per hour, with three traffic lanes to occupy if needed. If a problem developed with one of the trucks, all the lanes quickly filled with trailers swerving to avoid a collision with those in front of them. In a situation such as that, Nelson would hit the brakes, stopping us just short of the convoy trucks immediately ahead of us.

Complications arose when a convoy traveled directly on our heels. If they held at least a half mile behind us, there would be no concerns. At sixty miles per hour, they could safely slow their thirty semi trucks enough to come to a complete stop before making contact with our convoy.

One hundred meters proved a little more difficult to envision a positive outcome. The convoy following us would not have enough room to stop if a problem occurred with one of the trucks traveling in our convoy. In a split second, we would be squashed like road kill by the semi trucks following on our tail.

"Man, they're really close," I shouted over to Nelson.

He looked at me with a big smile on his face and gave the thumbs up. "I got it covered, Lew."

Nelson drove exceptionally well. He appreciated fast cars and could repair just about everything that might go wrong with them. He possessed that natural ability to understand anything mechanical. The humvees proved little if any additional challenge. He handled the gun truck like an outlaw on the back roads.

Suddenly, a cloud of blue smoke appeared when the seventh truck up from the rear locked its brakes and brought all trucks following to a screeching halt.

Nelson quickly jerked the steering wheel to the left, pulling us out of the center traffic lane, through the left lane, and stopped us on the shoulder next to the median strip and behind our trucks. The lead gun truck from Road Hunter Two, traveling in the left lane, pulled sharp right just narrowly missing our gun truck and taking the center lane we previously occupied. The deafening rumble of the trucks sounded like a freight train passing as their convoy followed them one by one around us.

I reached for the radio handset. "One-Six, One-Six Alpha, this is One-Six Bravo. Pull the convoy over. We have a truck stopped on the left-hand side of the road. Over."

Road Hunters Two and Eight jammed the radio with traffic describing the near miss. With the unnecessary chatter walking on my radio transmissions, my attempts to contact our team miserably failed.

"Break! Break! Break!" I transmitted over the radio once more to clear the traffic. It did no good. They ignored me and continued with their light banter.

In order to get through to the team, I would need to walk on their radio conversation, otherwise, the rest of the convoy would continue without us. I keyed the handset. "Break, Break, Break. One-Six, One-Six Alpha, this is One-Six Bravo. Pull the convoy over. We have a truck stopped on the side of the road. Over."

With the passing convoy moving dangerously close to the passenger side of the humvee, Nelson and a 201st soldier in the backseat opened the doors on the driver's side to check on the truck that stopped ahead of us. Just as suddenly as it stopped, the truck charged ahead with the other six trailing closely behind. The guys jumped back into the humvee and slammed their doors. Nelson shifted the transmission into gear and we darted off after them.

Ping. "One-Six Bravo, this is One-Six Alpha. Do we need to stop the convoy? Over."

On a dead run, the trucks raced as fast as they could move to join up with our convoy. We had no way of slowing them down. Nelson pushed the humvee to top speed cruising in the left lane in an effort to catch the small detachment of seven trucks. Directly to our right sprinted team two's convoy in the center lane. Their lead gun truck traveled ahead of us next to our main convoy's last truck.

I keyed the handset. "One-Six Alpha, this is One-Six Bravo. Negative. Maintain your present speed. The trucks are moving and we will be joining the convoy momentarily. Over."

Ping. "One-Six Alpha. Roger. Out."

The radio quickly sounded. Ping. "One-Six, this is Road Hunter Two. You have a huge gap in your convoy. You need to slow down to fix that gap and allow us to pass. Over."

A long hesitation engulfed the radio as we waited for the LT to respond. The command vehicle may have experienced radio problems so Hanson answered the call.

Ping. "Two, this is One-Six Alpha. This is not your convoy.

One-Six Bravo is in the position to make that determination. One-Six Bravo, what is your call? Over."

From prior radio traffic, I knew of team two's aggressiveness in wanting to pass us from the beginning of their mission. Now, our gun truck began rounding a long curve in the highway and I could not identify the last truck in the main convoy. Team two occupied the middle lane making it impossible to determine which of the trucks belonged to them and which actually belonged to us.

The unintended pass quickly turned into a potentially dangerous mess. With safety a major concern, allowing them to pass so they could move clear of our convoy seemed to be the only alternative.

"One-Six Alpha, this is One-Six Bravo. Slow it down five to ten miles per hour and allow team two to pass. Over."

Ping. "This is One-Six Alpha. Slowing down five to ten miles per hour. Roger. Out."

The main convoy body began slowing down but our seven-truck detachment continued accelerating to catch them. We could not contact the truck drivers and inform them to slow. Our gun truck, in following, caught team two's command humvee, which passed us earlier. In an attempt to join the main convoy, the little detachment began passing team two's command vehicle along with the other trucks in their convoy.

Ping. "One-Six Alpha, this is Road Hunter Two. Over."

Ping. "This is One-Six Alpha. Over."

Ping. "You're not supposed to speed up when a convoy is passing. You need to slow down so we can complete this pass. Over."

Ping. "This is One-Six Alpha. We have slowed down. Over."

Ping. "How can you be slowing down when all your vehicles are passing us?" he screamed.

From team two's perspective, our convoy did not slow down. As they watched the detachment race by, it looked as though our convoy actually increased speed.

Civilian traffic began merging with the trucks of both convoys. The truck drivers commenced changing lanes to maneuver around them and maintain the convoy speed. All three lanes quickly filled with convoy trucks, trailers, cars, small pickups, old Suburbans, and our two military humvees traveling bumper to bumper at sixty-five miles per hour. At that point, the two convoys no longer existed. The confusion forced everyone to fend for themselves.

Suddenly, a bobtail locked up its brakes directly in front of us. In order to avoid a collision with one of the other trucks, the bobtail driver cranked his steering wheel causing his rear end to slide around. Blue smoke instantly filled the air. The smell of burning brake drums and tires quickly followed. With his truck stopped perpendicular to the flow of traffic, he hurriedly crossed the lanes and veered off the road into the sand filled ditch to avoid being broadsided.

Without hesitation, Nelson jumped on the brakes of the humvee. We swerved left then right just nearly missing a semitrailer. I could taste the diesel exhaust in my mouth as team two's convoy trucks roared around us. Our gun truck, a bobtail from the small detachment, and team two's command vehicle along with half of their convoy came to a sudden stop.

Adrenaline continued pumping wildly as the sand and dust gradually settled onto the still highway.

I picked up the radio handset. "One-Six, One-Six Alpha, this is One-Six Bravo. Stop the convoy. We have a bobtail in the ditch. Over."

I passed the radio handset to Nelson and Leptien to confirm contact with the team as I stepped out of the humvee to survey the damage. The bobtail came to rest in a large pile of soft sand. The truck's duals produced a cloud of sand as the bobtail driver worked frantically to free his truck.

Team two's command humvee sat idling on the right-hand side of the road a short distance to the rear of the gun truck. Half of their convoy, bottlenecking the highway, sat motionless behind them. Iraqi civilians, unfortunate to be included in the chaos, stared at us through the open windows of their stranded vehicles.

The lieutenant in charge of Road Hunter Two strutted down the ditch with his 9mm pistol drawn. He pointed it at the hajji driver sitting in the bobtail who continued his effort to free his truck from the sand. The lieutenant's driver remained up on the highway next to their command humvee observing the massive confusion.

It puzzled me as to why they remained and did not leave with their convoy. Could this be their bobtail? All of them looked an identical white in color. I shouted over to the lieutenant, "is this your bobtail or ours!"

"It's yours!" both he and his driver concurred.

The lieutenant began yelling at the hajjis while waving his weapon at them. Sand continued to fly as the bobtail's dual tires spun forward then reversed. Two other drivers from a bobtail parked on the road came running down to assist.

The lieutenant looked at me and shouted, "We are not going to waste a lot of time trying to get this vehicle out."

His bizarre statement surprised me. He held no authority over this convoy or this bobtail. I turned toward my gun truck and yelled, "Leptien, did we make contact with the LT?"

"Yeah, they have the convoy pulled over a ways down the highway. They are waiting for us."

I turned back toward the lieutenant and yelled, "You need to get your convoy moving. The highway is becoming too congested and someone is going to get killed. We'll stay here and take care of the bobtail."

He looked at me, hesitated, and returned his pistol to its holster. Turning around, he stepped back up the incline. Thirty seconds later his convoy began moving out which gradually cleared the road for traffic to continue.

With the extreme softness of the sand, the remaining bobtail driver could not guide his truck down from the highway to assist. I instructed Nelson to maneuver the gun truck through the ditch and attempt to pull the bobtail out. Attaching chains to the humvee, the drivers heaved them across the sand and connected them to the bobtail. In less than five minutes, we returned to the highway and once again raced to join the convoy.

Our riders from the 201st received more than they bargained for during the ride-along convoy mission. A flat tire or engine trouble would have been good convoy experience for the first time on the road. Instead, they witnessed firsthand how events could quickly escalate into a dangerous situation. They learned something valuable to share with their Bulldog teammates. How it felt coming close to dying in a humvee accident, twice in one day.

We eventually pulled into Safwan while following behind the convoy. The trucks slowly crawled along as they moved to cross the border into Kuwait. Had we not let the two convoys that followed behind us pass, we could have been waiting at the MCT lot or possibly picking up a convoy for the return trip. Now, we sat at the end of a long line and it would be some time before we left.

The 201st sergeant occupying the seat directly behind me spotted a mentally handicapped young man sitting on a berm next to the side of the road. A boy in his early teens, he usually sat in the same area smiling, waving, and talking to the traffic as it passed him.

I overheard the sergeant quietly conversing with himself. "Oh, you poor boy. I feel so sorry for you. If I could help you, I would. I hope someone can help you. I feel so sorry for you…"

From the turret, Leptien glanced down into the backseat and watched him wipe tears from his eyes.

Sadly, some of us may have unintentionally dulled our senses for compassion. We became numb as we continually witnessed the daily pain and suffering these people endured. Constant pressure, excessive speed, inept drivers, and begging kids blended into a reoccurring collage of a day on the road.

We ended the mission at the border where we released the convoy. After clearing weapons, we removed our body armor and proceeded to the military fuel point. The military did not require wearing of the body armor when driving on the roads in Kuwait. Freedom from the extra weight on our shoulders provided a great relief. The breeze blowing through the windows of the humvee helped dry the sweat saturated throughout our DCUs. In the camps, all recognized those who wore body armor on a regular basis. They displayed the signature markings of white salt stains streaked across their uniforms.

We pulled into the fuel line and showed the 201st the process to obtain diesel fuel for the humvees. The fuel point consisted of an organized line of fuel hoses connected to a large bladder filled with diesel fuel. Civilian contractors maintained the responsibility for the operation of the fuel line. Most came from a military background serving at least a few years in one of the branches. We finished refueling and left to join the team at the MCT lot.

A few days prior, we had an interesting conversation with one of the fuel point contractors. As I began to refuel the gun truck, he approached us with his clipboard. "How are things going today, boys?"

"Same old crap, different day," Nelson replied as he signed the fuel sheet.

He talked with us about the heat, sand, and present happenings with the war.

"I suppose you will make enough money here to retire when you get back home." Nelson joked with him.

"Oh, no man, its good money but I'm planning on retiring with the help of the Iraqi dinar."

"The dinar? How is that?"

"I have a friend who exchanges dollars for dinar at the bank here in Kuwait. Currently the exchange rate is a little over 1,400 dinar for every dollar. When he makes a trip to the bank, I give him $100 to pick up dinar for me."

"Isn't that kind of risky?" Nelson asked.

"Yeah, it's all speculation. Once the Iraqi government straightens itself out, the exchange rate should go back to thirty-three cents as before the war. For every $100, I lay down now, I should see close to $50,000 down the road. Right now, my $2,200 investment will equal a million dollars if the exchange rate goes to where it should."

A different civilian contractor assisted us with fuel today. The retirement activities update will have to wait for another time. We drove to the MCT lot and found the team waiting for a push north to Camp Cedar.

That evening, the LT approached me and asked if I would write a report pertaining to the incident on the road with Road Hunter Two. He requested it as part of an after action review to present at a meeting in defending our position. With the leadership examining the occurrence, I looked forward to the possibility of setting some new convoy safety guidelines.

I wrote the report. It changed nothing. At the most, it gave those who remained in the camp an eye-opening snapshot of the daily hazards we encountered during convoy security missions.

CHAPTER 6

The Towers

A number of guard towers provided security for the camp while positioned around the perimeter of Cedar. The battalion assumed responsibility for two of the towers, tower five and tower seven. The towers stood quietly on the desolate far western edge of the camp, over a mile from the living area. With many in the unit unwilling to man the towers, the battalion tasked the Road Hunter teams with this monotonous chore.

After chasing trucks for days on end down MSR Tampa, the leadership offered us a short respite from the road and instructed us to rotate through tower duty shifts. Moss and I secured tower five or Tango Five as the camp security referred to it. Nelson and Boswell manned Tango Seven.

Tango Five sat secluded in the northwest corner of the camp. With the use of the tower binoculars, we readily identified Tango Four to the east and the vague resemblance of Tango Seven to the south. Tango Six did not exist. At one time, they may have planned for a tower in between five and seven but for manpower reasons decided against it.

The tower's cream-colored steel platform projected ten feet off the ground furnishing an elevated view over the top of the berm. Hardened with sandbags to offer extra protection, its half walls provided cover from small arms fire and shrapnel.

Staff Sergeant Kligel, the sergeant of the guard (SOG), held responsibility for guard tower security of the camp. He received direction from his unit, the 197th Field Artillery Brigade, a National Guard unit out of New Hampshire whose command the battalion fell under.

Tower duty, as always, began with an inspection.

"Fall in!" Kligel shouted.

63

Over a dozen soldiers, pulled from various units throughout the camp, formed into two ranks as he counted heads checking the presence of all those required to report for tower duty.

"You." He pointed to one of the soldiers standing in the ranks. "When you fall in at attention, shoulder your weapon and always point your barrel upward."

The soldier displayed a confused expression. "Our sergeants tolt us ta always keep it pointed at the ground so is no one gets kilt."

"I know what your unit said but this is tower duty," Kligel patiently explained. "We'll have an inspection of arms before we leave for the towers. I can't check your weapon if it's slung across your back and pointing down."

Always having a few new soldiers showing up for tower duty, we heard this routine many times before.

Kligel walked down the rows checking everyone's weapon, identification tags, and military I.D. cards. He rapped his bare knuckles against our body armor to see if anyone purposely removed the heavy small arms protective insert (SAPI) plates. Looking through some of the soldiers' personal bags, he suspiciously searched for magazines, books, and CD/DVD players, all of which the brigade considered banned from the towers. Religious reading material and an am/fm radio remained the only items allowed.

A quick briefing provided us with updated information relating to camp security, afterward, we loaded into the back of two humvees for transportation to the towers.

Kligel reported nothing significant during the briefing, just the usual warnings of snakes, rats, and rabid dogs around the tower bases.

Huge ruts filled the dirt roads leading to the towers, which furnished a jarring, uncomfortable ride. As we sat in the back of the open box humvee, a thick layer of dust quickly covered every inch of our bodies. We squinted our eyes and made small talk trying to avoid inhaling too much of the suffocating, fine powder.

Kligel stopped the humvee at each tower along the route exchanging guards and supplying ice for the plastic tower coolers. The faces became familiar over time and we often joked about the aspects of tower duty.

For some, this became their full-time job. They were tower

guards. The SOG transported them to the towers every day where they continually stared at the open desert in front of them for hours upon end. They searched for anything out of the ordinary, anything posing a possible threat. An important job, it symbolized the presence of security protecting the camp. On occasion, something unusual happened which livened the day with a sense of excitement but for the most part it proved a boring, miserable, and thankless job.

While on duty, we scanned the entire area within the range of our binoculars. To the west lay a massive berm with MSR Tampa located directly on the opposite side. To the north stretched a small road that ran parallel to the boundaries of the camp. Sparse civilian traffic traveled on the road during the daylight hours. Most of the vehicles moved along the road destined for the few mud houses scattered on the opposite side. A random herder occasionally wandered into the area moving his sheep in search of edible vegetation. The Euphrates River, not visible from our tower, flowed three to four miles to the north of the camp.

Each tower accommodated two radios. The tower-mounted radio provided contact with Hellfighter Base, which controlled security for the camp. A smaller hand-held fm radio maintained an informal contact with the sergeant of the guard and the other guard towers.

As the sky grew dark, we observed small sparkles of light illuminate across the landscape as the local Iraqis prepared their homes for the evening.

Moss reached down into the red plastic cooler. He searched through the ice and pulled out a bottle of water.

"They're starting to get a little cold. Do you want one, Lew?"

"Sounds good, warm or cold, it will do."

Water drained off the bottle's side and splashed across the tower floor as he handed it to me.

"I hope things stay as quiet as they are right now," Moss said as he reached back into the cooler and found one for himself.

As we gazed out and around the tower area, we talked of things happening back home. How our families firmly managed in our absence and how we missed them. We talked of what we would be doing when normally back home at this time of year, and of course, we speculated as to when we would be leaving. We discussed the politics of the unit, whom they picked for promotion and who missed out. We shared stories of Road Hunter missions and talked of those trying to get off the Road Hunter teams and those who may be stuck joining them.

As the daylight left us, we did less talking and more listening to our surroundings. The silence suddenly broke with the sounding of the tower radio. Ping. "Hellfighter Base, this is Big Dog South. Over."

Ping. "This is Hellfighter Base. Over."

Ping. "We have a suspicious looking object here in the ROM, a possible IED."

Ping. "What does it look like? Do you have a description?"

Ping. "It is a truck battery that has been sitting here for the past three to four days. It's recently been moved and now has wires strung to a tire and also wires attached and connected to a light bulb."

Ping. "What is the location of the IED?"

Ping. "Let's see, we're about a mile north of the south ROM gate. It's about one hundred meters off the road."

Ping. "Do you have a grid coordinate on that?"

A long hesitation silenced the radio.

Ping. "Hellfighter Base, this is Big Dog South. Negative on the grid coordinate. Nobody here has a GPS (global positioning system). I can pull a grid coordinate off of the map if you like."

Ping. "No, that won't be accurate enough for the IED form. We're sending a humvee down to the ROM with a GPS."

Ping. "Roger. Out."

Moss and I discussed the presence of the huge amount of garbage scattered throughout the ROM. It would not be difficult for someone to place an IED anywhere out there and not have it discovered.

The hand-held radio sounded. "SOG, this is Tango Three. Over."

"This is SOG. Over," Kligel answered.

"This is Tango Three. Would you come back here? I want to make a citizens arrest."

"A citizen's arrest, why is that?" Kligel asked.

"When you drove by our tower, you threw some trash out

onto the ground. I want to make a citizens arrest for littering."

"It's OK to throw it on the ground," Kligel laughed. "This whole country is a trash can."

"Negative," the tower responded, "this whole country is a shit hole."

Moss and I laughed at their conversation over the hand-held radio. In a sad way, they were not far from the truth.

The tower radio sounded again. Ping. "Hellfighter Base, this is Big Dog South. Over."

Ping. "This is Hellfighter Base. Over."

Ping. "We've got those coordinates for you. Prepare to copy."

Ping. "Go ahead."

The security in the ROM listed a series of numbers over the radio. Hellfighter Base disagreed with the accuracy of the coordinates. They filled the next five minutes discussing the use of the GPS until finally both agreed upon a grid coordinate they felt looked close enough.

Ping. "Big Dog South, this is Hellfighter Base. Did the EOD (explosive ordinance disposal) show up with the IED robot?"

Ping. "Roger. He's here right now. They said this robot is not going to work very well so they sent for another from Tallil."

Ping. "The one you have won't work?"

Ping. "Roger. It's not the right type they need. Right now they're chasing camel spiders with it."

Ping. "Let me know when the other IED robot arrives."

Ping. "Roger. Out."

The radio traffic continued off and on throughout the shift. Eventually they decided to destroy the suspected IED with a direct hit from a shotgun blast.

We heard small arms fire in the distance created by the feuding families living in the area. They preferred to shoot at one another during the early evening hours. At times, they lit up the night sky with tracer rounds. We searched the area with the night vision goggles but did not see anything of significance to report.

Near the end of the shift, we spotted the headlights of a humvee traveling down the tower guard path. Our relief arrived to replace us. As the humvee pulled up to the tower, Sergeant Glen Geditz stepped out. A member of the battalion, he performed the SOG duties for the night shift. Our replacements took over and we traveled back to the tents to get some sleep. Tomorrow would quickly furnish another day of tower duty.

The next day, Nelson, Leptien, and I walked to the chow hall with Hanson to eat a hot meal before reporting for tower duty. The alternative consisted of an MRE in the tower. With adequate opportunity to eat MREs on the road, we ate hot meals when the chance provided. The dining facility bustled with the noon meal. We timed our arrival to coincide with the last few people of the initial long line entering the chow hall. That way, we would not have to wait long, if at all.

We picked up Styrofoam plates and plastic silverware stacked by the doorway then walked through the serving line pointing at the various cuisines we wanted to eat. The hajji servers closely watched our movements in order to dish the correct foods onto the plates. The door suddenly opened and closed behind us as the sergeant major walked in.

"Oh no," Hanson mumbled as he left the line and disappeared into the busy dining facility with a half-empty plate.

"Sergeant Lewandowski, does he work for you?" the sergeant major asked as he pointed to Hanson before losing sight of him in the crowd.

Not scheduled for tower duty, Hanson had not shaven in the past few days but the sergeant major singled him out for a different reason. He did not approve of the scope on Hanson's M-16 rifle.

Some of the guys brought their own personal riflescopes along with them to Iraq. It helped with the accuracy for single shots if needed. For some reason, the sergeant major felt not everyone should use a scope with their rifle. A rule came down allowing only those, who shot a perfect forty out of forty targets during their last M-16 qualification, the privilege to use a scope on their rifles.

Hanson has qualified in the past shooting forty out of forty targets but for some odd reason during our last qualification, he did not hit as many silhouettes as he usually does. I normally shoot Expert as well but experienced the same problem. They just would not fall down. Hanson felt more comfortable with the scope on his weapon than without it so he left it attached.

"Negative, sergeant major," I answered. "He doesn't work for me. He's a staff sergeant. He outranks me."

I nodded toward Nelson and Leptien. "These two work *with* me though."

Nelson and Leptien remained silent and continued through the line avoiding becoming part of the conversation.

I could sense the sergeant major had hoped to hear otherwise. Since our deployment, I have noticed many immediately jumped on a man if he screwed up and hesitated to praise him if he did well. Unless you were one of the few favorites in the unit, they were going to jump on you and often. He did not say another word as he picked up his plate and utensils, and followed us through the chow line.

We returned to the tent to prepare for tower duty and found Boz sitting comfortably in a chair and waiting for us. Upset with the eight-hour tower guard shifts, he wanted to return to the two four-hour shifts we previously worked.

The battalion's towers remained the only two towers on the camp that worked in four-hour shifts. The other towers worked eight or twelve-hour shifts. The guys became discouraged pulling tower duty for four hours only to return later to finish another four-hour shift. When through with the first shift, they found it difficult to become relaxed knowing they would return in a few hours to finish another shift. They felt it better to complete it in one eight-hour shift. Besides, it took an extra hour's worth of time each shift to prepare with inspections and travel time to and from the tower. We spoke with the battalion leadership about this but they refused to change the shift lengths.

The guys on tower duty took it upon themselves and organized a plan to work one eight-hour shift instead of the two four-hour shifts. The SOG favored the eight-hour shift, which would eliminate an extra inspection and trip to the towers for him. It worked very well with the exception of one person. Boz did not buy into the idea.

We picked up Moss as we left for the TOC to report for tower duty. Boz still felt upset he worked an eight-hour shift during the previous day. He did not look forward to doing it again.

"Boz, why don't you want to do the eight-hour shifts?" Moss asked.

"It gets too hot out there. I can't stand out there in the heat for eight hours," Boz explained.

"How about the night shift?" Moss continued. "It's not as hot at night. You shouldn't have any problems with the heat then."

"No, that won't work either. I can't stay focused out there for eight hours. Four hours is just right for me."

"It works out for everyone else but you. Would you just please try it for one more shift?" Moss asked. "That's all we're asking. Give it another try?"

"OK," Boz agreed, "I'll do one more eight-hour shift. After that, we are going back to the four-hour shifts. If not, I'll have to talk to the LT. He'll make you go back."

He may not have been physically or mentally capable of performing tower duty for eight hours straight. Like many of the others, he knew his own limitations and did what he needed to protect his health and wellbeing.

He shared with me how the commander told him to travel up north with one of the batteries that received a new mission providing security for a captured enemy ammunition site. Boz can be outspoken at times on various matters, which upsets some in the leadership. They thought this provided a good excuse to lose him for a while. With one of his military vocations being that of a cook, they decided he should accompany the battery to help prepare meals. He did not know if he could handle it so he threatened to urinate in the food if they sent him. They dropped their plans and let him stay.

Kligel briefed us on information he received from new intelligence reports. Along with the usual snake and rat items, he informed us of the nerve agent, Tabun, a chemical used during the eight-year Iran-Iraq war of the 1980s. He explained how intelligence suggested it might now pose a threat.

Tabun? We had not heard this through our unit's chain of command. Then again, we did not hear much at all through our chain. At times, we found it difficult to tell the accuracy of information. Without a steady reliable source, you could only listen to the communications put out and then analyze it as time went on. Kligel explained some of the effects of the nerve agent and told us what to look for. We climbed into the back of the humvee and left for the towers.

After leaving Nelson and Boz at Tango Seven, Kligel dropped Moss and I once more at five. As always, the dusty ride did not disappoint us. We knocked away the heavy coating from our equipment and manned the tower.

Kligel pulled away with the humvee full of soldiers and attempted to drive through a deep mud hole next to the tower. The rains had stopped falling many weeks ago and this seemed to be the only remaining mud hole left in the camp. As he slowly crept through the water, the humvee became stuck in its center. Amused at the challenge, Kligel rapidly worked the transmission, rocking the vehicle back and forth. He and the tower guards exploded with laughter as the mud flew through the air. By the time Kligel broke free from the hole, the spinning wheels covered the humvee and its occupants with the thick muck. We heard the laughter continue as they drove on to the next tower.

We spent the remaining hours of daylight swatting flies and sweating. As the sun slowly sat over the berm to the west, the stars began to brighten one by one in the late evening sky. With only the occasional rumble of a lone vehicle traveling on MSR Tampa to break the silence, it sounded peaceful being in the towers and away from the constant whine produced by the generators at the heart of the camp.

I gazed at the dark sky through the night vision goggles. Billions of stars, invisible to the naked eye, filled the green tinted eyepiece. Through the goggles, the universe became as brilliant as the lights of a large city in the night.

The sky lit up directly behind us with green star cluster bursts followed by illumination parachutes.

"Someone's having fun in the ROM tonight," I told Moss as we watched the sky brighten.

"Nelson and Boz will call that one in," Moss speculated. "The ROM is located just a few miles south of their tower."

At that moment, we heard Nelson's voice over the tower radio. Ping. "Hellfighter Base, this is Tango Seven. Over."

Ping. "This is Hellfighter Base. Over."

Ping. "We are observing green star clusters over the ROM. Over."

Ping. "Roger. They are expending some outdated flares."

Ping. "This is Tango Seven. Roger. Out."

We stood silently watching as a variety of flares trailed into the air and painted the night sky with a vivid display of pyrotechnics.

Later that evening, Hellfighter Base informed the towers of a controlled burn scheduled to take place at the front gates of Cedar. During the afternoon, a fuel tanker from one of the convoys developed a massive leak as it approached the front gate. The tanker completely drained its contents filling one of the outer ditches with diesel fuel. Setting fire to the ditches during the evening became the best method to remove the fuel.

The front gate stood a few miles away from our position but we could easily see the fire's flames dancing high into the night sky. The fuel burned for some time and provided another spectacular show.

As the fire slowly died, the radio sounded. Ping. "Hellfighter Base, this is Big Dog South. Over."

Ping. "This is Hellfighter Base. Over."

Ping. "We had a local national show up at the gate with a gunshot wound. It looks like he might need more attention than we can provide."

Ping. "What's his current condition?"

Ping. "He has a gunshot wound to the leg and he has been cut up and beaten pretty bad. The combat lifesaver has him on an IV"

Ping. "We'll have some medics escorted down to your location. It sounds like they may want to transport him directly to Tallil."

Ping. "Big Dog South. Roger. Out."

Moss shook his head. "The Ali Baba are busy tonight."

I nodded in agreement.

We scanned the area around the tower and watched through the night vision goggles as a few wild animals crossed through the wire. They foraged for food at the base of the tower where in the daylight a scattering of garbage signified others tried feeding them as well. While the animals ate the small portions of leftover MREs, we made slight noises, watching them scamper away to return later for more.

The shift ended and the SOG transported us back to the tent

city on the dark and dusty path. We were through with tower duty for another week.

The next day we drew the gun trucks from the motor pool and prepared to leave the front gates. The team took its turn in escorting the interpreter to the ROM. While there, he interpreted the convoy briefings to the drivers as to the expectations for the next day's convoys. A few local Iraqis provided the interpreting services to the military as needed. They lived nearby with family members transporting them to the gates of Tallil where we retrieved them.

Waiting by the gates, we sat watching as the interpreter arrived in a small, white car. Abrahiem, our interpreter for the day, had provided interpreting services since the arrival of the coalition forces at the beginning of the war. Carrying a handful of booklets containing Iraqi stamps and currency that he assembled for sale, he passed them around for the guys to examine which some quickly purchased. He became quite a businessman during the past year. Knowing the value of a U.S. dollar, he profited on his access to soldiers who willingly parted with them.

We traveled the ten-mile stretch of road to the ROM where trucks lined both sides of the highway and waited for escorts to Navistar. Some of the drivers rested in their vehicles with their doors wide open attempting to cool themselves with the slight afternoon breeze while others sat or slept on cardboard placed upon the pavement. Many gathered in small groups around worn, wooden stools they substituted for tables. Most had not bathed or seen a razor in several days. After transporting supplies to various camps throughout the country, the drivers waited patiently at this last stop before returning to Kuwait.

Before leaving with a security escort in the morning, the drivers were required to attend a convoy briefing. The briefing explained the specifics of the convoy such as the speed, distance of the intervals between the trucks, procedures in case of a breakdown, and so forth.

We drove up and down the ROM informing the drivers of the meeting. With the extreme heat of the afternoon, they were not motivated at all, as they slowly wandered to the command vehicle. Those who previously heard the information refused to attend and remained by their trucks. They knew the briefing's scripted contents would not change.

Some of the drivers sat waiting in the ROM for the past few days and felt eager to leave. Paperwork delays or mechanical problems kept them from departing with previous military escorts.

Abrahiem interpreted in Arabic as the LT gave his briefing to the group. Some questioned the convoy speed. Why did the guidelines state to drive no faster than fifty miles per hour during the briefings, but on the road expectations changed to travel at speeds in excess of sixty miles per hour? The LT laughed and nodded his head in agreement without giving an answer to their questions.

Some complained about the distribution of food and water. They were hungry and thirsty. Many had not eaten food or drank water all day. The LT explained they should wait for the movement control team for this. The MCT people would accommodate their needs.

I glanced up and down the ROM. It appeared as though the MCT people had already left for the day. We carried additional supplies so I offered a suggestion.

"LT, we have extra MREs and water in the back of the humvees. Why don't we give these people something to eat and drink?"

"No, it's not our problem," the LT began explaining. "The MCT will take care of them. They should be able to get what they need from the movement control people."

He knew as well as I did, the MCT were no longer there and the drivers would not receive a thing until the next morning.

"Is there someone who we could contact to take care of the drivers?" I questioned him.

The LT looked at me. I could tell by the way he hesitated that he did not want to deal with the problem.

"Yeah, I'll call to see if someone could come down and help."

We left the ROM and returned to Cedar. Scotting reminded the LT about contacting someone regarding food and water but the LT refused to notify anyone. He felt the responsibility lay with the MCT to handle the problem.

Hearing of this later, I became upset and found it hard to understand the reasoning behind the inaction. Previously there with food and water, we could have easily provided for those people. Our supplies consist of the exact same rations the MCT furnished. Why would anyone refuse to help the drivers?

Later that evening, Top, the unit's first sergeant, approached me and asked if I would visit with him and the captain. They needed to discuss an important issue with me.

I could not think of anything they would need to talk about. If not related to the food and water incident earlier in the day, there existed no other concerns that I knew of.

After a late meal, I walked over to see the captain and the first sergeant. Both sat at makeshift desks assembled in the rear of their tent. Assorted boxes and paperwork sat piled randomly on the floor. I noticed the bright colored labels of powdered drink mixes and snacks packed in some of the boxes—care packages sent to the troops from people back home.

They started with the usual small talk. How each of us managed to get along in Iraq. I sensed a slight uneasiness in the conversation, when they quickly pressed to the point.

"Um, well, Lew, some things have changed and we are going to have to put you in the specialist's cook spot," the captain said as he cleared his throat.

"Yeah," he continued, "you're going to have to be reduced from a sergeant to a specialist."

This surprised me. I exceeded the standards at the noncommissioned officers course and occupied my sergeant's position for some time now.

"Why would I need to take the specialist spot, sir?" I asked. "You already have people who have been through the school and well-qualified to fill that cook position."

The captain and Top exchanged brief looks. Something did not seem right.

"Well," Top continued, "you aren't fully qualified for the fire direction computer position you are presently in. They haven't approved your clearance yet so you can't hold the position any longer. We have to move you to the cook position. I wish there was something we could do about it but there isn't."

A full-time national guardsman, Top knew the ins and outs of the system. If a solution existed that allowed me to retain my stripes, he would know of it. He helped many others advance in their military careers.

Still, the reduction did not sound right. "Are you sure about this, Top? Before leaving home station, you said I would not have any problems with this. You told me, I had over a year to become qualified and it would not concern this deployment at all. Why has this all of a sudden changed now?"

"It was that way back then in the armory but things have changed here," the captain answered. "There is nothing we can do about it now. I wish there was. Yeah, it sucks, but we have to reduce you to a specialist."

The captain presented me with a counseling statement, prepared in advance and ready for my signature. The document detailed my reduction in rank to a specialist and my resigning of the computer position to become a cook. I found the whole matter difficult to understand. I held the position of a field artillery computer operator during my initial enlistment twenty years ago and again accepted the same position upon returning to the guard unit. I enjoyed performing the job and have always done very well with it. Now, in the middle of a war in Iraq, they were reducing me to a specialist and placing me in a cook's position. Why? We have had nothing to do with field artillery operations on this deployment. Even the cooks did not help in the kitchens. Some performed convoy security operations along with the rest of us.

"Now, this won't change your position at all on the gun truck," the captain explained. "You will still do convoy security as you have been doing. You know as well as we do that if you don't agree with this, you could stretch this out for a couple of months if you wanted to. You would only be delaying the inevitable though."

Top continued where the captain left off, "If you want to, you have thirty days to request a reduction board to look into the matter. Once the reduction board is formed, it could take another thirty days to wrap it up. They would just conclude that you should be reduced. Yeah, you would only be delaying the inevitable."

"Yeah, yeah, it sucks." The captain handed me a pen. "There is nothing we can do about it though."

As far as the process went, it did not matter if I signed the statement or not. According to their explanation, no further options existed, so I signed. I thought of how it would have a negative impact upon my pay but I worried more of losing my rank as a sergeant. I have been a noncommissioned officer for many years now and felt proud of it. In less than thirty days, I would become a specialist. I left their tent thinking of how somewhere, someone may have put out incorrect information and I would be penalized with their mistake. The Judge Advocate General (JAG) lawyer at the brigade headquarters might be my only hope for a chance to clear this up.

The captain and Top did all they could to help. They did not want to see me lose my stripes. The JAG would certainly know if a mistake existed somewhere up the line. If he found an oversight, it would be good news for all of us. I needed to talk with him as soon as possible.

CHAPTER 7

Sniper in the Berm

"They cannot do that to you! They cannot fucking do that to you!" the JAG attorney angrily shouted.

After discussing my impending reduction in rank with some of the administrative personnel in the unit, at their suggestion, I approached the brigade JAG officer for help. At first, he refused to look at my situation. He represented the battalion and his stance would be for them and against me. After convincing him my interests were simply in looking for a correct answer and not in getting anyone into trouble, he accepted. I returned today after a tough day on the road to learn what he found.

"They are trying to pull some National Guard games on you. That won't work for them over here. You are on active duty now. Those games don't work anymore."

Rumors circled in the unit of a sergeant's promotion promised to another soldier. Top assured the soldier he continued to work hard at finding a means to get him some stripes. It surprised me, this soldier failed to attended noncommissioned officer schools in the past and he had difficulties passing the army physical fitness test, a pertinent requirement in promotions. In addition, he did not need a sergeant's rank in the work he performed. Not on a Road Hunter team, he worked as a radio and telephone operator for our leadership in the camp. I thought my chances for a positive outcome were weak until now, when I sat and listened to the JAG who seemed more upset about this ordeal than I did.

"I asked them. How are you going to assemble a fucking reduction board out here? Where are you going to find soldiers to sit on the board? If you are able to somehow accomplish this, who is going to represent you? Not me, I will have no part of this."

The JAG discussed the matter with the captain and Top. It

79

sounded as though he explained to them in detail how they made a major mistake and what they needed to do in correcting it.

"Anyway, they cannot reduce a sergeant in rank, only a lieutenant colonel can do that. What were they thinking?"

"Should I wait a few days for them to talk with me before I approach them about a change in the reduction?" I asked.

"That would be my suggestion. Give them a few days. If you have any problems with them, contact me. I will refer you to a JAG officer out of Tallil. She's an excellent attorney."

I left the JAG officer's tent feeling a great relief. The captain and Top could not reduce me in rank and they knew it. It upset me they attempted this. I trusted them. Not only did it cause unnecessary stress but it also distracted me from focusing my attention on the convoy missions. A favor of a promotion to their friend could have resulted in my or someone else's death. As I explained to the JAG, my intentions were not in getting anyone into trouble. I just wanted to walk away from it with my sergeant stripes on my collar. I would be pleasant about this and allow them to set things straight honorably.

The cool shower felt good after a long, hot day on the road. I stood by the sink and placed my things into my shaving kit when another soldier began running water into the basin next to me.

"Our Intel people suggested we sleep in our DCUs," the 201st soldier informed me. "They said Cedar is supposed to get hit either tonight or tomorrow night."

"I was not aware of that." I looked down and rinsed out the sink. "Our leadership has not said a word about it."

As I gathered my things together, the soldier filled me in on the information his unit provided him. I knew of the camp security plans given to us upon arrival. If an attack on the camp occurred during the night, we each had a designated position on the berm to occupy. If no attack, we would awaken in the morning and take a convoy mission as usual.

I left the shower trailer and hurried back to the tent for a team meeting.

"Is it OK to shoot someone dressed in black pajamas and wearing a green armband or headband?" the LT quizzed us.

"Yes!" came a unanimous reply.

This description identified those of the Mahdi army. With the recent surge in hostile activity, leadership provided us information describing the Mahdi army and ordered us to kill them on sight. The Mahdi army became loyal to Muqtada al-Sadr. Al-Sadr criticized the occupation by the American and the coalition forces. For this, the military banned his newspaper located in the Sadr City district of Baghdad and tried arresting him. He now held responsibility for violent protests in the Shiite south, which the Mahdi army quickly embraced.

Earlier, while checking e-mail, I read the news stories on the Internet news Web sites. They reported twelve marines killed at Fallujah during the past three days. A few days before that, they reported four American truck drivers mutilated there. Their bodies dragged through the streets and hung on a bridge.

In our area of operations, the Italians came under attack in the city of An Nasiriyah as well as the British in Basra.

Two days ago, I rode along with Road Hunter One-Five on their assigned task to retrieve the interpreter from the front gates of Tallil. As ordered, we transported him back to the battalion TOC. The officers wanted to interrogate him as to the recent Mahdi events in and around An Nasiriyah.

I thought back to the first time we escorted him to the TOC at the beginning of our convoy duties in Iraq. The staff officers were excited to meet him. They greeted him with a handshake and stood for pictures to e-mail to their families back home.

This occasion seemed not as bright. Stoic faces sternly questioned him. Not expecting this, he looked very nervous. He informed them of the two factions in the city who hated each other and quarreled for many years. He also explained how the people were not fond of the Italians who performed the coalition patrols there. It seemed the Italians were a little rough in their methods.

The following days showed fewer convoy escort missions scheduled than usual. Some of the private contractor convoys continued hauling supplies but the KBR trucks would not roll at all. Their drivers experienced problems with small arms fire, IEDs, and attempted kidnappings. The conditions on the road became too dangerous so they declined to take any unnecessary risks.

Without a convoy mission, the team patrolled MSR Tampa.

Radio reports of Mahdi dressed riders on motorcycles carrying RPGs kept us alert. I joked with the guys in the gun truck of how the first contact with the Mahdi militia will probably resemble hunters shooting at the first pheasant on the opening day of season.

We occupied this time exploring the access roads the Ali Baba have been know to travel as well as examining some of the bridges we passed under each day on Tampa. The insurgents littered the bridges with strategically placed piles of debris. Rocks, bricks, guardrail sections, and large bolts sat ready in piles to throw by hand at the passing convoys or civilian traffic. It would have been ineffective to clear the piles away. They were easily replaceable with the same material commonly found along much of the highway.

"Lew, the steering column broke," Nelson yelled.

He shook his head in disbelief as he lowered the steering wheel to his lap and then raised it back to its correct position. I contacted the other two humvees and we pulled over to initiate repairs.

We set up a semi-secure perimeter around the vehicles and monitored the passing traffic as Bloom, our mechanic, began work on the column. The morning felt particularly warm lacking even the slightest movement of air. Without the constant breeze circulating through the windows of the gun truck, sweat began rolling underneath the confines of our heavy body armor.

A young shepherd boy noticed the gun trucks parked along the highway and gradually moved toward the road. With his sheep wandering off, he sat on the curb at the road's edge and rolled a small, dark piece of rope in his hand as he curiously watched us.

Scotting and McMillan rummaged through the rear of the command vehicle and found a spare MRE and a bottle of water to offer the young sheepherder. Stopping work on the steering column every so often, Bloom made nervous off-color remarks, which drew only a few halfhearted laughs. Scotting and McMillan slowly approached the boy and held out the brown plastic MRE bag and water. The boy quickly stood up and hesitantly reached for it.

"Boom!" Bloom shouted and then began to laugh.

Startled, the boy ran back a few steps from the road.

I had enough of the humor. Bloom may have been apprehensive about stopping, and attempting to mask his unease.

"Just fix the damn steering wheel," I yelled.

Apparently, the LT felt the same. He also jumped on Bloom.

After a little coaxing, the guys persuaded the young boy to take the food and water.

With the steering column temporarily repaired with two zip ties, we once again continued patrolling down Tampa.

As we passed a civilian traffic accident, a group of Iraqis stood on the road motioning for us to pull over and help them.

When Iraqis came upon a traffic accident, they stopped their cars along the highway's shoulder to assist. We commonly saw at least two dozen men dressed in white robes walking around the wreckage of a vehicle. Studying the damage, they talked with one another as they pointed to the various twisted pieces of automobile.

On occasion, an accident victim's body lay on the shoulder of the road but most of the time it appeared as though no one suffered serious injury. Wanting assistance, the Iraqis stepped out into the traffic lanes and waved at us to stop but we drove around them and continued with the mission. When possible, I threw a bottle of water to help them. A slight toss rolled the cool water next to their feet.

As we proceeded down the highway, I spotted the bright red crescent of a civilian ambulance approaching us in route to the accident scene. Had we not passed the vehicle accident earlier, the ambulance would have been cause for alarm. Our Intel reported ambulances as suspect for possible vehicle borne improvised explosive devices (VBIEDs). As a means of gaining trusted access to protected areas, the insurgents filled stolen ambulances with explosives or armed militia. Under the cover of an emergency vehicle, they drove up next to checkpoints and moving convoys, and opened fire or detonated their explosives.

The steel cable used as a gate prohibiting entry into the MCT yard that normally draped across the front entrance lay stretched upon the ground unintentionally leaving the access open. With easy admittance into the lot, we quickly pulled into the yard, bypassing Navistar, to check if there were any pushes available for escort. The trip down proved encouraging to us. If we were fortunate enough to find a convoy ready to leave, it could end up being a short day.

The lot looked empty with the exception of a few stray trucks waiting for their paperwork to clear. With no convoys ready to leave, we parked the gun trucks in the yard and began the long wait. The clear sunny morning gradually brought a slight breeze to cool us in the heat. We sat in the humvees and talked about things happening back home. How our families were adapting. What we missed most.

Two British land rovers pulled up next to the gun trucks in a cloud of dust and sand. We acknowledged each other with a smile and a wave as we normally did. A few of the Brits wandered over to look at the alpha gun truck. Interested in the .50 caliber heavy machine gun mounted in the turret, they pulled out their cameras to take pictures.

As I stepped out of the bravo truck, one of the soldiers, a sergeant in the group, stopped to talk with me. I gave him a tour of our beat-up humvee.

I asked about their vehicle, the land rover, a simple looking truck. Its design dated back to World War II. A smaller vehicle in size, it compared to the old U.S. jeep. The rear compartment looked compact with little room for but a few soldiers to occupy. When we approached the British traveling down the highway, no more than two soldiers usually rode in the back area. Providing little if any protection for its occupants, the rear lay open with nothing but a sand brown camouflage material draped over the top and sides to conceal its riders.

"It's like papier-mâché," he shook his head in frustration as he explained. "The whole damn thing is made out of papier-mâché, no protection at all. It's a deathtrap."

Our fiberglass doors would not provide any more protection from IEDs but their land rover seemed much worse. It actually had nothing but camouflage netting.

We walked back to the gun trucks. The Brits snapped pictures of themselves on the humvee. They took turns exchanging cameras and posing. Some in the gun turret next to the .50 cal. and others sitting on the roof or standing beside the humvee.

The sergeant handed me his rifle. "Have you seen one of these before? It's an L85IW, SA80 series, same caliber as your M-16."

I could feel a difference in the weight compared to the M-16.

"It's slightly heavier than what I'm used to but it feels comfortable."

"Yes, it's a little heavier, but very accurate."

I offered my M-16 for his examination. He declined, having

trained with the M-16 as with a variety of other foreign weapons.

Behind us, the alpha humvee's engine roared to life. Hanson allowed a few of the Brits to take it for a short drive around the yard. With smiles on their faces, they looked as though they enjoyed themselves as they tested its maneuverability.

In the past, we complained a great deal about the gun trucks, how they were not suitable for convoy operations. The humvees may have had power but they did not provide the speed needed to catch the civilian vehicles that we chased, nevertheless, as the British sergeant pointed out, the humvees were much better than their land rover.

Our intended short stay lengthened and slowly crept by. We waited over three hours for a convoy without receiving a call. The time finally arrived to leave. Road Hunter One-Seven received a mission at the last minute so we followed along as extra security during the return trip to Cedar.

As team one-seven readied the convoy for movement, we drove the alpha and bravo gun trucks into Safwan to secure a few of the questionable areas. We parked the bravo truck next to the cement brick maker to pull security. Reports indicated some locals recently threw rocks from that location. The alpha gun truck moved farther down the road to pull security on the opposite side of the Jiffy Lube.

The Jiffy Lube, as we called it, stood on the main road intersection as we turned from Safwan in route to the bridge extended over MSR Tampa. The local Iraqi businessman, who owned the small cement block shed, bartered in oil and lubricants to those traveling by. The waste oil saturated the dark stained soil around his building indicating his services were in high demand. A passerby printed the words "Mr. Lube" on a piece of brown cardboard and hung it above his doorway.

As we stopped next to the brick maker, I opened the door of the humvee and stepped out to secure the area. Nelson remained in the driver's seat and Leptien provided security from the turret with his SAW. The convoy would be moving by shortly. We would leave as soon as it would pass or possibly earlier if we received a call on the radio requiring security elsewhere. It became quite hot since our arrival earlier in the morning. As I stood next to the gun truck, I could feel the sweat slowly beginning to roll down my lower back and legs.

Some of the Iraqi civilians roamed about in the distance performing their daily business. Others observed us from open windows in the mud brick houses while a few of the kids poked their heads from behind some of the buildings.

Ping. The humvee radio sounded. "One-Seven, this is One-Seven Alpha. We are approaching the border. Over."

Ping. "This is One-Seven. It's about time. Roger. Out."

The convoy moved on its way and would be passing by shortly.

Some of the children gradually began walking toward us. As they approached, they steadily picked up speed. I discovered from my experience on the road that the best method in holding the kids off the highway and away from the trucks when the convoys passed lay in keeping them occupied.

"Marhaba," I greeted them.

The kids smiled and began speaking in Arabic. They asked if I spoke Arabic. I shook my head. A few of them spoke English, some a little better than others. More children started to appear. They seemed to come out of nowhere. At least a dozen children gathered around us by then.

"Ma asmak?" I asked each one as I shook their hands.

They told me their names. Some were brothers and sisters. Most were good friends. They indicated this by holding out their hands and wiggling their two index fingers together.

They were very talkative and teasing. I asked them questions. Where they lived and where they went to school? Do they play soccer and chess?

They asked many questions as well. "What was my name? Did I like it there?" They asked the names of my two companions in the gun truck whom they briefly talked with and teased.

They questioned parts of my uniform and gear. One of the boys eyed my miniature thermometer and attempted to grab it. Another of the older boys pulled his hand away and scolded him.

Looking down the road, I saw the convoy approaching. I reached inside the humvee and pulled out a package of Tootsie Roll suckers that I previously purchased at the PX for the kids along the road. They smiled and laughed as I handed each one a piece of the candy. I gave some to a grandmother, who walked over to join the crowd and talk with me. I explained to her that if she did not want the candy she should give it to some of the children who were not present.

"Let's go, Lew," Nelson yelled.

The convoy finished passing the gun truck. I opened the door of the humvee to step in. The children did not want us to leave. One of the little boys grabbed onto my leg to keep me there. I smiled and gently pushed him towards his grandmother. She nodded and held onto his shoulder.

We darted off to join the convoy. The kids waved and yelled thanks as they walked back to their homes with Tootsie Roll suckers in hand.

I grabbed the radio handset. "One-Six Alpha, this is One-Six Bravo. Over."

Ping. "This is One-Six Alpha. Over."

"What is your location? Over."

Ping. "We are still sitting up here a little ways past the Jiffy Lube. Over."

"We're at the end of the convoy and should be at your location shortly. Over."

Ping. "Roger. The convoy is still passing us. We'll wait until you get here. Over."

"Roger. Out."

We continued following behind the one-seven bravo gun truck at the end of the convoy. The streets looked quiet. Not many kids stood begging by the sides of the road. It may have been too hot for them during the mid afternoon.

"Look at that idiot." Nelson shook his head and laughed.

As we turned the corner by the Jiffy Lube, we approached the rear of a gun truck stopped along the side of the road. I looked up and noticed their gunner, standing on the roof of the gun truck, urinating over the side and onto the ground next to their vehicle.

Less than fifty feet away stood a series of Iraqi homes. When a military vehicle stops next to a house, its occupants usually rush to the windows and watch the activity. I witnessed no one at the windows.

A few days later, we waited once again at Navistar for a push north. I looked at my watch. Five hours had painfully passed since we arrived with a convoy. The mission down to the border went so well, quick and without incident, we thought we would experience a fast turnaround and return to Cedar in record time. That proved not to be the case. There were no missions available. No convoy trucks ready to leave.

The guys threw the football until their arms were sore. They read and reread the *Stars and Stripes* many times. Some talked while others slept but we all sweat in the dry heat.

I remembered a conversation at Camp Virginia I had with a soldier from the 3/18th. He waited in our tent to talk with one of the guys out busy performing various tasks. Thinking they both knew the same girl back home, he wanted to share stories with him.

"He won't be returning for anther two hours," I informed him.

He lay down on a cot. "That's OK, I'll wait."

"Wait?" I laughed. "He won't be back for another two hours. There must be something you want to do. You're going to get awful bored just sitting around here and doing nothing."

He smiled and slowly placed his weapon on the cot behind him. "I'm used to it. I'm used to waiting hours and hours, even days and days, just waiting for something, anything to do. Usually we are waiting on the leadership. We wait for them to make up their minds. You'll see what I mean."

I understood what he meant now. There were occasions when we could not move fast enough and then there were times such as these, when we waited endlessly. The system became an established, step-by-step process but not everyone abided by the same time schedule. We might be waiting on the person three steps up the line instead of the person right next to us.

As we prepared to leave, the LT received a message from the TOC at Cedar requesting we remain an additional thirty minutes past the standard leave time. Wanting to get back as soon as possible, we left the camp and drove across the road to the MCT lot in search of a push north. The sooner we located one, the sooner we could leave. Entering the lot, we found none of the trucks organized or ready to move. The situation looked unpromising.

Once again, the time passed and we prepared to leave when the LT received a call from Trade Center South. A convoy mission stood ready to depart just outside the MCT lot. The alpha gun truck and the command vehicle left through the gates to locate the column of vehicles.

As we slammed the humvee doors and began following, a captain from the MCT yard suddenly appeared as if from nowhere and leaped in front of the gun truck. I reached forward and braced myself against the windshield as Nelson hit the brakes to avoid running over him. We came to a quick stop less than a foot away from the captain. He looked extremely upset.

"Where the fuck do you think you're going?" he yelled.

I did not understand why he stood there shouting at us. He must have confused us with someone else. We had never seen him before. I knew we had a mission waiting and this captain's actions hindered us from proceeding with it. We needed to get to the convoy immediately and start moving down the road.

"You're not going anywhere. You shut that fucking humvee off right now," he began pointing at us as he continued yelling.

I jumped out of the humvee and took a few steps toward him as he walked up to me. His fuming eyes glared at me through an angry strained face.

"I know what you're trying to do. I know what you're fucking trying to do. You're not going to play games with me. Not today. Not ever. I was in OIF One (Operation Iraqi Freedom I). I know what you're fucking trying to do," he continued.

"Sir, I don't know what you're talking about. We need to get going. We have a mission waiting for us outside the gates."

"I was in OIF One. I was in OIF One. I know what you're trying to do. You guys laid around all fucking afternoon and now you want to leave without taking a convoy. You're going to wait here and take one. You're not leaving without one."

I pointed outside the gates. "We have one, sir. That's where we are going. We have a mission to go north with a convoy."

The captain glanced over my shoulder and noticed the other teams preparing to leave. He stepped toward their trucks and continued yelling as a major from the MCT building appeared and walked up to the gun truck.

I looked at him and briefly explained, "Sir, we have a convoy waiting outside the lot. We need to go now."

He nodded his head as indication to leave. I could tell he did not totally agree with the captain's excessive methods.

I jumped into the humvee and instructed Nelson to step on it. Not sure if we should be leaving, he briefly hesitated as he stared at me in silence. We were in the middle of having our rear ends chewed. Was it wise to leave now?

"Step on it, he's nuts! We have a mission waiting for us and we don't have time for his nonsense. He can babble at the other teams."

Nelson agreed and stomped on the gas. A cloud of dust trailed behind us as we sped through the open gate. I watched the captain's reflection through the dusty side mirror as he glanced at us and then continued yelling at the two teams who prepared to leave.

The clock indicated we were well past the extra time ordered to remain when we finally joined the team just outside the lot. Parked next to a group of trucks, they attempted to locate its convoy leader so we could depart.

"Where have you guys been?" Boz asked.

We described the adverse meeting with the captain and explained how fortunate we were to have gotten away when we did.

The convoy leader approached us along with a civilian employee of the MCT lot. They informed us not all the trucks would accompany us during the mission. They needed to confirm the driver's paperwork, prepare them to go, and stage the trucks. The whole process would take at least another half-hour.

This delay would place us traveling with thirty trucks in the dark. We could not provide adequate security when unable to see beyond the headlights. After waiting an extra half-hour at the direction of the battalion TOC, the convoy leader now told us to wait longer and one could certainly bet it would be at least another hour before the trucks were completely ready to roll out.

After explaining the dangers of traveling after sunset, the LT informed them we could wait no longer. We were leaving now and would take all the trucks that were ready.

The convoy leader became upset. "No, you will wait here until we are all ready to go!"

He continued yelling as the MCT employee talked on a hand-held radio with his people back at the lot. We started the gun trucks and the LT indicated once again to the convoy leader we were leaving. Those wanting to come, leave with us now. Displeased with the decision, the convoy leader slowly shook his head in disgust.

Departing without a convoy, we would patrol back to Cedar. We fell in behind Road Hunter Ten, who with the help of the friendly captain, ended up with a ramshackle push hastily assembled in the MCT lot. They would have serious problems with their mission. The lieutenant contacted team ten over the radio and we agreed to follow them across the border and help provide security for their convoy as we traveled back to Cedar.

The three humvees in our team were about to cross into Iraq when a gun truck raced beside us. It darted in front of our team, cutting off the last gun truck in team ten's convoy and blocking anyone from crossing the border. The quick moving gun truck stopped in the middle of the road, swung a loaded .50 caliber heavy machine gun around, and pointed it directly at us.

Not knowing what to make of the aggressive action, I opened the door of the humvee to question the LT, stopped in the command vehicle directly in front of us. As I stepped out onto the pavement, the irate captain from the MCT lot, accompanied by another soldier with his weapon locked and loaded, brushed past me in route to the lieutenant's vehicle.

Furious we did not stay and wait for the convoy, the captain began arguing with the lieutenant. He refused to listen to reason and ordered the LT to direct our team to return to the lot and retrieve a convoy. He gave orders to his soldiers to shoot us if we attempted to cross the border. This man was definitely insane.

I could not believe the events unfolding before my eyes, I half-expected CNN or the press to jump out and begin extensive coverage. This absurd occurrence briefly reminded me of one of the stories you hear about on the news and shake your head at. "Deranged Captain Threatens to Kill American Soldiers Detained at Iraqi Border".

We waited as the lieutenant, captain, and the battalion TOC via satellite telephone worked out the details. Fifteen minutes later, we crossed the border trailing team ten's convoy. With a concern about the lack of safety in the dark, someone at the TOC finally stood up and made the right decision.

We traveled along with team ten, assisting with their mission. As we anticipated, there were many breakdowns to contend with providing an arrival at Cedar well after dark.

Upset with the incident at the border, the leadership requested written statements from those who witnessed the actions. The request pointed down a familiar path. Nothing would ever become of the incident. They began following a process whereby a report needed filing somewhere up the chain. At the most, that is all it would ever amount to, a filed report. Besides, the incident resulted from the unsound actions of an officer. How far would it actually proceed before someone stopped it?

"Aren't you going to write something, Lew?" one of the guys asked.

"No, I'm not writing anything. I didn't see a thing."

"I agree with you, Lew," Scotting spoke up. "I didn't see a thing either."

"You guys are going to spend many hours writing out statements and nothing is going to become of it," I explained to them. "They won't do anything to him."

"You're probably right, but I'm so damned mad at what he did to us today, I'm going to write something just to get it out of my system."

The others felt angry as well so they wrote. It took them many hours to complete the statements. They could have used the valuable time to take care of personal issues or catch up on some much needed rest.

The following day, there were no problems with the MCT lot at Navistar. They operated as though the whole incident never occurred at all. We kept a cautious eye out for the captain but did not see him anywhere.

Over the next few days, incidents involving the Mahdi army continued in the south. New rules stated we could no longer "just shoot" at the Mahdi army on sight as previously directed. Now, orders instructed us to only engage them if they carried weapons. If unarmed, we were to leave them alone and continue on.

Our convoy stood waiting on the right-hand side of the road with the usual flat tire problems. Nelson, Leptien, and I provided security at the rear of the convoy while the command vehicle assisted with the repairs. The MCT people gave us the last push out of Cedar earlier in the morning. With no other convoys behind us wanting to pass, it would be a quiet wait.

A late addition to the convoy, a non-tactical vehicle (NTV), sat idling directly in front of the gun truck. A newer extended cab pickup, it carried civilians and contractors. When the convoy stopped, I informed the driver as to the nature of the breakdown. All of the doors flung open as its occupants stepped out to relieve themselves. They claimed to be from Macedonia. We suggested they remain in their vehicle but they insisted on talking with us for a few minutes as they stretched their legs. Pulling digital cameras from their coat pockets, they took pictures of themselves standing next to the gun truck and us.

A few local women dressed in black abayas appeared from the empty desert and began walking from truck to truck begging from the TCNs. Some of the drivers threw snacks and juice boxes out of their windows hoping the women would move on and leave them alone.

"Imshi. Imshi," Nelson yelled as he chased after them.

They quickly disappeared only to return later up the line continuing to beg from the drivers.

"Can't you keep them hajjis away from the trucks, Nelson?" Leptien laughed.

"These people are crazy. They're nuts. Why don't they listen?" Nelson replied as he followed them up the truck line.

"You're yelling at them to leave and their stomachs are screaming to stay," I joined in with a slight laugh.

"Look at Boz." Leptien pointed. "He's having a tough time catching that one."

Glancing up the column of trucks, we watched amusingly as Boz chased after an older woman who limped along while steadying herself with a cane. After catching her and politely escorting her away from the trucks, like the others, she returned and continued to beg. They meant no harm. They were only hungry.

With the tire finally changed, we left the roadside women and continued with the mission. As we drove, I noticed a dark red van swerving to the side of the road in the opposite northbound lanes. The driver, an Iraqi civilian, displayed a concerned expression as he began waving and yelling at us to stop.

"I wonder what he wants," I shouted over to Nelson.

"They all want the same thing," he said. "They don't take care of their cars and then when they have problems, they expect us to stop and fix it for them."

This occurred quite often. When people experienced car problems, they usually attempted to pull us over for help. It would have been nice to assist everyone who needed it but stopping with a convoy would be unsafe.

When possible, I threw a bottle of water to them. If we could not stop, then at least they had something to drink while they waited for help. At times, the water filled their needs. They poured the liquid into the car's radiator to cool their overheated engines. It provided an adequate amount of assistance to move them a little farther down the road.

The radio sounded. Ping. "One-Six Alpha, One-Six Bravo. Get the heck out of here!!"

The frantic call originated from the LT in the command vehicle. Along with his urgent message, I heard automatic weapons fire over the radio.

I turned to Leptien and Nelson, and yelled, "The command vehicle is being fired upon! They have contact! Keep your eyes open!"

Nelson yelled back, "Right or left? Which side, right or left?"

From the sound of the radio transmission, the lieutenant seemed too occupied to provide a detailed description of the contact. I picked up the radio handset but we did not have enough time. Right or left, at sixty miles per hour, we were almost there.

"He didn't have time," I yelled. "Keep your eyes left, I'll take right, Leptien, either one."

Being right-handed proved difficult to shoot through the passenger side window of the vehicle. I pulled my right leg up into my chest and turned my body in the limited compact space. Moving my right shoulder back, I firmly steadied my weapon. I sat ready to fire.

For a split second, the thought raced through my mind that the gun truck retained its original fiberglass doors. We did not drive an up-armored vehicle like some. I just exposed more of my unprotected body to the sniper. That did not matter now. My position offered at least a better angle to return fire.

In eagerly scanning the berm, I saw no one. Suddenly, the side of the road next to the humvee lit up with automatic fire. Dust and sand danced into the air. A sniper in the berm fired on us. Had he raised the barrel of his weapon a fraction of an inch higher, he would have riddled the side of the gun truck full of holes.

Continuing to scan the desert, I could not locate him. I searched the berm for a silhouette, someone running, a white or red keffiyeh head wrap, anything indicating someone out there. No one, not a thing, it felt like one of the most frustrating moments of my life. I possessed a magazine full of ammo and I could not find the shooter to return fire.

"Do you see him?" I yelled up to Leptien.

"No, I can't locate him anywhere!"

We had taken fire and the sniper had gotten away with it. The adrenaline continued to rush though my body.

I turned to Nelson. "We were shot at, man!"

Nelson did not look amused. He shook his head and stared straight ahead at the convoy trucks as we continued down the road.

I felt proud of Nelson and Leptien. Under fire, they maintained their discipline. Leptien could have expended a box of ammo blindly into the berm but he did not identify a target so he held back. Nelson maintained a steady speed and position with the convoy while searching for the sniper with his rifle through the side window. Neither one of them remotely fell apart.

I picked up the radio handset. "One-Six, this is One-Six Bravo. Over."

Ping. "This is One-Six. Is everything OK back there? Over."

"We received some small arms fire from a sniper in the berm but no one is hurt and everything seems to be running fine. How about with your vehicle and alpha? Over."

Ping. "Alpha had nothing. From what I can see with our humvee, we were hit once but everyone is OK. We are going to check things out when we cross the border. Over."

"Roger. Out."

Upon arriving at Navistar, I immediately reported the specifics of our contact once again to the LT. He did not seem genuinely interested. It did not matter. I only followed through with the process.

The Road Hunter teams examined the damage to the command vehicle. The round entered through the roof of the humvee just above the passenger's door and exited behind the driver. With Boz driving, Scotting returned fire from the backseat.

Team one-seven's leader seemed slightly shaken over the whole incident. Reaching for a package of cigarettes, he pulled one out and began again his habit of smoking. The others shared his legitimate concern. In returning to Camp Cedar, we would all pass once more through the same area of the contact like ducks in a shooting gallery.

The wind picked up for the return trip. Fine sand and dust began filling the air. With no convoys scheduled to travel north, we patrolled MSR Tampa back to Cedar. As we traveled, we received word that a security patrol searched the area where the sniper fired at us. They reported two dead bodies. Scotting seemed relieved to find they were the result of a hijacking and not his returned fire.

The sand in the air significantly reduced our visibility. At times, we encountered difficulties in establishing the outline of the alpha gun truck. They spotted a suspicious vehicle directly in front of them and took off in pursuit only to lose them in the blinding sandstorm.

Clearing our weapons at the berm in Camp Cedar, we heard the LT contact the alpha gun truck over the radio. The Lieutenant instructed them to proceed to the TOC after he received a message from the commander requesting they meet with him when we returned to camp.

We drove the gun truck to the TOC to meet up with the team. As they stepped out of their vehicles, the LT quickly waved us by.

"Keep going. Keep going," he yelled. "There is no need for you to attend."

Fine with us, we needed fuel. We drove to the fuel point and filled the gun truck for the next day's missions.

I prepared a handwritten, request for a reduction board statement to present to the captain. Neither he nor Top approached me regarding a possible change in their plans to reduce me in rank. In an earlier conversation I initiated with the captain, I hinted as to him possibly talking with the JAG regarding the reduction. In suggesting it, I hoped it might jar a positive response. It did not. He simply stated he would talk with the JAG and get back with me. He never did.

With a thirty-day time limit to request a reduction board, I had no other alternative. The time arrived to move ahead with a formal request.

Their plans were not difficult to decipher. They were up to their National Guard games once again, as described by the JAG officer. Once the thirty days expired, as stated in my signed counseling statement, I would more than likely retain no recourse. They would reduce me in rank from a sergeant to a specialist. They would give my stripes to another soldier as a favor, a perfect example of the old stripes-for-buddies program.

With the captain and first sergeant sharing the same tent, I could possibly catch both of them together. I knocked on the door. Both were present and invited me in.

"Sergeant Lew, what can we do for you?" the captain greeted me.

I stepped across the dusty plywood floor and stood next to their desks. Both sat quietly in their chairs and prepared various paperwork under a fluorescent light fixture attached to the steel tent post.

I handed the written statement to the captain. "I am requesting a reduction board, sir. Here is my formal written request."

The captain's chair creaked loudly as he slowly sat back and stared at the piece of paper in my hand.

"Ah, ah, ah...." He glanced nervously over to Top and then back.

"Ya know, Lew, ah, ah.... we don't have to reduce you in rank," he went on. "I was just thinking. Why take the money away from you and give it to someone else. It just doesn't make sense."

He cleared the papers from the top of his desk and placed a manila folder in front of himself. "I tell you what we'll do. We'll tear up the counseling statement. You can keep you stripes and it will be like this whole thing never happened."

His suggestion indicated the total opposite from what he attempted to maneuver all month. Although pleased he finally made a decision, I felt a little upset this whole situation occurred in the first place.

"You mean, just like that?" I asked. "Tear up the counseling statement and it never happened?"

Something did not feel right. After what they tried to pull with this reduction, how much could I actually trust them now? I attempted once again to hand the request to the captain.

"I still want to give you this request for a reduction board, sir," I continued.

Top broke into the conversation. "That won't be necessary. We'll just tear up the counseling statement and you won't have to give us anything."

"You can do whatever you want with the counseling statement," I explained. "I just want to follow through with the process and hand this request to you. I don't want anyone to come back later and say I didn't present a request for a reduction board."

The captain reached across the desk and took the request from my hand. "OK, fine, I'll put it in the file with the counseling statement and tear everything up together."

"Once the request is in your hands, I have no control over it. You can do whatever you like with it, sir."

"I'll be a witness to the fact that you gave the request for a reduction board to the captain," Top added.

I thanked both of them for their time and left.

The request did not proceed anything as I thought it would. They dragged their feet on this for the past month. I felt sure they would take the request and sit on it for a few more weeks before finally making a decision. Maybe I called their bluff or maybe they had some other angle they were working. I knew one thing. They would not let the issue die easily. They promised a promotion to a soldier in the unit and one way or another, they would promote him. At least I knew where I stood with them. I now moved a little farther down on their list, possibly the bottom.

As I walked back to my tent, I wondered how many of the other guys received the shaft since we left home station. How many of them did they actually lie to, walk on, and kick to a lesser spot. I knew of one senior noncommissioned officer (NCO) forced into a reduction in rank just before our deployment. The circumstances surrounding his reduction were just as questionable. I would talk with him to see if I could help in some way and then maintain an awareness for others experiencing similar problems.

CHAPTER 8

Illusions of Help

Ping. "One-Six Bravo, this is One-Six. Over."

I reached up and keyed the radio handset pinned between my ear and helmet chinstrap. "This is One-Six Bravo. Over."

Ping. "You'll be coming upon a group of Iraqi civilians along the roadside. Stop and check them out. They seem to be concerned about something. They were waving and yelling at us. If there are any problems, let me know. Over."

I had a visual on the small group directly ahead of us and motioned Nelson to pull the gun truck over next to them.

"This is One-Six Bravo. Roger. Out." I ended the call as the gun truck rolled to a stop.

"Ali Baba! Ali Baba!" they yelled and screamed, pointing to a berm a few hundred meters off the highway.

They looked shaken but no one seemed in need of major medical attention. The women and children wiped tears from their eyes as the men approached me.

One of them spoke a little English. He and his family were Dutch citizens visiting their relatives in Iraq. He explained how they drove down the highway and came upon a man standing in the traffic lanes waving at them as though he needed help. As they stopped their two cars, the man pulled a gun from behind his back. Another man, concealed along the road ditch, suddenly appeared behind them. The two thugs ordered the families out of their vehicles and began tormenting them. When the thieves noticed our gun trucks approaching, they took both cars and drove off across the sand to the other side of the berm.

I stood at the edge of the road and scanned the desert sand. Two sets of tire tracks led toward the berm where the civilians aggressively pointed but the Ali Baba were nowhere in sight.

I reached into the gun truck and grabbed the radio handset. "One-Six, this is One-Six Bravo. It looks as though there has been a carjacking. No one is hurt but they claim the Ali Baba are on the other side of a berm adjacent to the highway and holding their vehicles. Over."

Ping. "This is One-Six. Hang on, we'll pull the convoy over and come back to investigate. Over."

"This is One-Six Bravo. Roger. Out."

The command vehicle arrived as the civilians continued pleading with me to retrieve their cars.

I provided the lieutenant with the remaining details of the situation. "They said there is a ditch filled with water on the other side of the berm and the Ali Baba cannot cross the water. The thieves have nowhere to go. They're just sitting there waiting and hoping we'll leave."

He walked over and listened to the group's story. Without saying a word, he returned to the command vehicle to establish contact with the battalion back at Cedar for guidance.

The guys gradually became upset with the delay in taking action. Leptien threw his arms in the air. "Lew, what the hell are we waiting for? What's the big deal? Why don't we just drive over there, shoot the bastards, and get this over with?"

"I don't think there would be any shooting involved," I replied. "They would more than likely run away abandoning the vehicles. We're involving the battalion now, its hard saying how long this is going to take. They're a little slow when it comes to making a decision. Just be patient, the Ali Baba are not going anywhere. We'll get them."

Twenty minutes passed and we still had not moved. The hot afternoon sun beat down upon us as we waited along the roadside. A slight breeze, felt by the movement of air produced by an occasional passing motor vehicle, provided the only means of relief to cool the sweat on our faces. The guys and the civilians became restless at the inaction.

"I think I see one," Boz shouted as he pointed past Scotting and toward the berm. "A head popped up and went back down again."

The lieutenant stepped out from the command vehicle and

approached us.

"Hey, LT," Leptien called down from the turret of the gun truck. "Boz just saw one of the Ali Baba on the berm. Let's go pay them a visit."

The lieutenant glanced at the berm and then back at us. "Negative, this is not our problem. This is a matter for the Iraqi police to handle."

Faces drew blank expressions as we stared at the LT in disbelief.

"What? Not our problem?" I asked. "Since when did it not become our problem? How can the battalion make a decision like that? Are you sure they understood the situation correctly?"

He hesitated as he looked back toward the berm. "I was not able to make contact with Cedar. We'll wait here for a while and see if the IP show up. They can handle it. It's not our problem."

The Dutch civilians did not take this decision very well at all. The man's face dropped as the LT informed him of the plan. His family also produced the same surprised look as the man interpreted the conversation to them.

The lieutenant walked back to the command vehicle while the man trailed at his heels unsuccessfully pleading for help.

"LT, Boz just saw the Ali Baba," Leptien yelled as the LT passed us. "They're on the other side of that berm. Why can't we go get them?"

The lieutenant stopped and sternly explained, "it doesn't matter if we see them or not. We are not going to leave the highway. When the IP show up, we are leaving." He walked back to his humvee and sat in the passenger seat to wait.

The man, now at his wits end, stopped next to me and again begged for my help in retrieving his vehicles. His family lost their transportation, clothing, and everything they carried with them. They were unsure as to what would happen next.

I looked at the small group standing on the shoulder of the highway. The women and children continued to weep as the men comforted them. We did not help their horribly bad day one bit by stopping.

"I am very sorry we cannot help you get your cars back. The Iraqi police will have to assist you when they arrive. I am sorry but we received our orders and there is nothing I can do about it now."

He angrily shook his head. "Why? Why do you not want to help us? Aren't you Americans? Aren't you the United States Army? Don't you help people who are in situations like this? If *you* can not help us, then there is no one who can."

I did not know what to tell him. We were all very upset with the decision. If it were up to us, we would have taken action. The five of us were ready to race across the sand in the gun truck and engage the Ali Baba but that would not happen today. The LT gave the order. We did not agree but we needed to follow it. We were to do nothing.

The man pointed at my M-16. "Please, can I use? If you can do nothing, then at least allow me to take care of the Ali Baba. Please?"

"No." I shook my head at his request. "I am sorry but I cannot let you use it. I would be responsible if something were to happen to you."

He looked frustrated with all of us. If he had possessed his own weapon, I would have let him proceed. I would have even followed him over to the berm.

Leptien kicked at the equipment in the back of the gun truck. He felt upset like the rest of us. "What the hell is wrong with the LT? Why the fuck are we even here if we aren't allowed to help when people like these actually need it?"

Nelson shook his head. "Get used to it. This isn't the first time we fucked someone over and I'm sure it won't be the last."

The Iraqi police eventually approached our position on one of their patrols. Noticing the humvees parked on the side of the road, they stopped their pickups next to us to investigate. A great concern came over them when they discovered the involvement of the Ali Baba.

We left the civilians with the IP and rejoined the convoy. As I looked in my side mirror, I watched the civilians staring at us as they climbed into the back of the Iraqi police truck. The police did not attempt to pursue the Ali Baba. If we did not bother to do anything about it, they certainly were not going to attempt to retrieve the cars, at least not without our help to protect them. They turned their pickups around and drove back toward the Iraqi police station.

We felt disappointed with the decision. There were no explanations as to why we did what we did. We could do nothing about it but follow orders.

We sat relaxing in the tent back at Cedar during the early evening after another difficult day on the road when we heard a knock on the door. A friend of ours visiting the camp, a lieutenant, decided to stop by and see how the convoy missions were treating us. He explained how his battery provided ammo site security in the Az Zubayr area south of Basra. It was interesting discussing what the other batteries were doing in Iraq and how they were adjusting to their missions.

In our lighthearted conversation, he explained how they provided security for contractors who detonated confiscated ordinance at ammo sites. They told their own unique stories of dealing with the hajjis. The Iraqis they encountered were mostly scavengers who searched through the blast area looking for pieces of shrapnel to sell as scrap metal. One morning, they arrived to find a pair of sandals sitting where one of the locals attempted to take more than he could handle.

"Don't you get sick of them hajjis hanging around?" one of the guys asked the lieutenant.

"No, if we get bored, we line them up for donkey cart races."

"Donkey cart races?"

"Yeah, we have the hajjis line up in a row with their donkey carts and watch them race the carts to a finish line. The winner gets an MRE and a bottle of water. We tape the races to watch later. It's hilarious."

The guys laughed. "You got that on tape?"

"Yeah, we tape lots of things." He pushed himself back resting comfortably in a nylon folding chair. "We decided we would tape something every day to document our tour so we carry the camera along with us to the ammo site and find something to tape."

I shook my head. "No, you don't do that to these people and then tape it, do you?"

"Oh relax, Lew, its not hurting anything," one of the guys said with a few more agreeing.

"Donkey cart races, that's funny," they went on. "What else do you have on tape?"

He laughed. "We got one hajji having sex with his sheep."

"No, you're kidding." The guys asked in amazement.

"Well, he's not actually doing it. He's standing behind one of his sheep and making the motions like he's having sex with it." The lieutenant extended his arms and thrust his hips forward.

"Stupid hajji." The guys laughed. "Why did he do that?"

"We just told him that we would give him a bottle of water if he did it and he did."

I could not believe what I heard. "Does your commander or first sergeant know about these tapes?" I asked.

"Yeah, they know. At the end of the day, we all sit down and watch what we recorded."

"Isn't that kind of dangerous to keep around?" I asked. "What if the colonel or sergeant major found out about it?"

"Oh, they know about it."

I sat up in my chair and looked at him. "Know about it? And they're fine with it?"

"Yeah, when they come down to Azzy for their visits, we get together and watch the videos to show them what we have been doing. They think it's hilarious too."

"See, Lew, its OK," one of the guys spoke up. "If it doesn't bother the colonel or sergeant major, then why should it bother you? There is nothing wrong with it."

I sat back in my chair and silently listened as the conversation continued. Nothing wrong with it? It reeked of wrongdoing. This would never have happening if the leadership did not encourage it. These poor people have nothing. They spend their time scavenging in order to provide for their families. They would do just about anything if it meant food on the table and they were not above humiliation to get it. Some took advantage of this and it did not bother them. After all, to them, these people were only hajjis.

We shared stories of the road into the late hours. At the end of the night, we unanimously agreed upon one thing. The lieutenant felt comfortable with their mission and pleased they were not performing security escorts. We wished we possessed their mission and were not performing security escorts.

The next few days on the road, the guys occasionally brought up the amusing ammo site security stories described by the lieutenant. They grudgingly compared the convoy missions we performed to other work they could be doing elsewhere.

As we traveled down the road, the lanes congested with civilian traffic as we approached the Iraqi police station. The convoy moved steadily along at sixty miles per hour without any problems. I examined the traffic through the sand and dust in the air as the vehicles raced by us in the right-hand lane. All the cars and their occupants started to look the same after awhile. Some of the kids waved. One extended his middle finger. I smiled and waved back. He probably picked up the hand gesture from one of the convoys they previously passed on the road.

The traffic seemed heavier than usual. We had difficulties keeping track of all the vehicles moving by at speeds in excess of seventy miles per hour. A white Chevy passed by with its occupants smiling and waving. I returned the wave. I continued observing the traffic as it flowed by when I glanced up toward the white Chevy a little ways ahead of us. The passenger sitting in the backseat held up an AK-47, as if repositioning it, and then quickly returned it to the floor.

I keyed the radio handset. "One-Six, this is One-Six Bravo. Over."

Our humvee could not produce the speed required to catch the vehicle. The LT would have to attempt to stop it.

Ping. "This is One-Six. Over."

"Be on the lookout for a white Chevy Caprice heading your way, possible AK-47 in the backseat. Over."

Ping. "I'll keep my eyes open. Roger. Out."

The white car became lost in the mixture of civilian traffic. Many of the other vehicles traveling on the highway were white in color as well. My only chance in identifying the exact car resided in if it somehow fell back to our position.

I keyed the handset. "One-Six, this is One-Six Bravo. The white Chevy should be close to your position by now. Do you see him? Over."

Ping. "Negative, they all look the same. We may have lost him. Over."

"This is One-Six Bravo. Roger. Out."

The convoy team traveling in front of us overheard our transmissions and the radio traffic picked up with warnings of AK-47s. The other teams were on the lookout but we never located the white car.

Upon arriving at Navistar, we placed our team on the list to receive a convoy mission north. With the extra time, I checked my e-mail at the CyberZone Café, a pay as you go Internet service. Like everything else, the price seemed expensive but well worth having the access. I read through my e-mail from Donna and my folks. They and my two children were holding up quite well and all seemed fine back home.

I returned to the humvee and found we still had not received a call from Trade Center South with a convoy north. After reading the e-mail from Donna, I wanted to talk with her just to listen to her voice. I looked through my bag and found my cell phone. We purchased cell phones during our arrival at Camp Virginia. They had just one problem with their use. The phones could only access the network while in Kuwait. They were useless a few miles north of the border.

I limited my calls to once per week, if time permitted. Although I wish I could have called more often, it became an expensive phone call to make. I found some shade and privacy in one of the numerous concrete shelters next to the humvee parking area that the camp used as barricades.

"Hi, Babe, it's me." I placed my hand over the phone to keep the wind from distorting the call.

"Hi, I thought it may have been you. You're the only one who would call me at three in the morning."

"Sorry about that. I call when I can and I never know when that may be."

"That's all right, Babe, you know you can call me anytime. I understand it's tough to call."

We discussed the items she sent in the e-mail but as usual, I let her do most of the talking. The sound of her voice comforted me. I sat, closed my eyes, and pictured her in my mind as I listened.

A Blackhawk helicopter began circling above us searching for the makeshift landing zone located adjacent to the parking area.

"Is there a helicopter flying around?" She asked.

"Yeah, it looks as though it might land next to us."

A long hesitation dampened the conversation.

"Are you still there?" I asked.

"Yes, Babe, I'm still here. When we talk on the phone, it seems as though you are back home, as if I can get in my car, drive right over, and see you. Hearing the helicopter pulls me back to reality."

"Don't let it get you down, the time will go fast," I reassured her. "We've already been here close to four months now and that leaves just a little over eight left to go."

"I know. I'm sorry, Babe. I love you."

"I love you too. I'm going to have to let you go now. They are popping smoke about one hundred meters from here. The helicopter is going to land and I won't be able to hear you anymore."

The helicopter began its slow descent with the thundering sound beginning to distort the phone conversation.

"I love you, Babe," I continued. "I'll call again when I can."

The phone speaker started cracking and cutting out as the noise of the rotors echoed throughout the concrete shelters.

"I love...Babe..." The conversation ended.

With the cell phone in my hand, I sat and stared at the mixture of purple smoke and dust swirling around the rotors of the helicopter and shooting into the air. I wished I could have talked with her a little longer but even that would not have been enough.

"Lew, lets go. We've got a convoy," Leptien yelled from the gun truck.

During the return trip to Cedar, a convoy of military vehicles approached us from the rear. Too spread out to retain control during a pass, their lead truck sat at our heels and waited for the others to catch up.

Suddenly, the trucks in our convoy came to a halt with trailers darting across the highway blocking all three lanes. The military convoy behind us had no time to stop. Locating a tight opening on the shoulder of the roadway, they quickly swerved their vehicles through at sixty miles per hour just narrowly missing us.

While the command vehicle handled the breakdown at the front of the convoy, we parked the gun truck at the rear to pull security. Once again, the temperature reached over 100 degrees. With the present date resting in the middle of May, the conditions would only worsen as we moved into the summer months.

"That son of a bitch isn't slowing down!" Leptien yelled as he pointed to a vehicle charging our way.

A white car raced toward us at an accelerated speed. Nelson, pulling security at the rear of the humvee, held up his hand to motion the driver to stop. The car did not even attempt to slow. Leptien began waving his arms in the air to get the driver's attention. The car continued holding its speed. Nelson finally pulled up his M-16 and aimed it at the driver. The car locked up its brakes. Smoke filled the air as the car screeched to a halt less than fifty meters from where we stood. Long, black skid marks striped the highway indicating the excessive rate at which it traveled.

Nelson shook his head. "That crazy bastard, I almost shot him."

"Don't worry, Nelson. I think he learned his lesson." Leptien laughed. "He probably has skid marks in his shorts just as long as the ones he left on the road."

A call came over the radio and the convoy began moving. The trucks slowly straightened themselves out and filed into the left lane. We signaled to the cars we held waiting behind us to pass around but they stayed where they were and followed.

We each grabbed a bottle of water before Leptien sat down on the plastic cooler. The turret sling wore raw spots into his legs so the cooler doubled as his chair. The cool water gushed down quickly as dry throats opened to quench our thirsts.

Ping. "One-Six, this is One-Six Alpha. Over."

Ping. "This is One-Six. Over."

Ping. "We just heard an explosion ahead of us with possible gunfire. Over."

Ping. "This is One-Six. Do you see anything? Over."

Ping. "Negative, not yet. Over."

Ping. "Keep your eyes open and let me know if you see anything. Over."

Ping. "One-Six Alpha. Roger. Out."

Ping. "Bravo, did you catch that? Over."

I acknowledged. "This is One-Six Bravo. Roger. Out."

I explained the radio transmission to Nelson and Leptien. We continued searching for anything suspicious, anything out of the ordinary. The explosion may have been a cunning diversion with insurgents hidden within the sandy berm.

Ping. "One-Six, One-Six Bravo, this is One-Six Alpha. There is a truck on fire in the median up ahead. Over."

Ping. "This is One-Six. Roger. Out."

"This is One-Six Bravo. Roger. Out."

We passed a lone bobtail parked on the median strip of the highway. Like many we came upon before, it stood silently engulfed in flames. The truck belonged to another convoy and broke down during their mission. They abandoned it and continued on. Some person or group set it on fire and then hid in the berm when they saw us approaching.

That evening after supper, Top stopped me as I walked back to the tent area.

"Lew, I think we found a solution that'll make everyone happy and you would be able to keep your stripes."

What did he mean keep my stripes? According to the JAG officer, I had no reason to fear losing them.

He began explaining how a sergeant's position opened in the motor pool. I would be the units 92 Alpha, responsible for dispatching the vehicles and controlling the ordering and distribution of the motor vehicle parts. I would not actually be doing the work but I could use the sergeant's slot to hold my rank.

"Doesn't that slot belong to Brooks?" I suspiciously asked. "He's held that position for some time."

"Yes, it did, but he's agreed to take a position slotted in another unit in order to get a promotion. His slot is now vacant."

"What about the other guys in the maintenance section, isn't there someone qualified to move up into that slot?"

"They have the school but they don't have enough time in grade to be promoted to a sergeant."

I accompanied Top as we walked over to his and the captain's tent. They had the paperwork prepared beforehand and ready for my signature.

Both of them sat with smiles of accomplishment as they repeated the details of their plan. I did not trust them. I did not want to resign my artillery computer position but I knew they would stop at nothing in order to open up my slot and hand it out as a favor.

I did not say a word and signed the statement. Maybe the harassment would stop. This would assure me my stripes until we returned to the States.

My estimated time of separation (ETS) had long passed. I wanted to reenlist and continue with the guard but not under their leadership. My only option resided in waiting until I returned home and receiving my discharge from active duty. At that point, I could join a different unit and remain in the guard.

For the time being, I had real duties to perform. During the next two days, the rotation pulled us from the road to fill tower guard shifts.

Beep...Beep...Beep. My watch alarm woke me at 1:45 A.M. for tower duty. Moss and I would be manning Tango Five again on the 3 A.M. to 7 A.M. shift. It would be our last four-hour tower shift until we rotated off the road again. The tower shift from the previous morning moved along uneventfully with the exception of a fire near the burn dump reported by Tango Eight.

The KBR dug out a burn dump at the western edge of the camp near the towers and away from the main living area and its residents. With a slight north breeze, the tower guards spent much of their shift choking on the smoke and noxious fumes emanating from its flames. When the smoke became intolerable, the camp security provided the solution of moving from the tower and taking position on the berm. Of course, that did not help. If the smoke drifted to the tower, it also hung on the berm.

After reporting the fire, a great period of time passed before they realized the smoke actually originated from the burn dump. It took them twice as long in deciding if they should send a fire truck to extinguish the flames. They finally decided to let it burn.

During the afternoon shift, we witnessed a controlled explosion by the Italians in the direction of An Nasiriyah. Detonating a cache of explosives found in the area, an enormous cloud of sand and dust hung in the sky and gradually dispersed over time with the assistance of a slight wind.

Upon finishing the afternoon tower duty, I went for a run on the dirt road around the inner camp area. Running twice around equaled seven miles and proved to be a good run. I usually ran the berm of the camp during daylight hours but in the darkness, I preferred running closer to the living area. Even without the sun, the heat felt overwhelmingly present. After my run, I rested and talked with the guys in the smoke area as I drank a bottle of water to rehydrate.

The guys were upset over the rest and recuperation (R&R) schedule. The first group would depart in the morning for two weeks of leave. They would actually be away three weeks to include travel time. The schedule indicated two officers, and an enlisted man on a family emergency case. The guys felt disappointed the unit allowed two officers to leave for R&R before any of the younger enlisted men in the unit.

The leadership explained that not everyone would receive the opportunity to go home for R&R. They devised a lottery where they randomly picked names for the R&R slots. According to the list, many of the officers and senior NCOs would leave for R&R before some of the younger enlisted men. The younger ones wound up at the end of the list with their chance of going very slim if not at all.

Moss, Nelson, and I picked up Boz at the TOC and the SOG transported us out to the towers. The night seemed relatively quiet. Moss and I made small talk as we passed the night vision goggles back and forth keeping an eye on the surrounding tower area.

Ping. The tower radio sounded. "Romeo, this is Hellfighter Base. Over."

A long hesitation followed as the command base waited for a reply from the roving guards.

Ping. "Romeo, this is Hellfighter Base. Over." The call repeated.

The roving guards consisted of two gun trucks patrolling the outside perimeter of the camp and the adjacent area. They searched for hidden mortar positions and detained those who wandered suspiciously close to the camp. In the darkness, they continued patrolling with the assistance of night vision goggles.

Ping. "Hellfighter Base, this is Romeo One. Over."

Ping. "Romeo, what is your location?"

Ping. "We are presently in the ROM."

Ping. "You are in the ROM?"

Ping. "Roger, we are in the ROM next to Romeo Two. Over."

During the daylight hours, there were times when the roving guard chased a local sheepherder away from the tower area. The shepherd moved his sheep over the large berm that separated the camp from MSR Tampa. He grazed them on the sparse weeds growing a few hundred meters from the wire.

On their rounds, the roving guards, in spotting him, raced over to his herd. They waved long pickax handles while screaming at him. He always attempted to persuade them to allow him to stay but eventually he moved his herd back over the berm from where he came. A half-hour later, he returned with his herd when the roving guards were no longer in sight.

The shepherd never bothered us and kept his distance from the camp. We did not consider him a threat and left him alone to graze his animals.

At times the roving guards traveled along the berm, next to the wire. They passed by the towers as they circled the camp. We acknowledged each other with a wave to indicate no immediate concerns. Some of the guards in the towers removed their body armor to alleviate the effects of the extreme heat. The roving guards noticed them without their armor and reported it for disciplinary action.

Ping. "Romeo One, this is Hellfighter Base. Are you in the ROM? Over."

Ping. "Roger, we are in the ROM."

Ping. "What is your grid coordinate? Over."

Ping. "Grid coordinates?" The sound of surprise echoed in the roving guard's voice.

Ping. "Yes, what is your grid coordinate?"

Ping. "Wait one. Over."

Headlights of two humvees suddenly lit up a little ways from the back gate of the camp. It was the roving guard. They were nowhere near the ROM. In fact, the ROM lay a good five miles south of their position. One of the humvees took off full throttle heading in the direction of the ROM while the other humvee drove up to the back gate next to Tango Four, stopped, and exchanged passengers with someone waiting there.

I grabbed the binoculars to see what I could distinguish with the headlights shining from the humvee and the moonlight glowing above.

"They dropped off some chicks." I pointed out to Moss.

"No." Moss stepped over to take a look.

"Yeah." I handed him the binoculars and reached for the night vision goggles to see if I could get a better view.

"We should call it in, Lew."

"No, Tango Four is located next to the back gate. They are probably in on it. Otherwise, they would have called in something over the radio. If we call it in, we wouldn't be able to prove anything. We will wait for Geditz to stop by on his rounds and tell him about it. Maybe they can set something up to catch them in the act."

Moss shook his head. "I can't believe it. Those guys are supposed to be patrolling the area around the camp protecting us but instead they're out there getting lucky."

I looked at Moss. "I don't know if I would call it lucky. Have you seen some of those girls?"

"Yeah, maybe we should call it getting unlucky."

We laughed as we watched the second humvee speed away from the back gate.

"That's just plain stupid. It's dangerous for them as well as us," I said. "Maybe they get off on the danger they are in while doing it, knowing they could have their throats cut or heads blown open at any time."

Ping. "Romeo, this is Hellfighter Base. Do you have those grid coordinates for me? Over."

Ping. "Negative, we are having problems with the GPS. We had to shut it down and restart it. Over."

Ping. "Give me the coordinates once your GPS is up and running. Over."

We could hear the first humvee shifting through the gears as it raced down the road directly in front of our tower on its way to MSR Tampa. The second humvee trailed a quarter mile behind.

They were not the first soldiers to pull this. Kligel shared stories of similar incidents occurring when he first took over as the sergeant of the guard. A regular army unit assisted with roving guard duties. In the dark, they stopped their humvee straight out from Tango Four. The tower guards watched through the night vision goggles as a female in the roving guard group stripped naked and engaged in sex with the others on the hood of the humvee. It happened quite often. The tower guards never reported it. The soldiers helping with the duties were not part of the brigade and the tower enjoyed the free show.

Ten minutes passed before the radio sounded again. Ping. "Hellfighter Base, this is Romeo One. We have those grid coordinates for you. Over."

Ping. "Roger. Ready to copy. Over."

The roving guard gave the coordinates to Hellfighter Base. Neither said anything more over the radio about the strange incident.

The eastern sky began growing brighter as the sun rose. I explored the sun's beautiful colors through the binoculars as it pixelated over the contrasting sand. With each passing minute, it grew into an enormous, orange ball suspended above the horizon.

The faint sounds of dogs barking echoed from the mud brick houses in the distance. Sheep and cattle began moving under the directions of their white robed masters. Diesel engines roared to life as convoys of supply trucks began their movements along MSR Tampa. The giant machine slowly awakened beginning a new day in Iraq.

CHAPTER 9

Life on the Road

"What do you think of the hood scoop, Lew?" Nelson pointed to the new addition attached to the humvee.

Painted flat black, a fabricated piece of sheet metal protruded over the air intake vent on the hood of the gun truck.

"I like it. When did they get the hood scoops in?"

"They didn't. They don't make hood scoops for humvees. Sergeant Diekman made it, just one of his many talents."

"Ron does nice work, it looks machine pressed, gives the humvee a supercharged appearance."

"It should keep the engine running a little cooler. We may even pull some more power out of it. We'll see how it goes."

Traveling with a KBR convoy of fuel tankers moving out of Cedar, we passed the front gates in route to MSR Tampa as the sun reached over the horizon. Once on Tampa, we maneuvered through the ROM entrance on course to the main six-lane highway.

"Man that really stinks." I took shallow breaths to avoid inhaling as little of the foul air as possible.

"It's worse than a barnyard," Nelson agreed.

The ROM began developing a pungent odor. Huge piles of garbage filled the ditches throughout the five-mile stretch. Urine, feces, and dead animals combined with high temperatures of over 100 degrees boiled the waste into a tremendous stench.

As we traveled down the six-lane, one of the tankers pulled out of the convoy and onto the right-hand shoulder of the road where he stopped. We drove in behind him to assess the problem. Leaning over one of the side fuel tanks, the driver examined the source of his trouble. Diesel fuel drained through a large gash from his fuel tank onto the ground. Not present when we left Cedar, it was unclear as to exactly what may have caused the puncture hole during

117

movement down the highway.

I yelled back to the gun truck informing Nelson and Leptien
of the problem.

Nelson picked up the radio handset. "One-Six, this is One-
Six Bravo. One of the tankers stopped back here. He is trying to repair a hole in his fuel tank. Over."

Ping. "This is One-Six. We'll pull the convoy over. Let us
know when he's ready to go. Out."

A bobtail driver pulled back from the main convoy to assist
the tanker driver with the breakdown. Both worked quickly to stop
the leak. Diesel fuel continued draining steadily onto the pavement
and flowed to the road's side pooling along its edge. Too large of a
gash to patch with a quick fix, the drivers worked to close off the fuel
line between the two tanks in an attempt to save the contents of at
least one. One partial tank would provide enough fuel to complete
the remainder of the journey to Navistar.

Soaked in diesel fuel, the drivers rolled back and forth underneath the truck desperately trying to make the repair. They worked
quickly but the problem proved a difficult mend.

The Iraqi police soon pulled up behind us in two small pickups and stopped. The chief policeman yelled to his men as he
pointed to position them around the tanker, bobtail, and the gun
truck. Some lay prone while others dropped to a knee as they assisted
us with security.

The chief shook my hand and began explaining how he strategically spread his men out to provide cover for us.

"Ali Baba!" one of the policemen shouted as he pointed
across the sand.

Parked less than a mile away, a vehicle rested peacefully next
to a berm. It looked no different from the other vehicles we saw on
the road. Something familiar about it sparked their attention. An obvious sense of fear showed within them as they quietly repositioned
themselves closer to the gun truck.

The drivers overheard the concerns of the IP and sat up from
underneath the truck as if preparing to leave.

"No, no, keep working. Everything is OK." I smiled and
motioned them to stay at it. They glanced at the waiting vehicle, hesitated, and then reluctantly crawled back under the truck to continue

their repairs.

Leptien moved his gun turret around to face the berm.

"These boys are really spooked about something out there," he commented.

"Ali Baba, Ali Baba," the policemen whispered quietly to one another as they continued pointing their AK-47s toward the berm as if expecting an imminent confrontation.

The chief reached his hands up to his eyes and touched his fingers to his thumbs on each hand. "Do you have binoculars?" he asked in broken English.

"No, I don't." I shook my head.

I wished I had carried a pair of binoculars. There were occasions where they would have come in very handy. Supply stocked binoculars to issue but they would have charged me $350 if the binoculars were ever lost or stolen. Like many others, I did not want to help the army buy its equipment. It proved far less of a financial risk to purchase a cheap pair at the PX.

"Tony, if we needed to, do you think you could reach out and touch them with the SAW?" I asked.

"No, not at that distance, Lew, if we drove just a little closer to them, I think I probably could."

Qualifying as an expert SAW gunner, Leptien's abilities in using the automatic weapon surpassed many of his peers. He carefully studied the target as the suspect Ali Baba patiently watched us from the berm.

"They're not bothering us right now," I explained to Leptien and Nelson. "We better stay with the tanker. Once they finish, we can get out of here."

I patted the chief on his back and smiled. "You go get the Ali Baba. We'll wait here and pull security on the tanker."

He did not appreciate my sense of humor and looked at me as though I were nuts.

"No, no, too far, too far," he replied.

As the police nervously sat securing our position, it seemed as if they remained for their own protection and not ours.

The drivers began speaking in Arabic as they pointed to the repairs. They were through and ready to leave. We shook hands with the policemen and left to join the convoy. The IP followed closely behind us until we were a safe distance from the location where the tanker broke down and the Ali Baba waited.

The convoy moved along at a quick speed without further trouble. As we drove, I thought of the conversation I had with Boz during breakfast earlier in the morning. He talked of his dissatisfaction with being on the team. The convoy missions were inordinately tough on him and with the high temperatures continuing to increase daily into the summer months, it would only become worse.

He spoke with the LT, the captain, and Top about his concerns but they refused to make changes to the teams. Others felt the same way, many who worked convoy duty wanted off the teams as well but no one willingly offered to go out on the road and replace them. Those working in the camp knew of the extreme conditions on convoy security and held tightly to their jobs.

An oil streak began appearing in the far right lane. As the convoy continued moving forward, the streak widened with the oil starting to pool next to the curb.

"Can you spot anything ahead of us that may be leaking this oil?" I yelled over to Nelson.

"No, not a thing, there sure is a lot of it though."

As we drove along, the spill worsened, until finally the source appeared.

"There he is." I pointed to a civilian tanker parked along the curb with oil gushing onto the highway from its rear valves.

"Take a look at this." I tapped Leptien on the back.

I readied my camera to take a picture. As we passed the tanker, an oil-covered man stood next to an assortment of soaked clothes piled in front of his truck. Wearing a small, oil saturated strip of cloth across his groin, he stretched his arms to the sky while clutching a wrench in his hand. I had difficulty determining if he stood there crying, praying, or both.

"Look at that poor bastard. He's a mess," Leptien commented.

I lowered my camera and returned it to my bag. I could not take a picture of the man in his pain. I felt sorry for him.

After releasing the convoy at the border, we continued on to Navistar to locate a push north. The MCT lot looked empty which meant we could be in for a long wait. At times, I did not mind waiting. It provided us an opportunity to eat at the dining facility (DFAC) and rest in the coolness of the movie theatre.

The theatre, a common tent providing movies on a big screen TV, stood in the PX area. An assortment of nylon and metal folding chairs scattered the sandy, plywood floor. Competing with the outside heat, two air conditioning units struggled to blow cool air into the wide-open tent space.

As we sat resting in the folding chairs, soldiers came and left as their time permitted. *Hidalgo* must have been the camp favorite. It seemed to be the only movie playing when we were there. It did not matter to us. Each time we visited the theatre, we could only view twenty minutes of the movie before a call came to pick up a convoy. In the course of a month, we eventually watched the entire film.

"Let's go guys. We got a mission," Boz shouted through the doorway of the tent.

We drove to the MCT lot to find our push north. With the temperature over 120 degrees, I picked up an extra bag of ice for the gun truck cooler.

A few of the guys gathered around an attractive, young, blond girl standing next to an expensive, shiny, black car. She looked out of place with her European designer clothes. After four and a half months of combat duty, we found her presence an unexpected sight.

My curiosity peaked so I approached her to find how she happened to arrive at this place. She seemed slightly intimidated by the attention she received from a half dozen young American soldiers with smiling eyes.

"What is your name?" I asked.

"Eva," she answered with a heavy accent.

"Eva, where are you from?" The guys listened tentatively as I talked with her.

"I am from the Czech Republic," she proudly declared.

"I hope you don't mind me asking, but what are you doing here?"

"I am traveling through Iraq," she excitedly explained. "I take trips when I want and I talked a friend into going along with me." She pointed to a young man walking out of the MCT building. "We are going to drive through Iraq."

Discovering Eva talking with us, the young man stopped outside the doorway and waited, unsure if he should come any closer.

"Do you know what it is like in Iraq?" I asked.

"I see it on television and want to find out for myself if it is that way."

"Believe me, Iraq is very dangerous. It is not a place for tourists. For your safety, I would suggest both of you go back home or possibly tour another country. It is not safe here."

She shrugged her shoulders and smiled. With our convoy mission ready to depart, I wished her and her friend a safe journey. We have experienced many strange happenings while in Iraq. This one fell in line with the rest of them.

The heat caused many problems with the return push to Cedar. Although we slowed the convoy speed substantially to avoid overheating the truck engines, flat tires plagued our progress.

"One-Six, this is One-Six Bravo. We have another truck pulled over with a flat tire back here. Over."

Ping. "This is One-Six. Another flat tire? That makes five flat tires during this convoy alone. It has to be a record. Over."

"This heat seems to be tough on the tires. I hope this is the last one we have to deal with today. The trucks are going to run out of spares soon. Over."

Ping. "We'll pull the convoy over and wait. Over."

"Roger. Out."

The Filipino drivers worked feverishly to change the tire. Sweat ran from their pores and dripped off their faces in the extreme heat. We were fortunate to have the Filipinos driving in the convoy. They did not miss a step and changed each flat tire with time to spare. I could not imagine the other TCNs demanding this much from themselves.

With the problem fixed, we started the convoy in motion and continued to Cedar. The tires held up during the remainder of the trip. Upon returning to camp, we enjoyed the tent's cool 100-degree temperature provided by the air conditioning unit churning away just outside.

In checking through the current stories on the Internet news Web sites, headlines told of the decapitation of a civilian truck driver by a group upset about the prison pictures scandal at Abu Ghraib. I thought of Eva and her friend whom we met at the MCT lot. With soldiers, contractors, and civilians facing death each day in Iraq, this place definitely did not cater to tourists.

The next day our team provided escort for the mail run to Tallil while we retrieved the interpreter. We finished our business at the air base and waited patiently outside the front gates for the interpreter to arrive. Eventually a civilian vehicle pulled from a dusty trail and parked across the road from us. Abrahiem stepped out of the small, white car. After exchanging goodbyes with his driver, he walked over to meet us.

He projected an air of animosity as I greeted him.

"I am very angry. I do not want to be treated the way that I was yesterday," Abrahiem demanded. "I do not want to be treated like that ever again."

Surprised at his comments, I listened as he went on.

"Yesterday, the American soldiers who picked me up were not respectful. They searched me and went through my possessions. They did this while my family watched. It embarrassed me in front of my family and friends who were there."

"This was another escort team that did this to you?" I asked.

"Yes, they are like you. They picked me up."

"Did they give you any indication as to why they were doing it?"

"No, and I do not want to be treated like that ever again."

I apologized and explained how the soldiers may have been suspicious. They would not have searched him unless they felt a concern for their safety. He seemed to understand but remained upset. In relaying the information to the LT, he did not seem concerned with the interpreter's problems.

We proceeded to the ROM to brief the drivers on the expectations during the next day's convoys to Kuwait. With Abrahiem riding along with Hanson and me in the humvee, I seized the opportunity to learn more about him and the people along the road.

An English teacher before the war, he offered his interpreting services to the coalition forces after the invasion. He lived in the city of An Nasiriyah with his family, wife, and two small children.

"Has your family always lived in Nasiriyah or around this area?"

"No, I am from Kuwait. My family is from Kuwait."

"Kuwait? How did you end up here?"

"After the first war with the Americans, they told us to leave. My ancestors are from Kuwait but my mother and father were born in Iraq."

He reached his hands up steadying himself as I applied the brake to avoid a large hole in the road.

"After the war," he continued, "the Kuwaiti government told all the Iraqis to leave their country. Because my mother and father were born in Iraq, they considered us Iraqi citizens as well. My mother, father, me, and my siblings were all forced to leave."

I looked over my shoulder at him. "You sound like a man without a country. Are you upset with the Kuwaiti government for kicking you out?"

"I am not without a country. I am Kuwaiti," he proudly explained. "Kuwait is my county. One day I will return to live with my family."

"Have you lived in any of the other Iraqi cities?"

"No, after leaving Kuwait, we moved here to Nasiriyah and stayed. I like it here. It is good here."

As we passed some of the Iraqis begging along the road, I waved to them and they responded with their thumbs up.

"Who are these people and where do they come from?" I asked.

"They are herders and farmers who live close to here." He pointed out into the desolate landscape.

"Did they beg along the road like this before the war?"

"No, when the American soldiers came, they find they can get more from begging."

"What about the vendors in the stands along the road?"

"They are from An Nasiriyah. They travel back and forth every day with their goods. Their lifestyle has improved very much with the American dollar."

As we approached the trucks waiting in the ROM, Hanson leaned out his humvee window and began yelling at the drivers. During the briefings, the team leaders explained the rules of the convoy to the drivers. When the drivers left in the morning with the convoys, things changed and the escorts subjected them to a completely different set of rules, the rules of the road.

"Do you want to hear a bullshit story?" Hanson yelled out the humvee window as we drove by the trucks. "Come and hear a bullshit story. Everyone, come and hear a bullshit story."

Hanson felt as displeased as I did with the hypocrisy of the convoy briefings. We were all just following the process.

During the briefing, one of the drivers brought up a concern about his missing truck.

"He says he has been here for many days now waiting for his truck." Abrahiem interpreted for the driver.

"Ask him what happened to his truck?" the LT inquired.

Abrahiem spoke in Arabic with the driver.

"He says it needed repairs so they took it to repair. He says he does not know if it is at Cedar or Tallil."

"Tell him he needs to go to Cedar or Tallil and ask about his truck."

Once again, Abrahiem spoke with the driver.

"He says he will not go to Cedar or Tallil. He says he is afraid he will be shot if he approaches the front gates."

"Tell him that I will check on it when I get back to Cedar."

By the look on the lieutenant's face, I could tell he offered another empty promise.

After the short meeting ended, we departed to return the interpreter back to the pickup point near Tallil. Driving between the rows of parked trucks in the ROM, I felt the adrenaline suddenly kick in. I discovered the humvee we drove to be one of the rare few with power plus speed. The engine roared as I pushed it to its limits. The rows of parked trucks quickly blurred as we raced by at speeds in excess of seventy miles per hour.

"Damn, Lew, you drive just like Dale Earnhardt, Jr.," Hanson nervously commented.

With an uncontrollable urge to pull as much speed out of the humvee as I possibly could, I held the accelerator to the floor as we initiated the exit turn from the main highway. Looking in the side mirror, I noticed our second humvee desperately trying to keep up so I slowed it down to an acceptable speed. The excitement vanished as quickly as it appeared and the wild ride ended. We left Abrahiem with his family and returned to Cedar.

I asked around and found which team performed the interpreter run on the previous day. After ending their mission of providing security at a captured ammunition site, the new Road Hunter team picked up convoy security duty.

"He was upset about that?" The team leader laughed. "I tell ya, Lew, it was the first time we've ever picked him up. We just did what we thought was right."

"I'm not saying what you did was wrong. I'm curious as to what might have happened to upset him."

"Actually, we didn't trust the son of a bitch," he explained. "No one would let him ride in their gun trucks unless we were sure he was safe."

"If we felt a concern, we would do the same," I concurred. "I think it was the embarrassment that really upset him. Next time I see him, I'll explain what happened. Thanks for talking with me."

"Yeah, no problem, Lew."

The Internet news sites told of attacks occurring the previous day in Iraq with one being in An Nasiriyah just a few miles from Cedar. A local militia quickly raised a group of one thousand strong to attack the coalition forces on patrol in the city. Firefights and RPG attacks were the order of the day there.

After supper, the LT stopped by the tent to inform the guys of meetings scheduled with two JAG officers for that evening and the next concerning the border incident with the disturbed captain.

"What? Why do we have to meet with the JAG?" one of the guys asked.

The lieutenant explained, "They only want to talk to those who wrote out statements about the incident. It's going to take some time to talk to everyone so they are meeting on both nights."

"When do we go?"

"Everyone will have to go at the same time. They'll let us know how they want to handle it when we get over there."

The guys groaned at losing more time over the incident.

The LT walked toward the door and then stopped. "Oh, and by the way, everyone has to write out another statement to hand in to the JAG at the meeting."

"See, Lew, we did the right thing." Scotting chuckled. "If we would've handed in a statement like everyone else did, we would've been stuck in this mess too."

I shook my head. "With all this extra time these guys are putting into this, I sure hope something works out to their benefit."

The guys pulled out paper and once again wrote about the border incident. With convoys scheduled for the next morning, their plan to rest that evening quickly faded. With any luck, the meeting would end early.

The next day, we left Navistar and drove the gun truck out ahead of the convoy to pull security in Safwan. Reports stated some of the trucks received damage caused by the locals throwing rocks. As we crossed the border into Safwan, I spotted two gun trucks parked along the side of the road. The soldiers stood out of their vehicles and next to three kids kneeling on the ground. The stern actions of the military police (MPs) indicated they might have caught the rock throwers reported over the radio.

We drove a little farther down the road and parked next to an intersection where we waited for the convoy to roll by. I stepped out of the humvee to pull security and hopefully deter others wanting to throw rocks at the trucks. As the sun beat down upon us, sweat slowly began rolling down my arms and dripping from the tips of my fingers onto the ground.

While waiting for the trucks to appear, a group of young kids moved toward us from the local mud brick houses. They seemed hesitant at first but eventually built up enough courage to approach us. As they moved around me, they laughed and asked questions in Arabic. I greeted them as I always greet the kids and found some who spoke a little English.

"George Bush goood. George Bush goood," they began shouting.

"America goood. America goood," they continued.

"Yes, yes, George Bush goood, America goood. Who's been teaching you this?" I laughed.

They stood and giggled while holding half-cupped hands to their faces in covering big smiles.

"What about Iraq?" I asked them.

"Iraq goood. Iraq goood," I shouted.

They stared at me and smiled. No one thought to teach them that phrase.

Leptien playfully stuck his tongue out at one of the little girls.

She returned the gesture.

"She has you figured out, Tony." I laughed.

Another little girl walked up from the group and began twirling and dancing in front of me. When she finished her graceful steps, I clapped my hands in appreciation. She returned her hands to her face and giggled.

In response to her performance, I extended my arms straight out from my sides and began hopping from one foot to another in providing them a little dance as well. Under the weight of the body armor and equipment, it felt difficult to move but I managed to make them laugh. The little girl and I exchanged turns displaying our dance steps as the group watched.

Laughing at my dancing skills, the other children began jumping up and down wanting me to do the same. By now, a large group of kids had gathered around to participate. Some of the little ones reached up with sticky hands, grabbed mine, and pulled me toward their houses insisting I come and play with them.

"No." I shook my head and laughed. "I need to stay here with my two friends. They will be upset with me if I leave them to go play with someone else."

Understanding I could not leave the humvee, they were content with staying where we were. One of the young girls began singing to me. Her beautiful voice, accompanied by some of the others, sang an Arabic song familiar to them. I gently clapped along to the rhythm of the music, which prompted the remainder of the group to join in with song.

As I stood motionless in the center of the choir of children, their powerful voices penetrated deep into my body with an unimaginable soothing harmony. I slowly closed my eyes and for one brief moment, I absorbed their incredible energy as it resonated throughout my soul. I no longer stood beneath my heavy body armor in the burning heat of the Iraqi sun. The dangers and anxieties of the war did not exist. Wading effortlessly through a serene field of tall lush grass, I felt at peace with the world.

"Hey, Lew, can you hear me?" Leptien yelled down from the turret. "I said here comes the convoy."

My eyes popped open at the abrupt announcement. The children had finished their song, the dream ended, and the war returned.

As the convoy passed, the command vehicle trailed and stopped next to the gun truck.

"We're missing ten trucks," the LT informed us. "They may have turned around at the border. Go back and check on them."

I explained to the children I needed to leave and thanked them for the song and dance. Some grabbed my hands in an attempt to keep me there but I eventually convinced them of our need to go.

We drove back across the border and through the checkpoints looking for the trucks. The task would not be as simple as driving straight through to the MCT lot. We followed the slow process of stopping in the staging area and clearing our weapons before moving through the maze of roads in route to the lot. Unable to locate the ten trucks, I contacted the LT over the radio.

Ping. The radio in the command vehicle sounded. "One-Six, this is One-Six Bravo. Over."

"This is One-Six. Over," the lieutenant answered.

Ping. "We've traveled the road all the way back to the lot and cannot find the ten missing trucks. Over."

"That's OK. We'll leave without them. Over."

Ping. "We are returning to the convoy. We'll contact you when we arrive. One-Six Bravo. Out."

Scotting became curious as to the strange task the LT assigned to us. "Hey, LT, why did you send the guys chasing around to find those trucks? We knew where they were. We saw them turn around at the border and head back to the yard."

The LT said nothing.

CHAPTER 10

Let Them Eat MREs

Looking through the cracked and pitted windshield of the gun truck, I curiously watched as the alpha humvee and command vehicle each turned around in the sandy roadway and drove toward us.

"Do they actually know where we are supposed to be going?" I asked Nelson.

Nelson drove off the path, turned around over the top of the narrow road, and followed.

"No, I think he's lost."

The team, scheduled for a midmorning weapons test fire, traveled to the firing range located south of the camp. The U.S and coalition forces used the test fire range to check the function and accuracy of their weapons. Maintaining a busy schedule since arriving in Iraq, we finally received an opportunity to test fire our weapons.

Ping. "One-Six Alpha, this is One-Six. I think we may have driven by it. The range should be up here somewhere."

Ping. "This is One-Six Alpha. Roger. We'll keep looking for it. Over."

We bounced though the many potholes and continued following in the trail of dust and sand. After a long, hot morning of changing oil and performing scheduled maintenance on the gun trucks, we were eager to get this over with and use the remainder of the day for personal time back at the camp.

Ping. "Stop here. This looks like a good spot. Pull over next to the berm on your right," the lieutenant instructed the alpha gun truck.

We pulled in next to the opening of a gravel pit and parked the humvees facing toward a large berm.

"I don't think this is the spot, LT," Hanson said as he exited his vehicle and approached us.

131

"It looks like a test fire range to me. We can test fire here and get back to the camp, unless you want to spend the rest of the day driving around."

"If this is not the right location," I spoke up, "then before we test fire, we need to check and see what's on the other side of that berm."

"Oh, you've got to be kidding me," one of the guys said.

"No, I'm not kidding anyone. I see tents and mud houses in the distance," I explained. "There may even be some kids playing just behind..."

Crack! Crack! Crack! The guys opened fire into the berm producing numerous bursts of sand and gravel. I was overruled. The few minutes it would have taken to crawl up the berm and check on the opposite side seemed like too much time for some to consider.

If the berm just became the only test fire range we have seen since arrival, I needed to check my weapon as well. I rotated my selector switch off Safe and fired a few rounds into the ground ten feet in front of me. My rifle worked just fine. As far as accuracy, I would have to hope its sights remained precise and not jarred from my zero with the daily handling of my weapon on the road.

Although instructed not to, many soldiers test fired their weapons into the wreckage scattered along MSR Tampa as they traveled down the highway. With children playing in the debris and men scavenging for scrap metal, the careless act could have injured or possibly even killed those living in the surrounding area.

Dogs were a large receiver of rifle lead with their huge packs roaming the desert. They became an easy target for those wishing to end their boredom during the convoys.

As we finished test firing our weapons, a red gravel truck drove up out of the adjacent pit. The driver stopped his sputtering, old truck behind us and caught my attention. He waved his hand in front of his face indicating his need of water. I nodded to him and walked to the humvee to locate a spare bottle.

"Don't give him any water, Lew," one of the guys yelled.

"Yeah, Lew, why do you want to give him our water?"

"We have plenty of water to spare," I replied. "He wouldn't have asked if he wasn't thirsty."

I walked to his truck and handed him the bottle of water.

Reaching a shaky hand down the side of his door, he took it from my hands and opened it. As he poured the cool liquid into his dry mouth, some of the water splashed from the bottle's opening and washed away the crusty, white salt covering his lips.

He closed his eyes and hesitated for a moment as he placed the half-empty bottle in his lap.

"Good?" I asked.

He opened his eyes and nodded as he turned the key in the ignition. I smiled and returned the nod as he shifted his truck into gear and left.

"Why do you do that, Lew? It only encourages them to continue to beg."

"He wasn't begging," I explained. "He was just a thirsty man looking for a drink of water."

With everyone's weapon operating as they desired, we picked up the brass casings and left for Cedar with much needed rest on the agenda for the remainder of the day. As we turned a corner near a small mud house on the dusty trail, two young children sat next to the decayed building and waved excitedly as we passed. A gunner, standing in the turret of a passing gun truck, turned and acknowledged them with a gesture of his own from both hands.

This lack of respect toward the civilians became commonplace for many of the soldiers. Whether out of nervous fear from their experiences on the road or an out lashing of anger from being in Iraq and away from their lives, it became their safety valve in dealing with the stress.

Upon returning to the tents, we sliced open a watermelon we left cooling in our small refrigerator. Two days ago, a small truck carrying a load of watermelon slowly passed next to our gun truck. In the past, we have seen these trucks and commented on how we would enjoy a slice of the fresh produce.

"Get his attention, Leptien," I yelled up the turret. "We'll see if we can talk him out of one of his melons."

The gentleman gladly stopped and offered us one of his round, green watermelons. He refused to accept payment for it but we insisted. Exchanged into Iraqi currency, it probably equaled enough to buy half of his supply loaded in the back of the truck.

As we sliced into the ripe melon, the sticky juices flowed

through our hands and onto the crushed rock between the tents. We commented to one another on the sweetness of the watermelon as we spit its seeds into the air. Others refused our offer of a generous sample slice.

"I wouldn't trust them. Do you know how they are grown?" they teased us.

We heard rumors of raw sewage used as fertilizer in the growing process of Iraqi produce. To contend with the possibility of food poisoning, we took precautions in cleaning the melon with bottles of fresh water. For our efforts, we stood with smiles and laughed as we enjoyed the ruby red fruit.

"I've got it." Specialist Dana Dargatz rushed into the tent holding a computer jump drive in his hand. "It was downloaded off the Internet."

"What do you have there?" Scotting asked.

"It's the beheading of the civilian contractor that the insurgents uploaded on the Internet."

The guys gathered around a laptop computer as Dargatz handed them the drive. I sat back in my chair and continued paging through my magazine.

"Aren't you going to watch, Lew?" Scotting asked.

"No, and I would suggest that you guys not watch it either."

"Oh, why is that?"

"Not because it's a gruesome clip but just out of respect for the contractor who was murdered. Besides, there is a very real possibility that any one of us could be in the same situation in the future. If you watch that clip now, you may be sorry you did later."

"There's the file," one of the guys indicated as they sorted through the drive.

They stared at the liquid crystal screen in silence as the video clip played. Their eyes widened and faces grimaced as the contractor's life came to a sudden end. With blank looks, they walked away from the computer without saying a word, the images of the grisly act now etched forever into their minds.

"Boy, I wish I wouldn't have watched that. That was a mistake," Scotting said as he walked back to his bunk. "Lew, why did you let me watch that?"

I laughed. "Who knows, maybe it was better the guys saw it.

It may help keep them on their toes a little more when they are out on the road."

"Yeah, but I didn't need to see it. I should have listened to you," he added.

"Even though technology provides it, some things just shouldn't be watched." I flipped though a few more pages of the magazine. "It only motivates the insurgents to do it again."

The time approached late afternoon and I needed to get my run in before the sun completely set. Upon arrival at Cedar, I found an unimproved trail running the inside of the berm that totaled approximately seven miles in length of which I did my best to run every other day.

At times, some of the others accompanied me on a partial run as I took them out, brought them back, and continued my run once more. The long runs within the berm were tedious at times so I enjoyed the company if only for a brief segment. I pushed myself to run hard underneath the hot sun. The run reduced the stress and cleared my mind. A scattering of feral dogs sat and watched as I leaped over the many deep ruts and pushed on. Occasionally, an Italian helicopter from Tallil Air Base buzzed closely over my head with its occupants acknowledging me with a casual wave.

After finishing my run, I walked the tent rows drinking a bottle of water to cool down.

"Jim?" Chaplain Lynn Wilson stopped me. "I was able to talk with the lieutenant colonel and sergeant major about that issue we discussed."

Pastor Wilson has been a good friend of mine for many years. Of the clergy I have met, I have found him to be the most sincere. He is truly genuine when it comes to understanding and practicing his beliefs.

During a conversation a few weeks back, I brought up the subject of the treatment of hajjis by the escort teams. Unaware the problem existed, he felt it an issue to convey to the attention of the leadership.

"They said there was nothing that could be done about it. They said it was due to combat stress," he regretfully reported.

"So they have known about this all along?" I asked.

"Yes, I would assume so."

In discussing the issue, we understood that neither of us could do anything about the mistreatment at the moment. Those above us wrote it off as combat stress and would allow it to continue.

I walked back to the tent and met some of the guys resting in folding chairs out front. As we talked, one of the 201st soldiers from the tents opposite ours approached us.

"Hey, take a look at these." He held out his digital camera.

"What do you have there?" one of the guys asked.

He pointed to the small display on the camera's backside. "Just take a look."

We quietly examined the photos as he clicked through each image.

"I took these pictures this morning," he explained. "Those are 155 millimeter artillery rounds. The hajji drove by us with these 155 rounds mixed in with shrapnel in the back of his little, white pickup."

"He's practically got a whole pickup load," one of the guys commented.

"Yeah, you know where he was going with those don't you?" he excitedly asked. "He was off to daisy chain the artillery rounds together and make an IED. We would have had a big surprise waiting for us tomorrow on convoys if we hadn't caught him."

With the day ending and convoy missions scheduled for the morning, we prepared to turn in for the night.

"Tent city is on fire!" Leptien and McMillan yelled as they burst through the door.

"I can't believe you guys are going to bed when tent city is burning." McMillan shook his head.

"How close is the fire?" I asked. "Do we need to evacuate the tent?"

"It's about five rows down. We're lucky the wind is from the west. If it changes direction, all these tents are going up."

We ran out through the door and stood in our nightclothes as we watched the flames shooting into the dark sky above the tent city. After quickly dressing, we hurried over to see if we could assist. An organized group of camp firefighters worked to control the blaze as a crowd of onlookers stood by with cameras to record the unfortunate event. The occupants of the tents escaped the fire without harm but their living quarters along with their personal possessions completely burned to the ground.

Back on the road after a brief time away, we proceeded down Tampa with a KBR convoy in route to Navistar. With tempers beginning to flare at the drop of a hat, we were cautious in waiting our turn for an escort mission earlier in the morning. A few days ago, we drove to the ROM and waited next to the trucks while they prepared to leave.

Road Hunter One-Seven's command vehicle rushed up and abruptly stopped next to us. Their team leader furiously flung his humvee door open and jumped out.

"Fuck!" he yelled.

He tore his helmet from his head and slammed it against the paved highway. As we watched the helmet bounce, he continued yelling.

"I looked all over for these MCT fuckers and couldn't find them anywhere."

Reaching down, he snapped up his helmet and threw it against the side of his gun truck. It sprung back toward him swiftly rolling across the highway and stopping next to his boot.

"We were supposed to have the first push out this morning but now we're fucked."

Finding our team waiting at the beginning of the truck column, he convinced himself that his team missed their position to take the first convoy to Navistar. Grabbing his helmet by its chin-straps, he picked it up off the ground and hurled it through the open passenger door of the gun truck.

"Ouch! Damn it!" his driver shouted. "If you want to get mad, then get mad, but don't take it out on me."

We calmed him down and reassured him his team still owned the first push out. We merely waited for them to get there and leave with their convoy so we could proceed.

Today, in traveling with a KBR convoy, we made great time as the trucks cruised along at sixty to seventy miles per hour. Arriving at the border, we released the trucks, refueled, and began the wait for the return trip north. We enjoyed ten minutes of peaceful eating in the Navistar dining facility before a mission came our way. Wolfing down the flavorsome food on our plastic plates and filling our pockets with what remained, we rushed to the gun trucks and left.

With the air temperature near 120 degrees, we poured many bottles of water down our dry throats as we chased behind the convoy. Switching with Nelson to drive, Leptien debated whether it would be cooler with the fiberglass doors removed from the humvee so the breeze could blow through the vehicle, or would the extremely hot air feel more like a blast from a furnace.

Ping. "One-Six, One-Six Bravo, this is One-Six Alpha. We're slowing down. There are camels crossing the road ahead of us. Over."

Ping. "One-Six. Roger. Out."

I keyed the radio handset. "One-Six Bravo. Roger. Out."

As the convoy slowed to a crawl, we watched as a massive herd of camels moved over the highway and filtered through the convoy. Similar to the buffalo roaming the plains of the historic Dakotas, the large number of camels filled the desert in every direction.

With the camels behind us, we picked up speed and continued with the mission to Cedar. As we traveled, one of the trucks began gradually slowing and eventually pulled over to the side of the road.

Weakened by the intense heat, his partially shattered windshield bowed inward from the force of the wind pressing upon it while he drove. Covered with small shards of glass swirling within the cab of his truck, the driver could not safely continue on.

"We're leaving the truck," the LT insisted as he assessed the damage. "He can't go anywhere with a windshield like that."

He looked at the driver and pointed to the truck. "Clean your truck out. We're leaving it."

"No. Please, sir. Please, sir," the driver begged for the lieutenant to reconsider his decision.

"What if we just kick it out?" I asked. "He could drive to Cedar without a windshield."

"I don't care. That's not up to me. Ask the hajji."

"Is it all right if I remove your windshield?" I asked the driver.

"Yes, yes, please."

I opened the passenger side door and climbed into the cab of the truck. Lifting my leg over the dashboard, I shoved my boot through the windshield. The sheet of soft glass folded around my foot, tumbled across the metal grill of the truck, and shattered on the highway. With my gloved hands, I removed the remainder of the windshield from its frame.

"Thank you, sir. Thank you. Thank you." The driver shook my hand.

"It's going to be a breezy drive for you. Do you have some glasses or goggles to wear?" I asked.

He shook his head. "I can still drive. I can still drive," he insisted.

"I've got some goggles he can have," Scotting said as he ran to the command vehicle to retrieve them.

The driver pulled the goggles over his eyes and wrapped his red cloth keffiyeh around his face for extra protection.

"Let's go!" the LT yelled.

The trucks started moving forward and we began racing down the highway once again.

Completing four days of security escort missions, we rotated off the road to pull tower duty once more. Before taking our shifts in the tower, we escorted the interpreter to the ROM for the convoy briefings.

"Can you take us to Cedar?" a truck driver asked in broken English as we waited outside the gates of Tallil for the interpreter to arrive.

Another miserable, hot day tortured us as we filled the backseat full of empty, plastic water bottles. An assortment of flatbed trucks sat idling by the gate while their drivers searched for a security escort to Cedar. Concerned the Ali Baba would hijack them in the few miles of road between the air base and the camp, the drivers hesitated to leave on their own.

"We can't officially escort you to Cedar. We are performing another task at the moment." I wiped the sweat from my forehead. "However, you can follow along behind us. No one should bother you there. If anyone would happen to attempt to hijack your trucks, we would be obligated to protect you. As we pass the Cedar road, you can turn off as we continue moving straight through to the six-lane."

"OK, OK," he replied.

"You're taking a chance though," I continued. "If for some reason you should break down. We cannot stop and wait for you. We will keep going. You would be on your own. Do you understand?"

He smiled. "Yes, I understand. When you leave, we leave. OK?"

"OK." I returned the smile. "I'll let you know when we are ready to go."

A few of the local kids bounced between the humvees looking for anything we would give them, mainly junk food and candy.

"Mista, mista, can I have? Can I have?" one of the young boys asked as he pointed to various items in the humvee.

I reached into a bag of individually wrapped Lifesavers that I purchased at the PX for the kids along the road and gave him a handful. As he pulled his overflowing hands from my window, two more sets appeared.

"Can I have? Can I have?" another of the boys asked.

"I just gave your friend a handful of candy." I pointed to the boy happily rushing away. "It was for all of you. Go see him. He will share it with you."

"Mista, he is not my friend."

I laughed. "With all that candy in his hands, he would make a good friend now, wouldn't he?"

Abrahiem arrived and we left for the convoy briefings in the ROM. According to our information, only one convoy stood ready in the ROM for an escort the next morning. Others would slowly trickle in as the day progressed. Most would arrive in the late afternoon and the early evening just before sunset.

I waved to the flatbed truck drivers. In watching for the signal, they suddenly sat up in their seats and began following along behind us. Vendors filled the road selling bottles of whiskey, cases of beer, pornography, DVDs, Iraqi flags, and military souvenirs. Standing partially on the road, they waved the items in the air for us to see in hopes we would stop and purchase from them.

Looking through my side mirror, I watched the two trucks separate from us as we passed Cedar's main road. They should encounter no problems at that point, at least not in the daylight. In the dark, the mile stretch leading to the front gates would be just as treacherous as the rest of the highway.

We entered the ROM and notified the drivers to attend the briefing conducted at our command vehicle in the center of their convoy. The drivers gave a halfhearted nod and slowly sauntered over to the meeting.

Assisting with many convoy briefings in the past, Abrahiem quickly organized the group and began giving the briefing in Arabic. The drivers asked questions with Abrahiem doing his best to answer.

"What are they asking you?" I questioned Abrahiem.

"They have many questions about food and water," he said.

As Abrahiem spoke, several of the drivers approached me. "Some of us do not speak Arabic. Can you tell us what he is saying?" they asked.

Not all the drivers originated from Arabic speaking countries, many spoke other languages as well.

"No, I don't speak Arabic either," I replied. "As soon as he is finished, we'll give another briefing in English."

"You are like us then." They laughed. "We can't understand a thing he is saying." They made babbling sounds in poking fun at the language and continued laughing.

According to the procedure, the lieutenant should have given an initial briefing in English followed by the interpreter repeating the brief in Arabic. The LT had problems with his briefings so Abrahiem's assertiveness pleased him.

As Abrahiem continued speaking, I walked over to the LT who stood quietly off to the side. "Some of these drivers informed me they don't understand Arabic. Do you think you could give another briefing in English when Abrahiem is through?"

He laughed. "Yeah, I guess I can do that."

I reassured the drivers the lieutenant would give another briefing in English.

"Do you have any food or water you could give us?" they asked.

It then occurred to me, all the drivers might be in need of supplies so I asked them, "do you need food and water now?"

"Yes." they said as they nodded their heads.

The interpreter had just finished his briefing. "Abrahiem," I asked, "What are the drivers saying about the food and water?"

"They say they do not have food or water. They say they have not eaten all day."

I looked at the lieutenant. "LT, let's give these people some food and water."

"No, they can get it from the fuel point," he insisted.

He turned to Abrahiem. "Tell them if they want food and water then they need to go to the fuel point and get it."

Abrahiem spoke to the drivers.

"They say they asked at the fuel point for food and water but were told they could not get it there. They say they were told to look elsewhere."

The lieutenant became upset. "Tell them the food and water is at the fuel point. We are through with the briefing. We're done. Let's get out of here."

I could not believe we were doing this again. "Do any of the drivers have food or water?" I asked Abrahiem. "Are all the drivers completely out?"

"Yes, they have no food or water," he replied.

The LT moved toward the command vehicle door in preparation to leave. With the commotion involving the lack of food heating up, he decided to skip the English briefing and take off.

I moved through the uneasy crowd and walked over to the command vehicle. Lifting the humvee's rear hatch, I found numerous cases of bottled water and MREs. These people were hungry and in need water. We left a group without food and water in the ROM a few months ago and I felt determined to do what I needed so it did not happen again.

"Form a line if you need food or water," I yelled as I motioned to the drivers.

As I began to hand out the supplies, Scotting, Nelson, and Boz quickly joined in distributing the food. They felt as I did in wanting to provide the drivers with something to eat and drink.

"Thank you, sir. Thank you, sir." The drivers expressed gratitude as they received the much needed handouts.

"We only have a limited supply so don't take more than you will eat this evening and tomorrow morning. There will be more when you arrive in Kuwait."

"I take for my friend, OK?" one of the drivers asked as he reached for additional meals and water.

"Yes, if you know of someone who isn't here and needs food, take extra for them."

"Thank you, sir. Thank you, sir."

The lieutenant did not say a word. Standing at the front of the humvee waiting to leave, he glared at us as we fed the drivers. I would probably receive a counseling statement or an article fifteen for disobeying him. There were numerous work details he could punish me with for doing this. I did not care what he thought. I would not let these people suffer when we possessed plenty of food and water to offer them.

CHAPTER 11

No Good, No More

Racing on the tail of the alpha gun truck, we were in route to Tallil after receiving orders to retrieve two U.S. mail trucks. The command vehicle remained at Camp Cedar to receive possession of the main convoy. If all worked as planned, we would meet at the intersection, one mile south of Cedar's main gate, and continue on to the Kuwaiti border with the convoy.

The early morning drive seemed no different from previous trips to Tallil. The humvee engines roared as the drivers held the pedals to the floor pushing the vehicles to their limits. I squinted through the bright rays of the sun slowly rising on the horizon as I attempted to locate the alpha truck somewhere directly in front of us. I felt an occasional quick brake followed by a sudden swerve left or right to avoid large holes in the shattered, paved road.

People began appearing along the road. The local peddlers stocked their roadside stands for the day's passing roadway travelers, while the children, lining both sides of the road, rubbed their tired eyes and waved to us in hopes of having food thrown to them.

We parked the vehicles near Tallil's front gate and watched the locals file through to perform various manual labor jobs at the air base. Some arrived on foot while many appeared in overcrowded compact cars and small pickups. Two air force security personnel, observing the traffic, sat on the roof of their humvee in the glow of the rising sun and ate a hot breakfast served on white Styrofoam plates.

After waiting over twenty minutes, I looked past the front gate and down the air base's main road for a sign the mail trucks were on their way but they were nowhere in sight. I walked over to Hanson's humvee where McMillan and Bloom sat arguing over food eaten by one and belonging to the other.

Hanson finished a sip from his soda and placed the can on the radio. "I don't think they are going to show, Lew."

I looked down the road again. "They should have been here by now. I don't even see a trail of dust in the distance."

"Yeah, I think they stood us up." Hanson picked up his radio handset and contacted the lieutenant. We waited long enough for the mail trucks and our convoy stood ready to move. Our new orders stated to return and hold at the intersection.

We arrived at the turnoff to Cedar and waited for the convoy by an assembly of concrete barricades. A variety of graffiti spray-painted in Arabic and English covered the sides. The words "Cedar II" stretched across the length of one with an arrow pointing in the direction of the camp. As we waited, escort teams passed through the intersection with convoys in route to MSR Tampa for trips moving both north and south.

The hajji cigarette vendors were out in numbers that morning. They stood in the ditches along the road and waved cartons of cigarettes at the truck drivers. Every so often, a convoy truck slowed and its driver shoved his arm out the window holding currency in his hand. The vendors sprinted from the ditches to the moving vehicles and exchanged the cigarettes for the money in one swift handoff.

A security concern existed with the cigarette vendors and their access to the convoys. Most sold cigarettes simply to earn money but it would not be difficult to place an explosive device inside a cigarette carton and throw it through the window of a truck. To discourage them from approaching the convoys, we yelled and threatened them as they ran to the trucks but they ignored us and continued with their sales.

"Hey!" I screamed as loud as I could.

Startled, they hopped a foot off the ground and turned to look at me. I had their attention now.

"Koft! Koft!" I yelled as I walked toward them motioning to pull back from the trucks and clear out of the ditches.

They retrieved their cigarettes hidden behind a small berm and hung their heads as they slowly treaded away from the road.

We positioned the gun trucks in the convoy as the LT passed through the intersection with the mission to the border. The morning breeze felt comfortable as it flowed through the open windows. The radio remained filled with the usual chatter of convoy breakdowns experienced by the other escort teams. Our convoy did not reserve immunity for this problem. Midway through the journey, one of trucks pulled over as the convoy continued moving along.

As the truck rolled to a stop, Nelson made radio contact with the command vehicle informing them of the situation as I jumped out of the humvee and ran up to the driver's door.

"What's wrong? Why did you stop?" I asked.

Unable to speak English, he opened the door of his truck and pointed to his clutch pedal while pushing it to the floor without resistance. His clutch was out.

"Keep moving. That is no reason to stop. You can take care of that in Kuwait." I motioned him to move forward.

He nodded, closed his door, and accompanied by the unpleasant sound of grinding metal rushed to join the convoy.

"He's good," I yelled to Nelson. "Tell the LT to keep going."

We were fortunate this time. The bad clutch incident being only a minor problem lasted less than sixty seconds.

Upon arrival, we found the border backed up with convoys waiting their turn to cross. As we slowly moved our group of trucks through Safwan, we stopped many times and cautiously waited before continuing. At each stop, I stepped out of the humvee and helped in securing the rear of the convoy.

During the long waits, some of the local kids approached the humvee searching for handouts. Mohammed, an outspoken young boy, seemed to be the ringleader of his small group. He helped pass the time by telling many stories about his friends along the road.

The bobtail driver, positioned in front of the humvee, motioned me up to his truck. An American contractor, the KBR hired him to assist with the truck drivers.

"I just received a call on the hand-held radio," he said. "There are kids up the line stealing from the trucks. They broke into the side compartments and took all they could carry."

We left the rear of the convoy and roared over the sand berm in the gun truck searching for the little thieves to retrieve the loot. Spotting a group of boys standing a short distance from the road, we drove over toward them to investigate.

They pointed to a large berm and yelled, "Ali Baba. Ali Baba."

They stood without tools or log chains so we safely assumed they were not the thieves. As we stopped, I opened the door of the humvee, pointed to the berm, and asked, "Ali Baba?"

Excited, all the boys spoke at once in Arabic. Through the confusing jabber, I interpreted they were upset with those who steal from the trucks. The wrongful actions of a few gave them all a bad name. The trucks began moving down the road. With the thieves long gone, I thanked the boys for their help and we rejoined the convoy for the slow moving ride to the border.

On the return trip to Cedar, we rotated positions in the gun truck. Leptien operated the radio, Nelson manned the SAW, and I drove. The change provided a slight variety during the long, hot day on the road. The team picked up a push of fuel tankers and we returned across the border into Iraq.

Once again, the kids swarmed along the roadside berm. Their begging brought them dangerously close to the massive tanker trucks' rolling duals, which could easily crush a small child.

An elderly man sitting in the shade beside a mud house yelled as we passed. He waved his shovel in anger at Nelson in the turret. The old man became upset with our interference of the kids, who begged for food to give to him. Nelson smiled and politely returned the wave.

We snaked our way onto MSR Tampa and pushed the convoy up to a good, fast cruising speed. As the breeze moved through the windows of the humvee, it slightly cooled us and dried the sweat rolling down our faces. According to my mini thermometer, the air temperature read close to 110 degrees and continued to climb.

This mission was the first convoy run into Iraq for the new Pakistani drivers. Their Filipino convoy commander assured me they would experience no problems. The Filipinos were excellent drivers. The Pakistanis were fortunate having this commander as their leader. If anyone could teach them properly, it would be him.

From the rear, the convoy looked steady as the vehicles moved along tightly at sixty miles per hour. As we neared the hajji mart, the traffic became heavier. Considered a resting point between An Nasiriyah and Basra, the half-mile stretch of Iraqi vendor stands catered to those civilians stopping along the road for food, drink, and supplies.

The locals built the rickety stands from mud bricks, corrugated tin, reeds, and anything they could scavenge from the area, in an attempt to provide shade and shelter. They constructed many directly on the highway's shoulder extending into the traffic lanes. The well-traveled exchange stood between two highway over-passes accommodating numerous civilian vehicles moving through and around the market.

As the convoy moved through the hajji mart, a civilian truck suddenly pulled out from the roadside and into the convoy's path. One of the tankers quickly swerved to the left avoiding a collision with the careless driver. In doing so, the fuel tanker rolled over onto its side covering all three lanes as it slid along the pavement. A massive shower of white sparks filled the air accompanied by a rapidly expanding cloud of dust and sand. The tankers following him hastily parted to alternating sides of the highway as they slammed on their brakes to avoid crashing into the fallen fuel tanker and one another.

"Oh shit!" Leptien shouted as he dropped the radio handset and braced his hands against the windshield.

"Hang on!" I yelled as I jumped on the brake pedal forcing us to a sudden halt.

For one moment, time stopped. Nothing moved. The world stood motionless. We were face to face with the wreckage of a tanker full of fuel, waiting, waiting for it to explode. I am here to attest that despite Hollywood's many spectacular depictions, a fuel tanker will not instantaneously explode when in a high-speed rollover, but it will catch fire.

Smoke slowly began drifting upward from the tanker with flames reaching closely behind. Leptien grabbed the radio handset and alerted the LT as to the truck accident. I drove the gun truck closer to the wrecked tanker checking for the driver. The flames engulfed the tanker, which showed little hope anyone could have survived.

Smoke and foul language filled the air as we checked the hajji stands next to the raging fire to clear everyone back in case the tanker would happen to burst and spray fuel over the area. Needing little coaxing, the civilians grabbed what they could carry and ran as fast as they could to get away from the shooting flames.

Nelson waved to the remaining tanker drivers, instructing them to form up by the bridge and wait for us. The bridge arched the highway a safe distance away from the fire and stood within immediate sight.

As I checked the last stand, I glanced toward the fire and noticed a miniature army man dressed in desert camouflage standing next to the burning tanker.

"Who the hell is that?" I yelled as I pointed toward the tiny soldier by the burning tanker. "We need to go up there and find out who that is, they may be hurt and in need of help."

Both Leptien and Nelson glanced at the burning tanker and back. "Lew, we need to provide security for the tankers at the bridge. We shouldn't leave them unprotected for this long."

I wanted very badly to drive up and grab that soldier but the few minutes it would have taken may have been disastrous for the trucks needing protection by the bridge.

I pointed at the remaining tankers and yelled, "Take the humvee back to the bridge and provide security for the tankers. I'll go see who that is and find out if they need help."

I took off running toward the burning tanker as Leptien turned the gun truck around and proceeded toward the bridge. I could feel the heat becoming more intense as I neared the massive flames. My body armor provided little protection from the heat. As I reached the lone soldier, he turned and gradually began walking toward me. It was Scotting.

"Hey, Lew," he seemed surprised at my presence and greeted me.

We were dangerously close to the burning fuel and needed to move away as quickly as possible. If the side of the truck suddenly split open, its fuel would drench our bodies and instantaneously engulf us in the fire's flames.

"Are you OK? Is everything all right?" I asked as I grabbed his arm and pulled him away from the fire.

"Yeah, look at this fire. Isn't it cool? I got some pretty good pictures."

At that point, I realized he was fine. He walked around the burning fuel rolling through the ditch to take pictures.

"Man, that wasn't a very safe thing to do, Gary."

"Yeah." He shook his head. "There was a few times when I got a little nervous but I'm fine. No problems."

"Lets get back to the gun truck and we'll contact the LT. We'll let him know you're OK. They may be worried about you."

As we hurried to the gun truck, I became upset thinking of his carelessness. I thought of how the fire could have burned him to death in his attempt to take a few pictures, not a pleasant story to tell his wife and family back home. One positive presented itself in his impulsive search for pictures, he provided an extra person to help pull security, and we were going to need him.

While I retrieved Scotting, both Leptien and Nelson arranged the trucks across the median strip in the southbound lane. With the wreckage burning in the northbound lane, this would be the only route to join the convoy once the fire let up. For now, the smoke and flames reached across the median into the southbound lane and stopped traffic in both directions.

In contacting the lieutenant, they found the tanker driver to be safe. He escaped from the fire before the flames overtook the cab of his truck. He suffered a few scrapes, bruises, and a sprain but otherwise seemed fine. I informed the drivers of their friend's condition and reassured them we would take good care of them. I stressed the need to stay alert until the fire let up and we crossed to the other side.

Looking around, I took a quick assessment of the situation. A fire separated us from the main convoy. The four of us were on our own with three fuel tankers, a bobtail, and one gun truck. Traffic started to congest on the highway behind us and the Iraqis were becoming extremely upset with the blocked road. This would be an excellent opportunity for the Mahdi army or some of al-Sadr's other followers to strike at us.

I yelled to the guys, "It's just the four of us on this side of the fire. Don't let anyone get close to the tankers. If something looks wrong, do what you need to do in order to protect us and the tankers."

I checked the chamber of my rifle and moved the selector switch off Safe.

"I see the ICDC coming this way, Lew," Nelson yelled down

from the turret.

The Iraqi Civil Defense Corps noticed the smoke from the fire and raced down the highway to assist. They should be friendly but one never knows whom to trust, especially in our present situation. Some of the ICDC and Iraqi police are known followers of al-Sadr.

The ICDC stopped their trucks on the opposite side of the median strip in the northbound lane. Two dozen men dressed in dark brown uniforms and all carrying AK-47s, climbed from the back of their pickups, and assembled onto the highway.

I did not want them any closer to the fuel tankers than they presently stood.

"Watch the tankers," I informed the guys. "I'll go talk with them."

The ICDC consisted of local volunteers organized by the Iraqis to help with various security tasks until their country's government formed and they established an army. The military did not authorize the ICDC to carry weapons until recently, when they issued them AK-47s. This particular group worked out of a new camp a few miles south of the hajji marts, located one hundred meters off MSR Tampa. The camp itself measured not more than fifty meters in diameter and consisted of a few tents with an Iraqi flag waving on a lone flagpole. Usually, when we met them on the road, they stopped and searched civilian vehicles for contraband while manning checkpoints along the highway.

I walked across the median strip, extended my hand, and smiled. A noticeable uneasiness blanketed them as they asked many questions pertaining to the fire. I knew a few words of Arabic but their questions came too fast. I continued to smile as I shook my head.

"Inglizia? Inglizia?" I asked hoping one of them would start to speak English. All shook their heads.

I did not want to explain the situation more than once and thought it would be best to talk with their senior ranking person. I pointed to the rank insignia on my Kevlar helmet and then at each one of them. They understood and pointed to a taller thin man approaching from their lead vehicle.

He reached out his hand and shook mine. Pointing to the

burning tanker, he nervously inquired, "Ali Baba? Ali Baba?"

The Ali Baba did not cause this. That I knew. I did not command the language skills to explain what actually happened. A civilian truck had pulled out from the market and the tanker swerved to avoid a collision.

They looked at me with anxious eyes hoping that it did not involve the Ali Baba. I held my hands together and placed them next to the side of my face. I tilted my head and closed my eyes. I then pointed to the tanker and shrugged my shoulders. They understood. The driver may have fallen asleep.

A look of relief came over them. Ali Baba did not cause this mess. With the good news, they shook my hand once more and smiled. I indicated I would return to my vehicles and they were on their own to do whatever they needed. They positioned themselves to set up a checkpoint where they could detour civilian drivers away from the fire.

Meanwhile, the smoke continued billowing as the fire roared. Some of the civilian traffic attempted to move around the blocked highway by driving off the road and through the sand. In desperation, they blazed their own trails as they climbed their vehicles up the side of the embankment to the overhead bridge. Many were bogged down in the sand with others assisting in pulling them free. With the traffic remaining heavy, the ICDC relocated a mile farther down the road to better direct the traffic away from the fire.

Time slowed to a disheartening crawl. We waited there for what seemed to be an eternity. The longer we remained, the bigger target we became. The mood started to become extremely uncomfortable on this side of the fire. The smoke continued rolling but the flames no longer reached as far into the southbound lane as they once did.

"Let the drivers know we are going to chance it and drive to the other side," I informed the guys. "Tell them they need to stay tight so we don't leave anyone on this side of the fire."

"Do you think its safe enough to go, Lew?" Scotting asked.

"Yeah, the flames have reduced so the heat should not be as intense. We won't catch fire if we charge quickly through the flames. Get ready to move."

I grabbed the radio handset from inside the gun truck. "One-

Six, this is One-Six Bravo. Over."

Ping. "This is One-Six. Over."

"We are going to try driving through the smoke to your side in the southbound lane. How does the southbound lane look? Is it clear of traffic? Over."

Ping. "Roger. It's clear. Good Luck."

"One-Six Bravo. Roger. Out." I tossed the handset back inside the vehicle.

"Let's go!" I yelled to the guys as I sat down in the driver's seat.

Leptien and Scotting jumped into the gun truck as Nelson waved at the drivers to follow us.

"You might want to hold your breath as we drive through the smoke," I suggested.

"Hold my breath?" Leptien asked. "Why?"

"Between the tires, wires, plastics, and fluids burning in that fire, the smoke could be very toxic. It could burn your airways and lungs. You may want to hold your breath."

Grabbing the steering wheel with both hands, I stomped on the accelerator and built up enough speed to charge the smoke and flames. Looking through the windshield, the smoke appeared extremely thick, so thick that I could not see the hood scoop mounted on the front of the humvee. I prayed there sat nothing on the other side of the smoke we would collide with.

We quickly pierced through the smoke and narrowly missed a British convoy waiting on the other side in the southbound lane. The inside of my nose burned from the toxic residue even though I held my breath.

I pulled the gun truck into the median strip allowing the tanker drivers to roll on around us and catch up with the main convoy parked a few miles ahead on the side of the road. I drove across the median to the command humvee, which sat next to the hajji stands, and checked on the driver from the burning tanker. McMillan, our combat lifesaver, had just finished treating him. The driver appeared a little shaken but doing fine.

The lieutenant contacted the leadership and waited for direction as to the disposal of the burning tanker. They finally instructed us to wait for the recovery team to arrive and allow them to take care of the wreckage.

Some of the hajji stands did not survive the fire and completely burned to the ground. Fortunately, none of the civilians were injured or killed. One of the stands, untouched by the flames, remained occupied by a man and his young son.

The man held out a bottle and smiled. "Pepsi, from Canada." He pushed the bottle into my hand. I appreciated his generosity in offering us something to drink but I felt it would not be right to take it. I smiled and shook my head.

While the others assisted the driver into the back of the gun truck, I handed him a bottle of water. He looked tired and beaten. Leptien, Nelson, and McMillan drove the gun truck up the road to join the convoy where they stayed to help pull security with Hanson, Boz, and Bloom. I remained with the LT and Scotting to assist with the Iraqi civilians and await the arrival of the recovery team.

"What now? What now?" One of the Iraqi vendors irately approached me. "Everything gone! Everything burned up!"

"Was that your stand?" I pointed to a pile of smoldering rubble.

"Of course it is. It is mine. Everything gone now, everything burned up."

"It was a bad accident," I explained. "We are all fortunate no one was seriously hurt."

"I have nothing now. Who's going to pay me?" He bent down and scratched zeros in the sand with a stick. "That is what I want. I want 100,000 dinar. You burned my business. I have nothing left. I want 100,000 dinar."

One hundred thousand dinar roughly equaled seventy-five bucks. In looking through the remains of his inventory, I would have estimated less than twenty dollars back home, maybe five there.

"I understand you lost your business and you want to be reimbursed for the damages but I don't make that determination," I politely explained. "You will need to talk with someone else. We are waiting for a group to arrive out of Cedar II to remove the wreckage. They may be able to help us at that time."

An expression of confusion shadowed his face. I pointed in the direction of Camp Cedar II.

"An Nasiriyah?" he asked.

"Yes, yes, An Nasiriyah," I confirmed. "Cedar is located in the area of An Nasiriyah. People are coming from there to clear this wreckage off the road."

Satisfied with the answer I gave him, he paced back and forth looking at the charred remains of his stand.

He pointed at me and asked, "Are you police?"

I half nodded.

"Are you police or are you soldier?"

"Both," I explained. "Depending upon the situation, we perform the duties of both."

Disgusted, he shook his head. "America no good!" he exclaimed. "They helped the Iraqi people, but no more."

I patiently listened as he began venting his anger and frustrations.

"America no good, no more," he continued. "Killing Iraqis at wedding." He referred to a recent air strike in western Iraq on a gathering of insurgents. "Iraqi prisoner abuse." He continued, referring to the abuse of Iraqi prisoners by U.S. soldiers at the Abu Ghraib prison. His long list of complaints sounded as though they came straight from the news broadcasts of Al Jazeera television.

"America no good, no more and should go," he shook his finger in the air and repeated.

I knew I could say nothing that would convince him otherwise. Over one thousand soldiers gave their lives during the past year so he could stand in front of me and spit in my face. He felt upset about losing his little stand. The stand provided his livelihood and now, it angered him that it no longer existed. He needed to take it out on someone. I happened to be the soldier he thought he could complain to. Yes, his comments upset me but I knew that generally, he lived a much better life now, better than over a year ago under Saddam Hussein's brutal regime. He felt angry because he wanted his stand back. He wanted things to be as they were a few hours ago when he laughed while conducting business with his many customers.

A few of the younger Iraqi men approached us as we waited. Some of them asked for handouts—water, MREs, porn, whatever we could give them. Having problems with a tooth, one man removed his hand from his mouth and displayed a set of blood covered fingers. Scotting dug through his personal bag and found some

Tylenol to offer. It provided little assistance but seemed enough to satisfy him.

"Let's go!" the LT shouted. "We are needed at the convoy. Alpha captured an Ali Baba."

"What about this mess?" I asked. "These people are expecting us to stay and take care of it. It won't look good if we suddenly leave."

"It's not our problem now," he explained as he sat down in the passenger seat of the humvee. "Recovery will have to handle this when they get here."

Looks of disappointment shown on the Iraqi vendors' faces as we jumped into the command vehicle and took off without saying a word. In talking with them, we gained their trust. Now, we left them with the burned remains of a tanker where their businesses once stood.

The convoy sat idling under a major power line two to three miles north of the hajji marts. The bravo gun truck stood out in the sand positioned a few hundred meters off from Tampa. Bloom secured the front of the convoy in the alpha gun truck while McMillan pulled security on foot in the rear. We drove out into the field and stopped next to the guys huddled together beside the bravo gun truck.

Excited about their catch, they snapped pictures of one another holding an AK-47 rifle. Their prisoner rested on his knees and seemed content as he sipped from a bottle of water they provided him.

I walked over to Boz who stood guard on the prisoner. "How did you guys capture him?" I curiously asked.

Boz straightened his glasses and leaned against the humvee. "He walked toward the convoy and just willingly handed over his weapon."

"Just like that, he gave himself up? Why would he do that?" I looked at the prisoner.

"I don't know. We tried talking to him but none of us speak Arabic."

We needed more information so I thought I would try my hand. "Did you guys search him?"

"Yeah, except for the AK-47, he's clean."

"Hold this for me. I'm going to talk with him." I removed my M-16 and handed it to Boz.

The prisoner, a young man in his late teens, wore a plain pair of pants and a shirt, not the common thawb robe we observed many others wearing. As I approached him, I retrieved my Arabic language guidebook from my pocket to help in translating.

In pointing at phrases in the book and using hand gestures, I found he worked for the power line company. His job entailed walking the power structures and checking the condition of the lines. During his daily routine, he came upon the Ali Baba shooting at the wire. The thieves took the downed wire to sell or trade to others. Needing help, he spotted the convoy parked along the highway and walked over for assistance.

From what I understood, the Ali Baba remained hidden in the berm about two hundred meters away from us.

"How many Ali Baba are out there?" I pointed to the berm and back to the Arabic numerals on the page.

He reached up and tapped the Arabic numeral indicating five.

After he finished examining the AK-47, the lieutenant walked over to check on the prisoner. I briefed him on my findings but he did not seem interested in the man's story or the Ali Baba hidden in the berm. The man did not carry a permit for the AK-47 so we were to confiscate his weapon and release him.

The LT approached the man for information to include on a report he needed to file at Cedar.

"What's your name?" he asked the man. "We're taking your weapon and you can pick it up at Cedar. Just approach the front gates and explain who you are. They will return it to you."

The man looked puzzled upon hearing the comments.

"He doesn't speak English," I informed the lieutenant.

"If he wants his weapon back, we are going to need his name." He looked at the man. "What is your name, name?"

The man looked at me for help.

I nodded and pointed to the LT. "Ma asmak? Ma asmak?"

The lieutenant jotted down the man's name as he spoke it.

"We're done here." He started toward the command vehicle. "Release him and let's get out of here."

"Sir." I stopped him. "We shouldn't leave this man unarmed.

Once we leave the area, he will most likely be killed by the Ali Baba waiting in the berm."

"No, we're taking the weapon with us." The LT insisted.

"He's going to need that AK-47 for his own protection," I continued. "He came to us for help. We should not leave him defenseless."

"It's not up for discussion. We're taking the weapon. If he wants it, he can pick it up at Cedar."

"You know as well as I do that Cedar is a long way from here and he will never get up there to claim his weapon."

Ignoring me, the LT walked over to the command vehicle and left for the convoy.

I indicated to the man he could ride along with us to Camp Cedar and retrieve his weapon. He understandably declined. He approached us for help and we confiscated his weapon. What else would we do to him down the road? He probably thought he stood a better chance with the Ali Baba. With a helpless look, he watched as we left him in the field and returned to the highway taking position in providing security for the convoy.

As the convoy began moving, Nelson reached down from the turret and tapped my shoulder.

"His buddies are picking him up, Lew," he informed me.

I glanced into the side mirror and watched a small pickup turning off the road and driving down into the ditch to retrieve him.

CHAPTER 12

Mohammed's Truck

I held the accelerator to the floor as we raced through the ROM following directly behind a KBR convoy. Nelson requested an additional day in the gun turret. He did not have his fill of the blistering heat on his face. Leptien felt ill. With a pounding head and churning stomach, he asked to man the radio. I enjoyed pushing the humvee to its limits and did not mind being behind the wheel.

"Hey! Hey!" a voice screamed from across the median strip.

I glanced over and saw one of the drivers running after us waving a handful of papers.

"It's Rena," I shouted. "He must have recognized our humvee."

"He probably wants us to give him a ride back to Kuwait." Leptien laughed.

I let up on the foot feed and began applying the brake.

"Keep going, Lew, just keep going," Nelson protested my actions.

"Yeah, Lew. Just keep going. I do not want that stinky bastard in here with us. I'm not feeling very well." Leptien rubbed his forehead. "If I have to smell his rear end all the way down to Kuwait, I'll puke."

It would have been fine with me to take him along. He did not smell any worse than the rest of us, nevertheless, we did not receive authorization for another rider in the convoy. As quick as the unit handed out counseling statements and article fifteens, I would be paying for quite some time if we gave him a ride.

I stomped the accelerator back to the floor to catch the convoy. He would locate a ride on his own through the MCT people. In all fairness, we could not hold Rena responsible for his predicament. The blame belonged to us.

The previous day we received a mission to escort thirty trucks full of groceries back to Cedar. The convoy moved at a slower speed than usual so some of the truck drivers became impatient and started passing one another. The rules stated no passing because of the tremendous danger it caused. The LT became furious. He began pulling out the violators from the convoy. One by one, he slowed them down until they fell back to the last truck of the convoy. He gave us orders to hold them in the rear to punish them.

One of the trucks constantly overheated. It moved no faster than forty-five miles per hour. Eventually, it fell completely out of the convoy and stopped next to the median strip along the highway. The LT pulled the convoy over a short distance up the road to wait for us.

Ping. "One-Six Bravo, this is One-Six. We don't have time to waste on him. He'll only slow us down. Escort him to the relay point up ahead. We are going to leave him there. Over."

"This is One-Six Bravo. Roger. Out."

This surprised me. In the past, some of the convoys traveled slower than this truck moved. There were no concerns with slow speeds then. Why now?

Nelson motioned the driver to follow us as we led him across a narrow, sandy path to the relay point. Located near the Iraqi police station, the relay point was one of many lining the highways of MSR Tampa. Manned by a few soldiers, it provided the convoy teams with a drop-off point to secure trucks until a recovery team retrieved them for repairs.

The command vehicle pulled in behind us as the truck stopped next to the concrete barricade entrance of the relay point. In a foul mood, the lieutenant began yelling at the driver. "Get down! Get down! Get out of your truck!"

The driver refused to move. One of the relay point sergeants also tried but failed. They became upset with him so I walked up to the cab of the truck and motioned the driver to get out. He shook his head at me as he did the others. Without a major mechanical problem, he may have thought we were trying to steal his truck. I motioned him again, this time very sternly, to leave his truck and come with us.

He reluctantly opened the door and stepped down onto the

soft sand. Rena Mohammed, the Egyptian driver, spoke no English. I directed him to climb into the back of the humvee as the lieutenant made arrangements to leave his truck. When the lieutenant finished, we drove back to the highway and joined the convoy.

We left him with one of the drivers whom he considered a friend. Rena tried speaking with the lieutenant but it did no good. The LT did not understand what he said so he ignored him. The convoy began moving. Rena, along with his friend, ran up to me with the same concerns they attempted to explain to the LT. I finally understood. He wanted a receipt for his truck. He worried he would be in trouble if he did not receive paperwork indicating we ordered him to leave the truck. There being nothing we could do out on the road, I convinced them to wait until we arrived at Cedar.

We released the convoy in the ROM and ended the mission. While waiting at the fuel point to fill the humvees, I noticed Rena ahead of us talking once again with the LT and getting nowhere. He asked for my help. I explained to the lieutenant about the receipt but I could tell he wanted nothing to do with the situation. I did not want to leave this driver without help so I motioned him into the gun truck. We left him in the ROM with one of the MCT people who promised to take care of his paperwork.

Now, watching him chase after us through the ROM, I felt the least we could have done was to provide him a ride back to Kuwait. This morning, he should have been traveling north with his convoy instead of begging for a ride. His luck would not change. He would soon see us again.

Two days later, after performing tower duty at Camp Cedar, we returned to the road. We retrieved a mission from the ROM to escort the last push of tankers to Navistar. The convoy started moving when we noticed not all the drivers wanted to join us.

Parked up the line, Hanson waved his arms through the air while cussing at the drivers, "Go! Go now! Go!" He wanted them to follow the rest of the convoy, which left for the fuel point to refuel before the trip south.

"Hanson," I yelled, "what's wrong? Why aren't they moving?"

Hanson looked furious. He had enough in dealing with them. "We're not waiting around any longer. Either they go or I'll leave them. They go now or stay." He stepped into his humvee and left to take up position at the front of the convoy.

I walked over to the drivers. They stood together next to their trucks and talked among themselves. One of them knew a little English but otherwise they all spoke Arabic. Their convoy commander remained up north in Scania. He held their passports and they did not want to leave without their papers.

"Do you want to stay?" I asked them.

The driver, who spoke a little English, sheepishly spoke up, "Yes, we want to stay."

The orders were not that they absolutely needed to come along. The orders were they either came along with us or stayed here.

"OK, stay," I said. If it did not make a difference to Hanson whether they stayed or went, then it made no difference to me as well.

They smiled as they walked back to their trucks to wait for their commander to return from Scania. It would be another night in the ROM for them. They would join a convoy tomorrow morning with one of the security teams escorting them to Navistar.

I started back for the gun truck when the MCT sergeant drove up next to us. She helped coordinate the movement of trucks through the ROM.

"What's going on here? Why aren't they moving?" She inquired.

I explained the situation, which upset her quite fiercely. She jumped out of her humvee and started cursing at them.

"You fucking retards, get the fuck out of here. Get going. You can't stay here."

They did not understand a word she screamed and continued talking within their group. This really upset her. She began waving her arms as she cursed but received the same results.

I knew they wanted to stay. Who in their right mind would want to spend another day and night in the ROM unless they absolutely needed to? Between the foul smell, flies, and heat, this place became an unpleasant nightmare. They must have enjoyed their convoy commander's company to desire to wait for him. He probably treated them as though they were human and not like a hajji. Not like a dog.

Seeing the sergeant's frustration, I decided they needed to come along with us. I knew it would be better for them if they did.

"Get in your trucks. Let's go," I yelled.

The drivers looked at me with a surprised expression.

"Come on. Get in your trucks. There has been a change in plans."

They quickly stepped into their trucks, started the engines, and joined the convoy refueling by the serpentine next to the ROM exit. I understood their concerns. They did not want to take off without their leader. They did not want to travel without a passport. Leaving with us must have been OK to some degree, otherwise, the MCT sergeant would have kept them there.

It surprised the sergeant to see them suddenly move. She looked at me as if to ask how.

"Maybe they don't understand what a fucking retard is," I commented as I stepped into the humvee. Nelson started the vehicle and we followed along.

We normally refueled the gun truck twice a day, the first at Navistar, to supply fuel for the return trip to Cedar. Once back, we refueled again, to provide a full tank for the next morning. We carried an extra five-gallon can of diesel fuel strapped to the rear of the humvee for emergencies. Fortunately, we had never needed to use it.

There have been a few times where we have not been able to refuel at the end of the day. On those occasions, we refueled in the ROM just before we left with a mission. This happened to be one of those instances. As the trucks refueled, we slipped into the fuel line at the end of the convoy and began filling the humvee's tank.

The air force managed the fuel point. They were pleased to see us and did not mind us refueling there at all. We helped them monitor the drivers. The convoy trucks normally accommodated two fuel tanks. They did not need more than one tank of fuel for the trip to Navistar. After they filled one tank, we directed them to move on. Some tried filling both tanks and would often siphon off the excess fuel and sell it.

Ping. "One-Six Bravo, this is One-Six. Over."

I grabbed the handset. "This is One-Six Bravo. Over."

Ping. "Are the trucks about through refueling? Over."

I looked at the remaining vehicles in the fuel line. "Roger.

There are a few left refueling along with us. All should be through shortly and ready to roll. Over."

Ping. "Bravo, you were supposed to refuel before we left Cedar. From now on, you will refuel when we return…"

In another foul mood, the LT chewed us out over the radio for refueling the humvee in the ROM. If it concerned him, he could have waited and discussed the matter with us when we arrived at Navistar or that evening when we returned to Cedar. That was not his style, no, not the LT. When he chewed into someone, he did not care who heard. He seemed to enjoy belittling people in front of others. This could have been from his inexperience in managing people or just his way of establishing authority. He was not alone in his style. I witnessed others, who held leadership positions within the battalion, doing this as well. If he had properly questioned us about refueling, he would have learned of our attempts to refuel and finding the fuel point closed. It would not have mattered though. We were not the first treated this way this morning and we certainly would not be the last.

"…Do you understand? Over."

"This is One-Six Bravo. Roger. Out." I ended the conversation.

We traveled down MSR Tampa and made great time. The only incident we encountered involved a few of the trucks joining another convoy. Actually, it concerned the same group of trucks we experienced problems with earlier in the ROM. The convoy escort team preceding us this morning experienced a breakdown on the road just ahead of us. Their convoy stopped for repairs on the right-hand side of the road. Discovering a convoy waiting along the roadside, the drivers thinking it theirs, pulled in behind to wait.

We drove up next to the trucks and Leptien convinced them they were in the wrong convoy and needed to follow us. They shifted their tucks into gear and left as quickly as they stopped. We eventually caught up with the convoy.

After crossing the border, we released the trucks and prepared for the return mission. Nelson took us into Navistar and parked the gun truck in line with the other teams' humvees. Alpha and the command vehicle arrived a few minutes before us and the guys walked off leaving Boz standing there to wait for us.

"The LT wants you guys to stay here and watch the trucks. He said it is your punishment for refueling this morning in the ROM. Besides, everyone else already left."

"Where is the LT?" Leptien asked. "Why didn't he tell us this himself?"

"He left with the others. He told me to wait here and tell you guys when you arrived."

Boz left for the computers to check his e-mail.

In the past, only one person from the team stayed to monitor the radios for a mission from Trade Center South. That person also kept an eye on the equipment in the vehicles so no one would walk off with it. Generally, someone always chose to stay and monitor the radios for one reason or another eliminating the need to appoint anyone.

With this considered our punishment, all three of us remained and waited. Otherwise, I could have sent Leptien and Nelson off to find some air conditioning. It did not make sense to us. Refueling earlier this morning should not be something requiring punishment. The LT obviously concocted this on the run. He felt upset about something and we were paying for it.

The temperature felt dreadfully hot as the sun pounded on us. We found a little relief in the shade of the humvee and next to the concrete barricades surrounding the parking area. My mini thermometer indicated 114 degrees and rising. We were in Kuwait so I pulled out my cell phone and called Donna. The time difference converted to 3 A.M. back home.

The hours slowly trickled by before Trade Center South finally contacted us with a push. We rounded up the guys and drove to the MCT Lot. The convoy waited staged and ready to leave. Some of the drivers gathered in a small group and stood next to their lead trucks. I walked over to talk with them and became surprised when I met Rena Mohammed, the Egyptian whose truck we left at the relay point a few days prior.

His face lit up when he saw me. I smiled and shook his hand. "Rena Mohammed, it is good to see you again."

He nodded proudly as I acknowledged him in front of his friends. The trucks soon roared to life. We passed the border, Safwan, and began cruising down MSR Tampa.

Team one-five left before us and stopped a few miles up the highway with a breakdown. As we came upon them, the radio sounded.

Ping. "Road Hunter One-Five, this is One-Six. Over."

Ping. "This is One-Five. Over."

Ping. "We're coming up behind you. Is there room to pass? Over."

Ping. "Yeah, we're all pulled over into the right-hand lane. The left lane is clear. Over."

Ping. "Sounds like you have one of those convoys that we normally get. Over."

Ping. "Yeah, if you want, you can stop and we'll trade. Over."

Ping. "Negative. We're not back yet. We'll probably see you again down the road. One-Six. Out."

As we passed team one-five, the guys exchanged the usual hand gestures. The temperature now read over 120 degrees. The red mercury in my mini thermometer pushed at the top of the tiny glass tube. It could not register anything higher. The air blowing in through the open windows felt like forced air through a furnace. The only relief came from drinking water, bottles and bottles of water.

We traveled a few miles down the road when one of the drivers pulled over with problems. He hit the brakes and came to a hasty stop leaving those behind him swerving to avoid a collision. In suddenly slowing, the other trucks veered into any open space available filling all three lanes.

"One-Six, this is One-Six Bravo. We have a truck stopped back here with all the traffic lanes completely blocked. Over."

Ping. "This is One-Six. Roger. We'll pull the convoy over. Out."

I stepped out of the humvee to open a driving lane so traffic could pass around us. With very little room for the trucks to maneuver, it would not be easy.

"One-five is right behind us. It looks like they'll be here in a few minutes," Leptien yelled down from the turret. He called team one-five on the radio and informed them of the situation. One-five stopped their convoy behind us and waited for an opening to pass around.

I ran from truck to truck instructing the drivers as to where they should move their vehicles. Each one of them knew the specific order in which they traveled and preferred not to deviate from it. They knew which truck they followed and they stayed behind it. I tried convincing some of the drivers to move ahead into other lanes but they refused unless the truck they followed also moved.

As I directed traffic, the convoy began moving. I jumped back and forth dodging the massive trucks, as they desperately tried returning to their correct positions in the convoy. As we left, we passed the command vehicle parked in the left lane behind two of the trucks. They continued to make repairs.

Nelson pointed back at them. "Why is the convoy taking off if the trucks aren't ready to go?"

It surprised me as well. The LT provided no radio traffic as to stopping the convoy so I picked up the radio handset. "One-Six Alpha, this is One-Six Bravo. Over."

Ping. "This is One-Six Alpha. Over."

"You might want to pull the convoy over. We still have two trucks on the side of the road back here. Over."

Ping. "Should I stop the convoy? Over."

I hesitated, allowing the lieutenant time to break in and provide direction.

Ping. "Someone better tell me what to do! I can't see what's going on back there! Pull it over or keep going?" Hanson screamed.

I keyed the radio handset. "One-Six Alpha, this is One-Six Bravo. Pull the convoy over and wait. We'll go back and check on one-six and the two trucks. Over."

Ping. "One-Six Alpha. Pulling over. Out."

Just as the convoy stopped, team one-five and their convoy passed around us on the right-hand side. The guys returned the gestures they passed earlier. The command vehicle, following our two trucks, trailed directly behind them. We were ready to try it again.

Team one-five traveled a little over forty-five miles per hour. Even though our convoy could capably move faster, the LT would not pass. He did not pass team one-five as they moved down the highway. The captain and Top exchanged turns commanding that team. They probably made him a little nervous. We matched their speed and crawled along behind them.

The vehicles in the convoy began leaping around a single

truck that gradually lost speed. The slower truck eventually fell back to our position. It belonged to Rena. His truck overheated and he could barely maintain the forty to forty-five miles per hour speed we traveled.

We stayed with Rena as he separated from the convoy and continued drifting farther back.

"One-Six, this is One-Six Bravo. Over."

Ping. "This is One-Six. Over."

"This is One-Six Bravo. One of the trucks is overheating and having a difficult time in holding the convoy speed. We've fallen away from the convoy. Any chance of stopping to fix this problem? Over."

Ping. "Negative. We'll slow down but we are not stopping. Over."

"Roger. Out."

As the convoy slowed slightly, we continued falling behind. It looked as though we would not catch up unless the convoy slowed down even further than they had. At our distance, the gun truck could not provide adequate security for the main convoy.

"One-Six, this is One-Six Bravo. You need to reduce speed again. We are continuing to fall behind. Over."

A hesitation lingered on the radio. Ping. "We're pulling the convoy over and switching the load to a different bobtail. Maybe that will make a difference. Over."

"Roger. Out."

We pulled to the left-hand shoulder of the road and waited for the extra bobtail to arrive from the main convoy. I talked with Rena and explained the change in bobtail. Without a load, his truck would be better capable of maintaining the convoy speed and return safely with us to Cedar.

The lieutenant became upset when he discovered which truck the problem involved. "That's the truck? That's the truck?" he yelled from his humvee window. "I can't believe it. That's the same truck we left at the relay point a few days ago and they still haven't fixed it. We should leave it here for the Ali Baba. That would teach the KBR a lesson. Maybe next time they would fix their trucks before sending them out on convoys."

It upset us all they returned the truck to the road without

making repairs. Unnecessary breakdowns and poor vehicle maintenance could cause a great deal of trouble to the point of someone
becoming injured or possibly even killed. We had no reason at all to
leave a good vehicle with minor problems on the road when it could
travel to Cedar under its own power. These trucks were expensive
and difficult to replace.

The lieutenant stepped out of the command vehicle and
walked over to the driver's side door. He looked up at Rena and
began to yell. "This is the same truck that we left at the relay point a
few days ago for this exact same problem. Why wasn't this truck
repaired?"

Not totally understanding why the LT stood screaming at
him, he stared down at the lieutenant without responding.

The LT walked back to the command vehicle while Rena and
the bobtail driver exchanged the load. The driver checked his con-
nections to assure he secured the load properly. With everything in
order, they were ready to join the convoy waiting a mile up the highway.

Rena shifted his bobtail into gear and began to proceed to the
convoy when the LT stopped him. "Clean out your truck and leave
it," he ordered.

Rena looked at him. His English was not the best but you
could tell that he understood the demand. Rena sat back in his seat
and stared at the lieutenant.

"You heard me. Get your stuff and get out. Take everything
you need. We're leaving the truck. The KBR can pick it up." He
stood there waiting for Rena to comply.

"Here come the Iraqi police," Boz yelled from the command
vehicle.

I looked down the highway and saw two pickups loaded with
blue shirts and AK-47s. They noticed the convoy parked on the highway and were on their way to assist with security.

I looked at the LT. "Sir, this truck can make it back to Cedar
on its own. Without a load it should have no problems."

"No, we're leaving it. It'll slow us down. We need to get going now," he insisted.

"Let's take it as far as it will go. If it blows, it blows. The way
it sits here, we're just giving the Ali Baba a perfectly good truck to

steal," I explained.

Boz waved the radio handset in the air. "They're calling for you on the radio, LT."

The LT shook his head and walked back to the command vehicle to check on his radio call.

The Iraqi police arrived. They pulled into the median strip and stopped in a cloud of dust and sand that appeared around them. Their pickups quickly emptied and they approached us holding out their hands in greetings.

Rena looked at me for help but I could do nothing now. With the final decision established, we needed to follow orders.

I nodded my head and waved him out of the truck. With a look of disbelief, he gathered his things and stepped to the ground.

The Iraqi police became excited when they discovered we planned to leave the bobtail. They communicated they would secure the truck for us so the Ali Baba would not steal it. Rena and I stared at the policemen. We did not trust them. One of the policemen finally gestured as to the turning of keys in the ignition with his hand. Rena looked at me. I grudgingly nodded. Rena held out the keys and smacked them down into the policeman's hand. He briefly stared into the man's face and then turned and walked over to catch a ride with the truck hauling his load.

"Ali Baba! Ali Baba!" One of the policemen yelled as he pointed to a car traveling our way in the southbound lane. The policemen suddenly dropped to their knees, drew up their AK-47s, took aim, and readied to fire. The cars on the highway quickly slowed with some pulling into the far lanes to get out of the line of fire. With a dozen rifles pointed at it, the car in question locked up its brakes and came to an abrupt stop. One of the policemen yelled to the others indicating the vehicle did not belong to the Ali Baba. They stood up and waved at the traffic to continue.

They seemed a little jumpy. Some displayed tense looks. They certainly feared the Ali Baba. After many incidents with the thieves, they did not take chances.

One of the policemen began arguing in Arabic with the driver from the truck preparing to leave. I could tell the disagreement involved leaving the bobtail. Both became angry at each other. I stepped between them to stop the squabbling before it escalated and began involving the others. I kindly motioned the driver back into his truck with Rena. He stepped up into the cab, shifted his truck into gear, and drove off to join the convoy. I looked at the policeman and sternly shook my head to establish he needed to leave the drivers alone.

"Ali Baba! Ali Baba!" Once again, all the policemen dropped to their knees, pulled their weapons up, and readied to fire at a suspected vehicle. After a half dozen cars came to a screeching halt, they passed the all clear with traffic once again returning to normal in the southbound lane.

Two of the policemen adjusted the interior of Rena's truck. Excited about driving, they displayed smiles extended from ear to ear. Actually, it did not matter if we handed them the keys now or if they came back five minutes after we left and took the truck. Either way, it belonged to them. I motioned to take it and leave.

The sound of grinding gears filled the air as they placed the truck into motion. The engine killed twice before they finally discovered how to operate the clutch. They turned it around through the median strip and started southward for whereabouts unknown.

After thankfully shaking hands with us, the remaining policemen returned to their pickups in pursuit of their new find. As the LT continued his conversation on the radio, the rest of us stood on the road's edge and watched in amazement as to what had just happened.

"Lew, I can't believe we just gave the IP a perfectly good truck," Scotting spoke up. "That was wrong. That was just plain wrong."

"There is nothing we can do about it now." I watched as the truck slowly disappeared down the highway. "The KBR will never see that one again."

We reached the ROM and found Rena standing along the truck rows waiting for us to arrive. Once again, without a truck, he needed our help. Without saying a word, I reached around and opened the back door of the humvee. He smiled, tossed his bag in, and followed. I explained to the MCT team that he lost his truck on the road. They were willing to arrange in finding him a ride back to Kuwait. Thankful for the help, he shook my hand before we left. I wondered if this would be the last we would see of him.

CHAPTER 13

Rules of Engagement

I rapped on the plywood door and stepped inside the tent. At 5:45 A.M. the interior of the tent looked just as dim as the outside early morning darkness. Experiencing an unfortunate mishap at Navistar the previous day, Boz would not be driving for the command humvee. While retrieving ice, Boz hurt his arm when he slipped and fell from the ice truck. His day off the road would include a long wait for x-rays at Tallil.

Scheduled to leave in fifteen minutes to collect a convoy, I had not noticed Boz's replacement, Sergeant Jason Severson, preparing his gear for the road. As with others who occasionally stood in on the convoy teams, they might not have informed him of the change so I thought I would check on him.

"Are you coming along with us today?" I asked into the dark tent.

With a small trickle of light from a distant generator beaming through the open doorway, I recognized the shadow of a head pop up from his pillow.

"I heard I was going but nobody gave me a time." He cleared his throat.

"Yeah, that sounds about right. We're not going to be leaving for another fifteen minutes. You don't need to worry about the vehicle, Scotting picked it up and it's ready to go."

He wiped the sleep from his eyes and began stirring. "OK, give me a few minutes and I'll be out there."

Locating a push in the MCT lot, we left Cedar with the escort mission to Navistar. As we drove, we enjoyed the early morning temperature of 100 degrees. It would be the cool point of the day.

As we traveled south on MSR Tampa, I noticed a 201st Bulldog security escort team on the opposite side of the median strip slowly picking up speed as they traveled north. With some of the Bulldog teams based out of Navistar, they traveled to Cedar each morning and returned to the border at the end of the day. Their route traced the opposite path of ours.

Unable to make repairs on a truck, they abandoned it along the roadside and continued with their mission. Bound for one of the camps in Iraq, the semitrailer now sat helpless and full of groceries. It felt shameful to watch them drive away and leave it, but like most, I am sure they had no other choice.

Their convoy moved down the highway no more than fifty meters when the locals stormed the broken down vehicle. Waiting nearby in anticipation of the event, it now belonged to them, free for the taking. Cars stopped, people ran from the fields, kids darted with bikes, and an old man hobbled with a cane, all swarmed around the truck's trailer eager to seize the treasure locked inside. Standing away from the back doors, they waited as a young man swung a steel bar against the padlocks in an attempt to shatter its clasps. The trailer door quickly opened and its contents spread across the highway for all to scavenge through.

The Bulldog team could do no more than we could about the looting with the exception of driving away and watching the chaos that always followed. I hoped some of the food would find its way to the bare tables of the poor who lived along the highway but most likely, the scavengers would sell it to provide weapons and explosives for the insurgency.

Continuing down the highway, dust and the smell of brakes saturated the air as one of the drivers pulled over with a flat tire. As the convoy stopped up the road, the driver quickly pulled out a jumbled assortment of wrenches and sockets to begin work on the flat. He desperately struggled with the wrenches but could not loosen the lug nuts. Some of the other drivers, who stopped their trucks behind him, also attempted to remove the tire but it did not help. The nuts had tightened themselves to the point where they would not budge.

The driver explained in broken English that he would not change the tire but would leave it on the trailer. Upon arriving in Kuwait, he would have more time and better tools to remove it.

After delivering his cargo up north and now returning to Kuwait with an empty flatbed, the flat tire would not cause a problem for his truck in traveling the remainder of the journey. We decided to continue on.

A little farther down the highway, Nelson spotted another flat tire on a truck directly behind the flatbed that previously stopped for the same problem. In calling the command vehicle, the convoy pulled over once again.

Nelson ran up to the driver's door. "Hey, you have a flat. You have a flat tire."

The driver stared at him through the open window from his seat in the truck.

"You have a flat tire. Come down here. Come down and see." He waved to the driver.

The driver stepped down and ran around to the opposite side of his flatbed to examine the tire. Speaking in Arabic, he pointed in the direction we traveled. Considering the dangers of the road and the convoy positioned almost halfway to the border, like the previous driver, he would also wait until he reached Kuwait to make repairs.

As we continued on, the flat tires started to wobble and jump, and eventually began burning themselves off the rims. Laughing at the trail of blue smoke, we watched as fragments of rubber flew and scattered about until the tires completely disintegrated.

After leaving the convoy at the border, we found a push ready for an escort to Cedar. Searching through an open case of MREs in the back of the gun truck, we grabbed a quick lunch to eat on the road and left.

The wind suddenly picked up with fine granules of sand quickly blurring the atmosphere. With the first truck of the convoy remaining visible to us in the rear, the sandstorm did not seem as severe as some we had encountered in the past. There were times we considered ourselves fortunate to identify trucks less than twenty feet in front of the hood scoop. The winds gradually subsided as we traveled north and the storm eventually ceased.

"There's another flat tire." Nelson pointed at one of the trailers.

The flatbed carried pallets stacked with bottled water. The extreme weight of the cargo noticeably compressed the remaining tires. I informed the lieutenant in the command vehicle.

Ping. "Roger. I spotted that bad tire awhile back. It doesn't seem to be hurting anything so let's keep on rolling. Over."

"This is One-Six Bravo. Roger. Out."

Nelson looked surprised at the LT's decision. "What? Keep on rolling? If another tire goes, we'll be in a hurt bag. We could end up with more problems than a flat tire."

Nelson accelerated the humvee moving us closer to examine the tire. Rolling free within its rim, the tire did not seem to be causing a problem at the moment. If the three remaining tires were good, it should be fine. We slowed the gun truck and positioned ourselves a half of a truck length behind the flatbed to monitor the tire.

Boom! A sudden explosion caused the three of us to jump out of our seats.

"A tire blew!" Nelson yelled.

Thank God. The blast did not sound loud enough to be an IED but we happened to be close enough to the tire where the noise scared the tar out of us.

Quickly realizing the bad tire belonged to him, the driver of the water truck pulled over as I contacted the lieutenant with the un-fortunate news.

With the trailer suspending an extreme amount of weight over the tires, the weakest one exploded and completely destroyed its rim. The two outside tires on the passenger side of the trailer were now gone, leaving the inside tires to support the load. The heavy cargo caused an imbalance to the trailer. Leaning to one side, the load severely compressed the two remaining tires, which upon closer ex-amination also looked in poor shape.

Furious with the breakdown, the LT searched for the driver. We were fifteen miles from Cedar and it would take some time to pull the damaged rims off and change both tires.

"Where's the driver? Where's the driver?" he yelled. "We're going to leave this truck here. Recovery can come out and retrieve it. We're not staying here to fix it."

It did not make sense to leave the truck. The water belonged to the troops in one of the camps up north who would certainly suffer without it. The truck broke down only fifteen miles from Cedar but it would take recovery at least another hour to arrive and retrieve it. If we abandoned the truck on the side of the road, the pal-lets of bottled water would completely vanish within ten minutes. We pulled security as we waited on the highway for word to return from the TOC as to the truck's outcome.

Accompanying the heat, the sand flies began swarming in great numbers. We bobbed and swatted as they flew into our eyes, mouth, and up our nostrils. The tiny bugs bit into our hands, wrists, and the back of our necks causing numerous, small welts. The road was not our only encounter with the flies. Those of us who performed tower duty were very familiar with the irritating bugs.

Sand flies carried a parasite that caused Leishmaniasis. Those contracting the disease developed open skin sores that would last for many months. In making matters worse, the disease produced high fevers that would not subside. Without a vaccine or preventative drug, those who became infected flew back to the States to receive a special drug treatment at Walter Reed Army Medical Center in Washington, D.C. with many who made the trip still hospitalized while receiving care.

"Fix the tire." The LT walked toward us with a bitter stare. "Tell the hajjis to fix the tire. The TOC said that the water is needed at Tallil."

With only one spare tire stored underneath his trailer, the driver required a second tire to help support the load. Nelson and Leptien transported the driver up to the main convoy and located an additional spare plus two un-consenting volunteers who would help with the tire change.

Finding the load unsteady, the drivers nervously hesitated before beginning the risky task. They slid underneath the trailer axle and hammered away at the damaged rim. The truck swayed back and forth, as they carefully applied pressure to the lug nuts. An extremely dangerous tire change, if one of the two remaining tires were to blow, the truck along with its load of water would collapse directly onto the drivers. We could have done little to save them.

As we pulled security, a pickup filled with Iraqi police drove up next to us with its occupants in search of water to quench their thirst. We reached into the cooler and provided each one of them with a bottle of cold water. They twisted the caps off and gulped the bottles half-empty. Speaking to one another in Arabic, they continued smiling at me as they sipped on the remainder of their bottles.

"Nabear? Nabear?" one of the policemen finally spoke up.

I did not understand what he said and looked up at Leptien who watched from the turret. Leptien shook his head. He had no idea what they said either.

"Nabear? Nabear?" the policeman asked once more as he and his companions smiled and nodded their heads.

I suddenly realized what they were after—NA beer, non-alcoholic beer. I began laughing. They wanted beer. They must have received some of the NA beer from one of the other teams where they had stopped to assist. I felt like a senior standing outside a liquor store talking to a carload of underage kids.

"You want beer? NA beer?" I laughed.

"Yes, yes, Nabear." They smiled.

"Mmmm." I rubbed my stomach. "NA beer goood."

They laughed at my response and continued nodding.

"No, I'm sorry," I shook my head to their disappointment, "We don't carry NA beer."

I acted as though I felt a little unsteady on my feet. "Nabear no goood," I said.

Understanding we possessed no beer available for them to drink. They laughed at my antics and drove off.

I continued to chuckle. "I would have never expected them to ask for beer."

"I thought they weren't supposed to drink beer," Leptien said. "Well, maybe it's OK if it's only NA beer."

"I'm sure they drink beer. They have more opportunities than we do to pick up alcohol along the highway."

After a long wait, the drivers finished with the repairs. Dripping wet with sweat and covered with a thick coating of black road dust from rolling on the pavement while wrestling the tires, they packed their tools and we began moving down the road again. Arriving at Tallil, we delivered the trucks carrying the needed bottled water, which completed the mission.

During the following days, numerous flat tires and a variety of engine problems persisted in aggravating our missions. With each stop, we continued scanning the berm and watching the passing traffic in providing protection for the drivers as they conducted repairs.

Upon returning to camp after a particularly hot and miserable day on the road, we unloaded the gun trucks and retired to the coolness of the tent. I removed my sweat soaked DCU top and hung it up to dry on a wooden tent pole inserted into the frame of my bed. It would not take long for it to completely dry and the white salt stains to appear.

As we sat and rested, Scotting and I discussed the events of the day.

"Lew, I almost shot the LT today," Scotting shook his head as he told me.

"Was he being that difficult?" I laughed as I slid my armor under my bunk.

"No, I'm serious. I had my weapon pointed right at him and I was this close to pulling the trigger." He displayed his thumb and index finger almost touching them together.

Scotting had my attention. He sounded very serious. It certainly was not like him to do something this extreme. I sat quietly for a moment and stared at him as I digested his surprising statement.

Leaning forward in my chair I asked. "What happened out there today, man?"

He began explaining how the incident occurred when the convoy pulled to the side of the road during one of the many truck breakdowns. Already in a foul mood, the LT instantly became upset and stormed toward the truck's cab. He demanded the driver get out of his truck and step onto the ground. The driver, sensing the lieutenant's tension, became frightened and refused to leave his truck. Infuriated at the driver's insubordination, the LT began beating on the driver's door with the butt of his M-16 rifle. The driver continued to shake his head and refused to move. Screaming and yelling, the lieutenant pulled the charging handle back on his weapon placing a round into the chamber. He pointed the loaded rifle at the driver and demanded he get out.

"Yeah, Lew, this was happening only a few feet away from me," Scotting explained. "I have seen the LT tear into the drivers before but it never went this far. I thought he was actually going to do it. I thought he was going to shoot the driver."

According to the rules of engagement, the military authorized the use of force, including deadly force, to protect civilians from crimes that were likely to cause death or serious bodily harm. This included the use of force on our own people.

With great concern for the civilian driver, Scotting pulled up his M-16 and aimed the barrel at the LT. Hoping the lieutenant would come to his senses and lower his weapon, he held steady as the intense rage continued. Shooting the LT was not something he preferred to do but if it looked as though the LT would pull the trigger on the driver, Scotting would have no other choice. He would need to protect the civilian driver.

"Yeah, I thought I was going to have to shoot him. I had a round in the chamber and ready to fire." He looked at the floor and shook his head. "I was relieved when he finally pulled his weapon away."

On the road, I have witnessed the lieutenant in his fits of rage so I knew exactly what Scotting spoke of. It did not surprise me that an incident such as this finally occurred.

"Gary, next time the LT starts harassing someone, give me a call over the radio," I advised him. "You don't have to tell me what's happening. Just say something to the effect that I am needed at the command vehicle. I'll understand what's happening and be there as fast as I can."

Scotting continued shaking his head. "The LT shouldn't even be out there. He should be off the road. I'm going to walk over and talk to the colonel and the sergeant major, and tell them what happened today."

I sat back in my chair. "I don't know if I would do that. They may not see things your way. They may be concerned that you pointed your weapon at another soldier, an officer."

"He shouldn't be out there, Lew. Someone is going to get hurt or killed."

"I understand what you are saying but they won't kick the LT off the team. They have no place to put him, besides, who would they find to replace him? None of the other senior NCOs or officers wants to be on the road. If they did force one of them out of the camp, chances are that person would not be that promising."

After discussing the matter, we walked to the dining facility for supper. Later that evening, Scotting came into the tent and approached me as we prepared to end the day with lights out.

"Lew, you were right. I know you suggested I not talk to the colonel or sergeant major about the LT but I did. You were right.

They did nothing."

"What did they say about the incident? You're not in trouble are you?"

"No, I'm not in trouble. After I told them what had happened, they told me I had done the right thing but they won't take the LT off the road. They told me to keep an eye on the situation and monitor things. If anything else happens I am supposed to let them know."

Understanding he did all he could with the incident, I again reminded him to notify me in the future if the LT got out of hand. The discussion ended the evening and the lights went out. The next day would furnish more breakdowns and struggles on the road.

With R&R rotation in full swing, Nelson and Leptien's slots eventually arrived. Excited to get home and see their families, both left within a week's time of each other. To help out, Scotting readily left the command vehicle and filled in as the driver for the bravo gun truck while Specialist Scott Long joined us in manning the SAW during the convoys.

While Nelson and Leptien were away on leave, the gun truck received a modification with an up-armor kit. At a gathering in Kuwait a few months back, a soldier questioned Secretary of Defense Donald Rumsfeld as to the reason for a lack of armored humvees in theater. After many months of the army's in-country leadership accepting the lack of armor as "just part of being a soldier", Secretary Rumsfeld finally stepped up and we received the much needed protection.

As I sat in the newly armored gun truck, I remembered a conversation between some of the guys back at Camp Virginia in Kuwait. After our arrival in theater, the battalion leadership debated a decision as to who should receive the limited amount of armor kits available to the units.

"No, you're kidding," Specialist Brad Jensen said as he shook his head. "No, you've got to be kidding me."

"Yeah, he said it," Specialist Mike Nei continued. "Now we know where we stand."

"I still can't believe it. Lew, did you hear that?"

"Now what happened?" I asked as I walked up to the tent.

"The colonel doesn't want any of us to have the up-armor. He wants it for himself. He said that it was easier to replace a spec. four than a lieutenant colonel."

"The colonel said that?" I scratched my head in disbelief.

"Yeah, ask Thyne." Nei nodded toward Sergeant First Class Mark Thyne who approached us in the middle of the conversation.

"Mark, is that true? Did the colonel actually say that?" I asked.

"Yeah, I couldn't believe my ears. There is only enough armor to up-armor a few of the humvees. They were discussing which vehicles should be up-armored. Some of the staff questioned whether it would be wiser to up-armor the humvees that would be performing the convoy escort missions."

"Why didn't they go with the escort humvees?" I asked.

Mark shook his head. "The colonel wanted his vehicle up-armored. He said that it was easier to replace a spec. four than a lieutenant colonel."

"What about the other armor kits? Who else is getting them?"

"They decided to give the armor to some of the battalion staff, battery commanders, and first sergeants."

"See, that's not right," Jensen said as he continued shaking his head. "The people having their humvees up-armored are not even going to be using them. Their humvees are just going to be sitting around a camp somewhere. Wouldn't it be better to give the armor to someone who actually needed the protection?"

Six months later, we finally received the armor, no more fiberglass doors. The armor no longer became a guaranteed means of protection though. In the same amount of time, the insurgents modified their roadside bomb making practices to penetrate the armor.

After escorting a humvee to Tallil, the team drove to the ROM to locate a push to Navistar. Directed by the MCT people, we found the convoy and prepared to leave.

Scotting drove the gun truck along the convoy line while Long stood in the turret awakening the drivers and directing them to start their engines. A driver stopped our humvee and informed us of three trucks with bad batteries unable to make the journey. One of the remaining truck drivers stared blankly at us as he sat comfortably on a small, wooden folding stool.

"You're not going with us today?" Long asked as we slowly drove toward him. "No, it looks like you're not going anywhere at all today."

Scotting stopped the gun truck next to the driver. I held the humvee door open and looked at him. Anticipating another miserable day in the ROM, the driver injected himself with heroin to numb the unpleasant experience. Loosening a strap synched around his upper arm, he slowly withdrew a needle attached to an empty syringe from his forearm.

"Don't you want to come along with us?" I asked.

A half smile slowly appeared under a set of glazed eyes.

"Are you going to stay here today?"

He slowly nodded his head.

"Yeah, he's staying, Lew." Long chuckled. "He won't be going anywhere for a while."

With many of the drivers needing fuel, the convoy began moving toward the fuel point to fill their tanks before leaving for the border.

As we passed by another Road Hunter team in the ROM, I noticed its team leader walking the truck line carrying a pickax handle over his shoulder.

During our initial training with the 3/18th, they suggested we use a stick or ax handle to motivate the drivers and intimidate the Iraqis along the road. They explained how in Saddam Hussein's military, those of importance carried sticks or pistols. In doing so, the people recognized the soldiers as upper class and connected. The common low ranking soldiers, who carried rifles, where not respected at all. If we wanted to get a point across, an ax handle provided the authority to do it.

It upset me to watch some of the escorts beat on the truck doors with wooden ax handles to awaken the drivers in the morning. Usually a rap on the door accompanied by a yell would spark them springing to their seats. I saw no reason why we needed to use Saddam's methods.

Ax handles were not the only tool used to get the driver's attention. A few weeks back we drove through the ROM looking for our push when I happen to notice another battalion's escort team members attempting to awaken a driver. As his convoy moved out, one truck remained standing as its driver slept. A soldier ran screaming to the truck and began butt stroking the driver's door with his M-16 rifle.

"Pull over next to him and stop," I ordered my driver.

An adrenaline rush fueled the soldier's rage and he required a hand back to reality, if not for his own good then at least for the safety of the driver. As we came to a halt, the soldier ceased his pounding and stepped over to the gun truck.

"Is everything OK?" I asked. "You look a little upset at someone."

"Yes, sergeant, everything is all right." He calmly smiled. "This hajji fell asleep back here and we're getting him back on track."

The truck suddenly started and with wide eyes the driver shifted gears leaping his vehicle forward in an attempt to catch their moving convoy.

"That's good," I reassured him as I watched the driver move up the road a safe distance. "We just stopped to see if you needed assistance but it looks like you have everything under control."

"Yeah, thanks anyway but we got it taken care of." He turned and rushed back to his humvee to follow their convoy.

After refueling the trucks, we passed through the serpentine and picked up speed for Navistar. The new up-armor on the humvee restricted the airflow. With smaller windows, the outside air did not circulate into the vehicle as before. Drinking more water proved the best solution to accommodate the change.

As we traveled down MSR Tampa, we passed the barricade that read "Barre Up, Down Respect Iraqis and Road Users".

Shortly after we began convoy operations on Tampa, the military placed reminders along the highway for all American and coalition forces to respect the Iraqis. Black lettering stenciled on six-foot tall concrete barricades read "Barrel Up, Slow Down, Respect Iraqis and Other Road Users". The markers prompted those riding in military vehicles to ease up on the civilian traffic and others along the road.

This improperly worded barricade remained untouched since placed along the highway six months ago. Every time we passed by, I told myself I would change it one day. I searched for spray paint in the motor pool and the supply tent but found it was in short supply and difficult to come by.

How did the insult to the Iraqi drivers wind up out there? They certainly would have inspected it after painting and before loading onto a flatbed for transport. Those who hauled and placed the barricade along the road surely would have noticed the inappropriate wording. During the past six months, no one has attempted to correct the distasteful joke. How does something like that happen?

Midway to the border, one of the convoy trucks pulled over. I quickly notified the LT who stopped the convoy for repairs.

Walking to the truck, I found the driver underneath the vehicle and working desperately to fix the problem. He indicated his fuel filters might be the cause of his truck stopping. The convoy's spare bobtail pulled in behind him with both drivers now laboring under the truck.

I grabbed the radio handset to inform the lieutenant of the situation.

"Here comes the LT." Scotting pointed toward the command vehicle racing our way.

"I wonder what he wants." I tossed the handset back into the gun truck.

The command vehicle swung in next to us and made a quick turn. The door flew open and the LT jumped out.

"Where's the driver?" he began yelling.

I explained the situation to him and that the truck should be ready to move shortly.

"Clean your truck out," he shouted at the driver. "We're leaving it here."

"Yes, sir. Yes, sir," the driver replied.

Ignoring the lieutenant's orders, the two drivers continued working on the truck as though they did not understand English.

"It's just the fuel filters, LT," I explained again. "They should have it fixed in a few minutes and we'll be on our way."

I could sense the LT did not seem interested in what I had to say. For some odd reason, he wanted to leave the truck. He continued yelling at the drivers to follow his commands. In defense of the drivers, I attempted again to explain the insignificance of the problem. The lieutenant's anger intensified.

"Lew, take your gun truck up and secure the convoy," he ordered.

"Yes, sir," I replied.

As did the drivers, I also dragged my feet in hopes of buying them more time to make the repair.

"Go up and secure the convoy now," he repeated.

We reluctantly left the drivers with the command vehicle and proceeded to the convoy.

"Why does he want to leave that truck?" Long asked.

"Who knows," Scotting answered. "He gets like this and its best to just get out of his way."

Wanting to leave the truck surprised me as well. Five days ago, we abandoned a truck on a trip to Cedar after an acceptable attempt to keep the truck rolling in the convoy. The driver performed many repairs but the truck would not continue. The brigade became upset upon hearing we left the truck full of supplies for the Ali Baba. They felt we should have somehow returned with it. After hearing of the brigade's expectations, you would think the lieutenant would want to hold on to every truck he possibly could.

"He got it started." Long laughed. "I bet that ticked off the LT."

Looking in my side mirror, I spotted the truck with the bobtail following closely behind moving up the highway to join the convoy. As we continued on to the border, the convoy trucks provided no more problems and maintained their speed and position for the remainder of the trip.

The return convoy consisted of a feeble mixture of dilapidated vehicles with many looking questionable as to if they were capable of making the journey. We waited some time on the highway at the border as the soldiers looked through the driver's paperwork. The guards turned one of the trucks back, which reduced the numbers needing security.

As we drove back through Safwan, I heard young voices yelling "Ali Baba, Ali Baba".

The boys stood on a berm pointing toward a group of young men gathered next to the road. In the middle of the group, the men restrained another whom they tightly wrapped in a bright blue plastic tarp and furiously punched and kicked.

"Slow down, they're going to kill him," I yelled over to Scotting.

I grabbed the radio handset. "One-Six, this is One-Six Bravo. Pull the convoy over. There are some civilians beating on another Iraqi back here. Over."

Per the rules of engagement, we were to protect civilians against harm from other civilians.

Ping. "Roger. We saw that. It's not our problem. Over."

"We can't just let them beat that man to death. We need to do something about it. Over."

Ping. "It's not our problem. We're not stopping. Out."

I tossed the handset back onto the radio. Looking through my side mirror, I watched as the small crowd tore into the bound helpless man.

I looked at Scotting. "It's not our problem? What the hell is he talking about?"

Scotting shook his head as we followed the convoy through Safwan. We left the man for dead. He would not survive the brutal beating they were giving him. We should have stopped, if not for the rules of engagement in protecting civilians, then at least for the sake of saving a human life.

With a mission to provide security for the convoy, the gun truck could not leave the convoy without the LT's approval. This stretch of road through the outskirts of Safwan was notorious for rock throwers and hijackings by the Ali Baba. If we stopped on our own, we would jeopardize the rear trucks of the convoy in an unsecured area.

Leaving Safwan, we snaked our way out onto the main six-lane. With all the trucks on the highway, we began picking up speed for the long journey back to Cedar when an explosion sounded up the road.

Ping. "One-Six, One-Six Bravo, this is One-Six Alpha. They're stopping traffic up here. It looks like there's a military vehicle burning in the southbound lanes. Over."

Ping. "This is One-Six. Roger. Out."

I keyed the radio handset. "This is One-Six Bravo. Roger. Out."

As the convoy slowly came to a halt in the left lane, I stepped out of the gun truck and held the traffic approaching us from behind. It could be a long wait. We scanned the berm and roadsides for possible IEDs and snipers.

Occasionally, military security stopped us around this area with the finding of explosives along the road. A week ago, a transportation company convoy held us at this same location. Having problems with one of their trucks, they pulled their convoy over to make repairs. As they waited, an IED exploded a short distance up the road from them. Had they not stopped when they did, they would have received the full impact of the blast.

Ping. "One-Six, this is One-Six Alpha. We've waited long enough. There doesn't seem to be any more activity around the burning vehicle. I'm taking off. Over."

Ping. "Roger. Let's get this convoy moving. Over."

Ping. "This is One-Six Alpha. Roger. Out."

One by one, the trucks in the convoy began moving. We eventually passed the burning wreckage. The frame of a two and a half ton truck stood smoldering in the southbound lane. There were no signs indicating an explosive device may have caused the mishap. The possibility existed that the truck may have accidentally caught fire while moving down the highway.

The remainder of the mission went smoothly without the usual rash of breakdowns. When we entered the ROM near Cedar, we separated the trucks into two groups with some needing escort to Camp Cedar and others the air base at Tallil.

We found Nelson waiting in the tent when we arrived. Returning from R&R, he looked tired and depressed. Most did. Before we left for convoys, I printed a "Welcome Back to Hell" sign on cardboard and placed it on the wooden door of the tent to greet him in our absence. After a day of unpacking and readjusting to the climate, he prepared himself to return to the road.

As we rested and dried the sweat from our clothes, Hanson walked into the tent to share some new information he received from the LT.

"There are going to be some changes with the drivers," Hanson informed us. "Nelson will be driving with us in one-six alpha and McMillan will be driving in one-six bravo."

This change surprised me. The LT did not discuss with me

the switching of the drivers. He seemed content with each gun truck's crew.

"I'm not losing Nelson," I spoke up. "Who decided this?"

"It's the LT," Bloom broke in, "he said that's the way he wants it."

"Why?" I asked.

"I don't know," Bloom continued. "You know the LT. He made his mind up and there is no changing it."

"That's not right," I said. "The gun truck crews have been together since the beginning. There have been no problems and there is certainly no reason to change positions. When is this change supposed to take place?"

"It starts tomorrow," Hanson answered.

"Something's not right." I shook my head. "I want to talk with the LT first."

CHAPTER 14

Shifting Drivers

"Lew, you're going to have to keep an eye on me." McMillan pushed himself across the green cloth driver's seat of the gun truck. "I have a tendency to nod off when I'm driving."

The LT made some hasty changes on the team at the request of Hanson and Bloom. With Nelson's excellent driving skills, they insisted he drive for them in the alpha gun truck and their driver, McMillan, move back to the bravo gun truck and become our driver.

The exchange happened without my input. I questioned the switching of drivers and found the decision not debatable. McMillan held his own as a driver for the convoys and I enjoyed his company. I did not worry about him at all. He would fit in nicely with Leptien and me. I felt upset about losing Nelson. The three of us experienced countless narrow escapes on the road. Like adopted brothers forced into a dysfunctional family we bonded while performing this demented job. It saddened me to see the original gun truck crew broken apart.

"Do you think you can keep an eye on me, Lew?"

"Don't worry, Chad," I assured him, "we stay busy back here keeping the trucks tight and the hajjis in line. You won't nod off."

"I'm serious, Lew. You can ask Hanson. I nod off when I drive. He had to watch me so I didn't fall asleep and kill them."

"I'm not worried. If you happen to nod off, you'll wake up quick enough when you hear the humvee wheels fall off the road into the left or right ditches."

"What? It doesn't worry you that I might fall asleep when I'm driving?"

"No, if you happen to fall asleep and put us in the ditch, I doubt you'll do it more than once."

"You're serious, aren't you?

I smiled and nodded.

"You're a crazy bastard, Lew." He shook his head.

"Scotting, did you hear that?" McMillan yelled up into the turret to Scotting who continued working with us while Leptien remained away on leave. "Lew's a crazy bastard."

"Yeah, you better stay awake," Scotting replied. "I don't want to end up in the ditch."

Over the next few days, we encountered the usual problems on the road with flat tires, truck collisions, and leaving a bobtail for the Ali Baba to steal. As we waited with a convoy mission for the drivers to exchange a disabled bobtail from its trailer, small pickups and cars began parking a short distance away. They pulled over to the sides of the highway and raised the hoods of their old, beaten vehicles imitating engine problems. We drove toward them with the gun truck chasing them away but like vultures, they slowly returned to wait in hopes we would leave the broken down bobtail.

After completion of the exchange, we continued with the convoy mission. I watched in my side mirror as the civilian vehicles swarmed the lone bobtail to strip it clean.

The rotation off the road brought us to an incident that resulted from an escort of the Tallil mail run. With Chaplain Wilson accompanying us, we made the usual stops at the post office and PX before returning, escorting the mail humvee to Cedar.

As the gun trucks rolled to a dusty stop near the berm, I stepped out to clear my weapon. Standing up in the humvee doorframe, I looked into the empty chamber of Scotting's SAW to double-check his weapon for possible ammo in the chamber.

"Clear!" I yelled as he angled it for my inspection.

As my driver and I checked each other's M-16 to assure the weapons looked cleared of ammo, a lieutenant colonel from the 197th brigade drove in behind us and quickly approached me.

"Good afternoon, sir," I greeted him. "Is there anything I can do for you?"

"Yeah, when you're done clearing your weapons, I want your group to go directly to the TOC." He turned and left as hurriedly as he appeared.

"Now what?" I stood there wondering as to what might have happened to anger him and cause this strange request.

"I think I might know what this is all about," Scotting said. "When we were driving up the main road to the camp, I took the ammo out of the SAW and cleared it on the road instead of waiting until we arrived at the berm to do it. He and his driver were behind us and might have seen me."

"That's it? That is what he's upset about? Why didn't he just tell us that at the berm?"

Chaplain Wilson spoke up from the rear seat, "Yes, it seems like such a trivial thing he could have discussed with us there."

"I'm sorry, Lew, but when I substituted as gunner with the captain's team, they always cleared their SAW on the road like that. I guess I thought if they were doing it and they were the captain's team, then it was OK."

"Clearing the SAW outside the camp shouldn't make a difference, Gary. There are times outside the camp when a person needs to check his weapon and clearing is a natural part of it."

"I'm going to come in there with you guys," Chaplain Wilson said. "If there is something I can do to help, I want to be there."

I sat back in my seat and closed the humvee door. "Thanks, Pastor Wilson, but I don't think it has anything to do with Scotting clearing his SAW on the road."

From what we heard in the ranks, our leadership did not get along very well with the leadership of the other battalions within the brigade. An uneasy competitive rivalry existed between them. The clearing of the SAW on the road provided an opportunity, although very weak, for the lieutenant colonel to slap the staff on their hands for the improper actions of their boys.

We parked in the rear of the TOC and walked into the air-conditioned office tent. The sergeant major and one of the staff officers waited with serious expressions.

"We were told to come to the TOC by a lieutenant colonel from the brigade," I informed them.

"We know." The sergeant major nodded. "We'll just wait for the lieutenant colonel to arrive."

The door suddenly swung open and he walked in. "Good, they're here. When we were following their humvee up the main road to the camp, their turret gunner cleared his weapon on the road instead of waiting until they arrived at the berm." His face showed a great concern as if we committed the ultimate wrong. "If their gun truck would have hit a pothole, he could have killed me and my driver or possibly someone else on the road. It was a dumb, dangerous thing to do."

According to the brigade and battalion standard operating procedures, when traveling down the highway, we left the SAW chamber clear of ammo. The ammo hung freely in the feed tray over a closed chamber. A round could not have possibly found its way into the chamber unless the operator manually placed it there. This safeguard prevented the SAW from accidentally discharging while the gun truck traveled down the road. The lieutenant colonel did not understand the operations of the weapon or the standard operating procedures.

When Scotting cleared his SAW on the road, he merely pulled the ammo belt off the weapon, removed its ammo box, and examined the empty chamber. It was as simple as that. At no time did a round enter the chamber.

The sergeant major maintained his serious disposition. "Sergeant Lewandowski, is it common practice for your gunner to clear his weapon on the road?" he asked.

I wanted to answer his question accordingly and leave. This was a waste of time and everyone knew it. There were no winners in the ridiculous game they played.

"Sergeant major," Scotting interrupted, "no one was ever in any danger. A round was never in the chamber."

The officers and sergeant major looked at him with a cloud of confusion beginning to fog their eyes.

"Here let me show you."

Scotting knelt down and placed his weapon on the floor demonstrating the process in clearing a SAW.

They slightly nodded their heads in a display of comprehension as they watched the demonstration but they certainly did not grasp his point.

The SAW was a relatively new weapon to the guard unit. Issued to us a few years prior, only a handful of people were then qualified on its functions. During training for deployment to Iraq, practically everyone received instruction as to its use in an attempt to qualify as many as possible on the weapon. While in Kuwait, in order to become accustomed to its operations, we competed between one another in timed disassembly and assembly of the weapon.

It quickly became apparent that many in the leadership were unfamiliar with the weapon. With their rank and stature, they may have felt it unimportant for them to learn. In my opinion, that provided no excuse. If they did not have time in the States or Kuwait to understand this important weapon, they certainly had time there. In between sending daily e-mail to their families and friends, and playing golf games on their laptop computers they could have picked up a training manual and a SAW, and familiarized themselves with the unit's procedures on handling it.

After Scotting's demonstration, he stood up and attempted to explain once again our innocence. I looked at him and shook my head indicating he should let it rest.

"I trust you'll handle things from here," the lieutenant colonel said as he pushed the plywood door open and left the TOC.

"Yes, sir, we'll take care of it," the sergeant major replied.

The sergeant major looked at me. "Sergeant Lewandowski, do you understand that weapons are only to be cleared at the berm?"

"Yes, sergeant major, all weapons will be cleared at the berm," I replied. "Shall we inform the other teams of this as well?"

Unsure of the slight sarcasm, he hesitated in his answer. "That won't be necessary. They know."

I nodded and followed the guys as we walked out the back door of the TOC.

"That's crazy, Lew," Scotting said. "Not only did the SAW not have a round in the chamber, it was never even pointed in their direction. I always aim it toward the open field when someone is following behind us or leading directly in front of us."

The driver laughed. "Did you see the look on their faces? They didn't understand a darn thing Scotting was showing them, did they?"

"It doesn't matter now," I said. "We played their game and now we're through. It's not worth wasting another minute of our time worrying about. There are more important things for us to be concerned with."

Leptien returned from R&R, and like the rest who made the heartbreaking trip before him, took some time readjusting to acquire the gun truck mentality of the road. After a day to unpack and settle in, he performed convoy missions from behind his SAW once again.

During one mission, a truck pulled over with a breakdown forcing the four trucks following to a sudden stop.

"One-Six, this is One-Six Bravo. One of the trucks stopped back here. Over."

Ping. "This is One-Six. Find out what the problem is. Over."

"This is One-Six Bravo. Roger. Out."

McMillan drove the humvee up next to the truck. I jumped out and ran over to examine what happened. The driver, unable to speak English, pointed to his fuel gauge as he attempted to start the engine.

"Leptien," I yelled, "he's out of fuel. Contact the LT and fill him in."

Leptien relayed the information up to the lieutenant who pulled the convoy over a few miles down the road.

Two drivers ran up to assist from their trucks parked behind us. To help fill the empty tank, they searched through their vehicles and located a plastic mop bucket and a rubber hose to siphon fuel from their own tanks.

The command vehicle raced to our location, turned a sharp semicircle in front of us, and stopped. The lieutenant threw his door open and stepped out of the humvee.

"Where is the driver?" he yelled.

I pointed to the man disappearing around the front of the truck's cab and then I quickly walked back to check on the two drivers siphoning the fuel.

The LT ran up and stopped him. "Why didn't you check your fuel before we left?"

Not understanding the question, the driver stood and stared blankly at the lieutenant.

"Where is your passport? Where is your passport?" he continued yelling into the man's face.

He had no reason to shout before investigating the circumstances relating to the empty tanks. The tanks may have contained a hole in them or the driver may not have received enough time to refuel his truck in the hurried frenzy before we left. On occasion, they leave at a moments notice even if not ready. Whatever the reason, screaming at him did not provide an answer. It would not fill the tanks and return us on our way.

We received instructions to confiscate the drivers' passports if serious problems developed with them during the convoy missions. The passports were important to them. They needed it in identifying themselves as they traveled. Without it, they would have difficulty in crossing the border and moving through the country. The threat of losing a passport frightened them into following orders.

The bucket and hose worked great in removing the fuel from the side tanks but not as efficient in pouring the fuel into the empty tank. Covered with diesel fuel, the drivers maintained a steady pace as the fuel splashed from the plastic bucket.

I returned to the front of the truck to fill the LT in on the situation. Confused, the driver did not understand the request as the lieutenant yelled louder. I gave the LT a serious look of disapproval. He understood I did not agree with his methods. Ending his shouting, he turned and walked away.

I smiled and nodded at the driver. "Passport, passport," I calmly explained.

The driver looked at me curiously and returned the smile. "Ah, passport." He turned and walked over to the open door of his truck, climbed into the cab, and retrieved his passport.

"Passport." He smiled again as he held it up for me to see.

The lieutenant became visibly angry. Along with the driver, I now made his list for the day. I did not care. I could see no reason to his approach. I shook my head and walked back the few trucks to check on the two who assisted with the fuel problem. Out of my sight, the LT began where he left off in berating the driver.

When a convoy pulled over with a breakdown toward the front of the column of trucks, our gun truck normally pulled security in the rear while the command vehicle attended to the problem. After discovering the abusive treatment suffered by some of the drivers, I attempted to end it.

During the breakdowns, when our gun truck remained at the rear, I instructed McMillan and Leptien to pull security while I ran the length of the truck column to check on the drivers. As I arrived at the command vehicle, the LT in seeing me would immediately cease his furious behavior and walk away. It was a tough, hot, unbearable run under the heavy body armor but my efforts dampened the abuse.

The two men continued siphoning diesel fuel from their side tanks with the small rubber hose. Both endured the difficult process as they hacked and spit the foul tasting fuel from their mouths onto the ground.

Worried they would suffer the same scolding as their friend if they took too long, they nervously poured the fuel from the bucket into the tank's small nozzle hole. Without a funnel, the fuel spilled out onto the sides of the tank and saturated their clothing. Diesel vapors hung heavy in the air as the fuel flowed off the tank, down their pant legs, into their shoes, and quickly spread across the hot pavement.

"Stop, stop, you need to slow down," I instructed them.

Both hesitated as they looked at me and nodded. They emptied the remainder of the bucket with less of the fuel flowing onto the ground. A sufficient amount of the fuel entered the tank to provide for the remainder of the trip.

I handed some hard candy and water to the drivers. "Here, this should help get some of that harsh fuel taste out of your mouths," I explained. It was not much of a reward but they were very appreciative in the gesture.

We arrived in the ROM at Cedar and stripped out two trucks with a destination for Tallil. The alpha gun truck led the rest of the convoy into Cedar while the command vehicle and our gun truck escorted the small detachment to the air base. One of the non-tactical vehicles (NTVs), a minibus that broke down earlier on the road with a bad tire, followed along behind us.

"Tell him to stay," I yelled up to Leptien. "He needs to stay at Cedar. He's not supposed to follow us."

Leptien waved his arms but the minibus continued tagging along.

"Looks like he's coming with, Lew." McMillan laughed.

In approaching Tallil, we weaved through the concrete barricade serpentine placed to slow traffic before entering the front gates. Giving us orders to remain outside with the minibus, the LT escorted the two main trucks inside the gates for delivery. Leptien waved to the minibus instructing the driver to stay behind us as we parked the gun truck roughly one hundred meters from the front gates.

I stepped out of the humvee and walked over to the bus to question the driver's actions in following us to Tallil. He explained he carried two passengers needing to stay at the air base. They were new workers for the Army and Air Force Exchange Service (AAFES) store. He transported additional AAFES passengers for the stores located at Cedar as well as Scania.

I keyed the radio handset. "One-Six, this is One-Six Bravo. Over."

Ping. "This is One-Six. Over," the LT answered.

"I spoke with the bus driver and he has a few passengers who need to stay at Tallil. They are employed at the AAFES Store. Is it allowable for them to travel into the gates and drop off the employees? It should only take them a few minutes. Over."

Ping. "Negative. Have them wait there to follow us back to Cedar."

"Is it allowable to have the bus remain with us and permit the two employees to walk into Tallil? Over."

Ping. "Negative. They shouldn't have followed along. We'll take them all back. Maybe it will teach them a lesson. Over."

"This is One-Six Bravo. Roger. Out."

It would have been perfectly fine for the bus driver to transport the workers into Tallil. They could have even walked through the front gates, either way, the gate security would have checked their papers before allowing them access onto the air base.

I walked back to the bus and relayed the decision to its occupants. They became very upset and began pleading with me to allow them to walk the short distance into Tallil. If I had known the LT would pull this, I would have skipped the radio call and told them to go. I explained to them that we could do nothing about it now.

Opposite the gates and one hundred meters in front of the gun truck stood two dozen Iraqis waiting by the road next to a berm. They looked as though they were workers from Tallil who after finishing their job for the day remained for transportation home.

In calming the occupants of the bus, they eventually accepted the decision. We discussed the flat tire they repaired on the road and the work they would be performing in the AAFES stores. As I talked,

I noticed four trucks loaded with the Iraqi Civil Defense Corps (ICDC) pull up next to the Iraqis opposite the front gates. Wearing camouflage uniforms and carrying AK-47s, they jumped out of their vehicles and joined with the others.

With the large number now formed, I thought it appropriate to acknowledge the ICDC presence so I caught the eye of one and casually waved. He returned the gesture and kept about his business. Looking back toward the gates of Tallil, I noticed the guards had stepped up security with weapons drawn and aimed in the direction of the crowd. I started to get a little nervous. There have been incidents at these gates in the past. With the gun truck and the minibus positioned between the groups, I hoped this was not one of those occasions.

I motioned the occupants in the bus to remain inside and directed them to stay low. Scanning the immediate area for additional concerns, I walked over to Leptien and McMillan who watched the activity from the gun truck.

"Are you guys catching any of this?" I asked.

"Yeah, something's going down."

I looked back at the front gates and noticed another gun truck pull up and position itself on line with their security.

"The air force just brought up another gun truck," I informed them as I shook my head.

Both turned and looked at the airmen preparing their position. "My pucker factor just went up." McMillan nervously chuckled.

"At the moment, things aren't looking quite right. We need to stay on our toes," I instructed them. "Pick your targets now so if things do fall apart fast, we're not all shooting at the same guy. Remember we have a minibus full of civilians to protect."

The uneasy situation produced a strange, warped feeling of excitement. We were right in the middle watching both sides gradually flex their muscles. I wanted to walk over to the front gate and ask if we should be concerned with the movements but I did not want to leave Leptien, McMillan, and the civilians. The gate stood only a short distance away but if the situation quickly turned sour, I did not want to leave them a man short.

Our best bet was to leave. It seemed like an eternity since this incident began. I picked up the radio handset. "One-Six, this is One-

Six Bravo. Over."

Ping. "This is One-Six. Over."

"How much longer are you going to be? Things are starting to look a little concerning out here."

Ping. "We are just finishing up and should be there shortly."

"This is One-Six Bravo. Roger. Out."

We could not predict how long shortly would actually be. At the moment, any amount of time sounded too long. I keyed the radio handset to check with the battalion headquarters at Cedar. "Pride Base, this is Road Hunter One-Six Bravo. Over."

Ping. "This is Pride Base. Over."

"Do you have any Intel on Tallil's front gates? It looks as though we may be in the middle of something that is just getting started. There are four trucks full of ICDC carrying AK-47s mixing with a few dozen Iraqi civilians on one side and the front gate has just reinforced security on the other. Over."

Ping. "I'll check on it. Wait one. Over."

As we waited for the TOC to check through their Intel reports, we continued planning our actions. Both sides seemed to hold steady as the Iraqis paced and the gate security maintained their show of force.

Ping. "Road Hunter One-Six Bravo, this is Pride Base. Over."

I grabbed the radio handset off the passenger seat. "This is One-Six Bravo. Over."

Ping. "Our information doesn't show anything happening at this point. Keep an eye on the situation and update us if it changes. Over."

"This is One-Six Bravo. Roger. Out."

We patiently waited and watched, expecting more Iraqis to arrive. Finally, we spotted the command vehicle behind us leaving the front gates. I signaled to the driver of the bus to start his engine.

As we approached the serpentine, a small, white Iraqi police pickup parked along the roadside suddenly darted in front of the gun truck. McMillan swerved hard left to miss him. We maintained our speed and quickly dodged around the vehicle. It may have been a coincidence with both of us leaving at the same time and the Iraqi did not see us. It could have also been a test of boundaries.

We arrived at Cedar without further incident and dropped the minibus off with the MCT coordinators. The bus would travel once more to Tallil in the morning with a different security escort.

After five days on the road, the rotation cycle brought us to a vehicle maintenance day with the addition of pulling tower duty.

On the mail run to Tallil, we parked the gun truck next to the finance building, a small, brown brick structure that survived the coalition bombings during the invasion.

McMillan and Leptien stepped out of the gun truck and shed their armor.

"You going to get some cash, Lew?" they asked.

"No, I'm fine. You guys go replenish your money supplies and I'll watch the vehicle."

As the guys rushed into the finance building, I stepped out of the humvee and removed my body armor as well.

A marine stood leaning against the front grill of a humvee parked next to ours.

"How's it going?" I asked in an attempt to make small talk.

He glanced at me but did not say a word. The marines operated an aircraft unit out of the air base. A lance corporal, he may have been part of their maintenance or security.

I placed my armor in the backseat and closed the door. "Do they have you watching vehicles too?" I asked as I walked up to the front of the gun truck and leaned against the side of the hood.

He stared down at a few rocks, slowly moving them back and forth underneath the toe of his boot. It seemed as though he did not want to talk, which made me more determined to pull a few words out of him.

"How much time do you have left here?" I asked.

He looked back up at me and opened his mouth. "Three months."

"That would be nice. We have a little over six months to go."

He slowly nodded. "Yeah, I have three months left of this hellhole and then I'm gone."

"You're active duty, it sounds like you could possibly be back here again," I said.

"No, not me, my time is up a few months after I get back

home. I'm getting out. I'm never coming back here again. This fuckin' place sucks. This fuckin' country sucks and these fuckin' hajjis suck."

"You're not a career man? You're not reenlisting?"

"No." He shook his head. "They would only send me back here again, and again, and again. No, I did my part and I'm done. I'm out."

As we talked, he seemed to loosen up and eventually produced a laugh or two. The guys returned from the finance building poking fun at each other and ready to visit the PX. In leaving, the lance corporal and I wished each other well in our tours.

We returned to Cedar and began the shifts manning Tango Seven in the southwest corner of the camp for guard duty. Intel over the past few days indicated a sighting of three small trucks, with mortar tubes, roaming the Camp Cedar area. The SOG instructed us to watch for suspicious activity involving pickups moving along the roads in the distance.

During the tower shift earlier in the morning, Scotting and I witnessed multiple controlled explosions toward Tallil Air Base conducted by the Italians. The plumes extended high into the air and hung motionless until gradually fading away with the breeze.

As the sun slowly fell over the berm, we set up the night vision goggles and prepared for the darkness.

"There is some tracer fire in the west." Scotting pointed to multiple dashes of colored light shooting blindly into the star filled sky.

"Feuding families at it again?" I asked as we watched the show.

"Yeah, they're playing with their toys again."

Planning on an uneventful shift, we listened to the radio as it kept us company quietly playing a variety of modern rock and eighties music over the Armed Forces Network.

I took my turn in relieving myself, not that I felt an urgency to go but it gave us an opportunity to stretch our legs during the four-hour shift.

In returning, I looked up at the tower as I approached its rear. The fire from the burn pit faintly illuminated the cream-colored structure. A white figure, possibly two, suddenly appeared out of the

darkness and soared above the top of the tower and into the perimeter of the camp. I hunched close to the ground as it narrowly cleared
the tower by a little less than six feet and flew over my head.

Hearing the swooshing sound of forced air as it passed, I
tried identifying the form. Small hang glider? Couldn't be. Why would
the insurgents use a hang glider to enter the camp? What could it be?
My mind raced to identify it. I had not seen anything like it before.

I quickly jumped up and looked in the direction where it may
have traveled. Nothing. Whatever it was, it had disappeared.

"Gary!" I yelled at the tower, "Did you see that?"

"See what?"

"The white thing that just flew over the tower."

Scotting stuck his head out of the back entrance. "No, I
haven't seen anything, Lew."

I pointed toward the camp. "I don't know where it may have
landed. Can you see anything out there that looks out of the ordinary?"

He had a concerned sound in his voice. "What now? Something white? Out there? No, I don't see anything different out there.
You're starting to freak me out, Lew. What did you see?"

What did I see? Actually, I did not know. I did not even know
how to explain it without sounding like a complete idiot.

Taking big strides toward the tower, I scanned the rutted road
and sand filled landscape behind us. In reaching the steps, I looked
up at Scotting. "Are you sure you didn't see or hear anything? It flew
right over the top of the tower. It was big. You couldn't miss it."

He stared at me and shook his head.

"What was it? What did you see?" he asked again.

It was not a hang glider that I felt sure of. It puzzled me. My
mind could not match what I saw with anything logical.

As I stared into the camp's perimeter, I began speculating.
Could it possibly be something unreasonable, something paranormal,
or supernatural? I was definitely not seeing things. The night was
young and I did not feel tired or fatigued at all.

Could it possibly have been an apparition, the ghost of a long
deceased Mesopotamian warrior? This area has seen many dead in
numerous battles over thousands of years. Maybe it was an angel, a
messenger sent by God to watch over the camp or us. Whatever it

was, it was big, white, and produced a sound as it moved through the air.

I scanned the area once more. The dim fires of the burn pit softly lit the slopes of the berm and tower roads. All seemed quiet. I looked up at Scotting. "It may have been some birds flying over," I replied as I climbed the steps into the tower.

Scotting's curiosity peaked. He did not believe I saw birds fly over. There were no birds native to the area or even the region that would have remotely matched my description. I did not know what else to tell him and thought of no better answer to give.

I looked out into the dark shadows and searched the area many times with the help of the night vision goggles but could find nothing. It vanished without a trace.

With the radio now switched off, we sat in silence as we listened and watched for whatever flew over to make a return appearance.

A half-hour later, Kligel, the SOG, drove up in his humvee with our relief.

"Anything exciting happening out here tonight?" the guys asked the usual questions as they replaced us in the tower.

I crawled down the steps. "Just some tracer fire to the west. The feuding families are at it again."

"Lew saw some white things in the sky," Scotting spoke up.

"No, I didn't see anything." I opened the humvee door and sat down in the front seat.

"What? Are you seeing things, Lew?" Kligel laughed. "They say you have been here too long when you start to see things."

I knew I would receive that type of reaction if I mentioned the incident. Without a rational explanation as to what happened, it would only amount to assertions of seeing things. Humor and doubt would plague me with my coherence in question during the remainder of my tour.

"No, I saw birds. That's all, just birds." I looked straight ahead through the dusty glass of the pitted windshield.

The guys discussed the happenings on their tower duty shifts as we traveled back to the tents. Through the side mirror, I watched the tower as its light orange glow slowly faded into the darkness. What did I see out there? Some could speculate shadows but I not only saw it, I heard it. Whatever I experienced was very real.

CHAPTER 15

Peacekeeper

"I'm off the road, Lew. I'm done." Nelson reclined back into his nylon folding chair and clasped his hands behind his head.

His statement somewhat surprised me. Like the other Road Hunter team members, Nelson occasionally talked of getting off the road. Although he mentioned it, through all the misery, he continued to accept the challenge and accompany us in the humvee every day, until recently, when the LT switched him to drive for the alpha gun truck.

Baffled, I stood there staring at him. I could not help but think of how an era had just ended. He, Leptien, and I pulled through many close calls while working together as a crew on the gun truck. The LT's recent changes in positions began to fragment the team.

"What do you mean, you're done?" I asked.

"I've been talking with Mac at the TOC and he said they could use me there to help out."

I sat down in my chair. "I'm glad you made it off the road but I hate to see you go. We've been through a lot together. You are an excellent driver. No one can handle a humvee like you can."

He hesitated as his eyes gently roamed around the tent and back again.

"When I was back in bravo with you and Leptien," he began explaining, "We were actually doing something on the road. We stayed busy driving up and down the convoy line keeping the hajjis straight. Things are different in the alpha gun truck. I place the needle on sixty miles per hour and stare at the road in front of me for three hours straight. I don't do anything. I can't take it."

I understood how Nelson felt. He needed to keep himself occupied with a meaningful task. Once you begin sitting still for too

long without anything to do, your thoughts begin drifting, the days
become long, and the end seems hopelessly out of reach.

"I would take you back in the bravo truck if I could," I explained, "but the LT won't budge."

"Yeah, that would never happen. The LT is set on his decision."

"What's he going to say about you leaving the team?" I asked.

"Frankly, I don't care what he says. He has no say in this one.
The decision was made by someone higher up the chain."

I envied Nelson in a way. He would shed his body armor and
Kevlar, and be rid of this madness. His life would now take on a sen-
sible schedule of hours where he knew exactly each task he needed to
perform and when. There were no surprises, just maintain your
duties.

As the team waited in the MCT lot the next morning for a
push to Navistar, I noticed one of the convoy trucks staging to leave
did not possess a windshield. With the truck driver working under its
suspended front grill, I walked over to talk with him about the
damage.

"Where're you going, Lew?" Leptien asked as he returned to
the gun truck from talking with the other teams.

"I'm going over to talk with some of the drivers."

"The hajjis? Why do you want to talk with the hajjis?"

I stopped and turned. "Just give me a yell if we get a push. I'll
be right over there."

Giving a slight half wave and a nod as indication he would
notify me, he opened the humvee door and sat in the gun truck with
McMillan to wait for the convoys to leave.

Standing in front of the truck's cab, I reached up and gently
wiped my hand around the rubber gasket that remained attached to
the frame where the windshield once existed.

"What happened here?" I asked the driver.

"Baghdad. Baghdad," he said while briefly pausing in his
truck maintenance routine to talk.

In hearing my voice, some of the other drivers gathered from
around the sides of their trucks. They greeted me with handshakes
and smiles. Excited to tell stories of their experiences on the road,
they all began talking at once.

Describing how his windshield shattered from bricks and rocks thrown by the Iraqis along the streets, the driver ducked and protected his face with his hands as if he were still there watching it all unfold in front of him. With the much needed safeguard from the wind and road debris now absent, he dreaded returning to the highway with the convoy.

"Do you have goggles for protection?" I asked as I covered my eyes with my hand.

He shook his head and motioned as to wrapping a cloth keffiyeh around his head and shrugged his shoulders indicating he had no other choice. Returning to his chores, he leaned under the grill of his truck and continued to empty water from a plastic bottle into the engines radiator.

A Nepalese driver stepped up from the small group and introduced himself.

"How long have you been driving convoys?" I asked.

"This once." He extended his index finger. "I done. I go home." He shook his head in submission.

"You're not going to drive convoys anymore?" I asked.

"No, I done. Come here. I show you."

He led me around the cab of his vehicle and pointed to damage caused by an explosion that detonated alongside his truck. Chipped paint surrounded multiple gashes cut deep into the thin metal skin of the cab. His passenger side mirror, partially attached to the door, contained a few jagged shards of glass as a reminder of its last reflection.

"RPG?" I asked.

"Yes, RPG. Look. Look." He pointed to a series of bullet holes staggered along the side of his cab. The 7.62 millimeter size holes resulted from AK-47 automatic rifle fire.

Spreading my fingers along the holes, I felt the rough outline of each indent and shook my head. "Baghdad?" I asked.

"Yes, yes, Baghdad." He nodded.

"Wow. You didn't have very good luck on your first convoy. Your next convoy will be much better though."

"I all done." He threw his hands into the air and shook his head. "I go home."

"You're not going back home, are you?"

"I go home," he repeated.

Reaching out, I shook his hand. "I understand why you would want to leave. Just remember that you delivered the supplies and brought the truck back in one piece. You did a good job. Don't let anyone ever tell you differently."

"Thank you, sir. Thank you." He graciously accepted my gesture of support for his decision.

Sensing they were eager to continue with their preparations, I wished them well and returned to the gun truck. A yell eventually sounded as an indication for them to leave and I watched as they fell in line within a convoy escort team destined for Kuwait.

After the long morning wait, our team finally received a convoy and left for the border. Upon arrival, we placed our name on the list of escorts in need of convoys and waited once more for a return push to Cedar. Trade Center South eventually contacted us with a mission to escort a convoy of bottled water trucks standing in the lot. Through a quick inspection of the trucks, we left two in the lot with low fuel in their tanks. The border guards turned back an additional truck at the border with paperwork discrepancies.

As the trucks waited to pass through the border checkpoint, we drove the gun truck ahead into Safwan to provide security until the convoy passed.

"Does this look like a good spot?" McMillan asked as he stopped the gun truck along the roadside. He parked next to a house known as a gathering place for rock throwers.

"Yeah," I said, "we'll pull security here until the convoy passes."

The main road and side streets were deserted. With the trucks held at the border checking paperwork, I opened the door of the humvee and stepped out to stretch my legs. As the sun beat down from over head, its tremendous power produced another extremely hot day. Sweat rolled underneath my armor and down my back as I stood and scanned the buildings for signs of life.

"Where are all your friends today, Lew?" Leptien laughed from the turret. "I don't see anyone around. It must be too hot."

"They probably saw you coming, Tony," I replied as I placed my boot up onto the doorframe of the humvee. "They know who you are and don't want to mess with you."

Suddenly, three young boys moved from around the building and started walking toward us. "Here come a few." Leptien nodded.

Ten steps behind them trailed more kids, which began the formation of a small crowd. In greeting me, they shook my hand with some saying they were my friend. Others informed me of the Ali Baba in the area. With the large number gathered, I closed the door of the humvee and treaded away from the vehicle.

The children were in a playful mood with some wanting to see my mini light and thermometer dangling from my armored vest as they asked dozens of questions.

As I talked with the kids, an older, gray haired man with deep facial wrinkles appeared from around the side of the brick building where the others previously emerged. Carrying a small, listless child in his arms, he made his way to me while pushing through the crowd of children. Speaking Arabic through a partial beard and very few teeth, he attempted to explain his grandson's need of medical attention.

Reaching down, the man lifted the toddler's clothing exposing the young boy's groin. Swollen and discolored, his genitals displayed the symptoms of a terribly infected circumcision. The ill boy's eyes rolled in their sockets as his grandfather pleaded for help.

"I am not a doctor. I am not a doctor," I repeated in hopes the man would understand I could only provide limited help if any at all.

He stood silently looking at me.

"I do not have any antibiotics. You need to take him to a doctor in Safwan," I pointed to the heart of the city as I explained. "Is there a doctor in Safwan who would see this boy?"

He seemed to understand a little of what I said. "No doctor. No doctor." He shook his head while extending the boy out in his arms for me to take.

We carried very few medical supplies in the combat lifesaver's bag. Other than an IV and bandages, the bag contained nothing of use in this situation. I felt as helpless as the grandfather did.

"Here comes the convoy, Lew," Leptien yelled as the convoy began rolling by.

"I need to go now," I explained to the man. "Take your grandson down the road to the border crossing and look for the

American soldiers." I pointed to the flag on my right shoulder and then to the border. "They may be able to help you."

Some of the soldiers based out of Navistar occasionally pulled security at the border crossing. They could possibly help him but the grandfather felt uncomfortable with approaching the border and wanted me to return the next day with a doctor. I told him I would try my best to help.

I walked over to the humvee and opened the door to get in when a young boy grabbed my leg. With a look of terror in his eyes, he clutched on and did not want us to leave.

"Ali Baba. Ali Baba," he cried as he pointed down a side street to a beat-up, old car that stood waiting on the sandy road.

"Ali Baba?" I asked.

He continued staring up at me with tears in his eyes and nodded.

"Come on, Lew, we've got to catch up with the convoy," Leptien informed me.

Glancing down the road, I watched as the last vehicle in the convoy rolled ahead of us. The boy definitely looked afraid of something in the car but the vehicle did not do anything that would cause us to take immediate action. If they fired a weapon or visibly hurt someone then maybe we could take off after them. At the moment, our priority lay with the mission to provide security on the convoy that just passed.

Holding onto the boy's shoulder, I gave him a slight squeeze and regrettably explained, "I'm sorry little guy but we'll have to get Ali Baba another day."

As I sat down in the gun truck and closed the door, McMillan rushed to join the convoy. The children waved as we left. In my side mirror, I saw the frightened little boy standing beside the old man holding his grandson. I wished we could have provided more in helping them. Under the circumstances, we did not have enough time or resources to assist. At times, it seemed the best course of action was not to even step out of the humvee.

Over the next few days, I searched for the grandfather as we passed through Safwan but could not find him anywhere along the road. Unable to supply me with medication for the boy without knowing the exact diagnosis, Lieutenant Sean Kenny, the unit's physician's assistant, instructed me to snap a picture of the boy's groin area for his examination. I could not locate the grandfather again and hoped that he found treatment for the boy elsewhere and did not need medical assistance any longer.

With Hanson leaving for R&R, the LT informed me that I would take the truck commander position in the one-six alpha gun truck until his return. Reluctantly assuming the duties, I began the monotonous routine of the lead gun truck crew.

Scotting received a promotion through finding a sergeant's slot available in one of the units back home and moved to the truck commander position of the bravo gun truck. The communication section requested McMillan's assistance at Cedar and replaced him with Specialist Chris Wright. With the openings for driver's in the alpha and command vehicles, the leadership forced some of the younger guys out of the camp and onto the road.

"Are you driving for Bloom and I today?" I asked Specialist Jeff Jungers as he sat down in the driver's seat of the alpha gun truck.

"I guess so," he grudgingly replied. "The LT kicked me out of the command vehicle and told me to drive for you guys."

"Don't worry, you'll do fine," I reassured him. "We'll take good care of you."

A convoy of KBR trucks pulled up to the intersection outside of the holding lot in Cedar and waited for their instructions to leave. I stepped out of the gun truck and walked across the gravel road to organize our departure with its commander. The KBR convoy commanders possessed an abundance of experience driving big rigs back in the States as well as in Iraq. Many went by colorful names such as Swamp Rat, Skinny, Batman, and Big Baldheaded Buddy.

"I go by Koma on the hand-held radio," the commander informed me with a handshake.

He switched on a small, hand-held fm radio and passed it to me. Customarily, the radio went to the military escort commander to maintain contact with the KBR commander. In the past, the LT preferred not to deal with the truck drivers and passed the responsibility to Hanson. With Hanson away on leave, I now took on the task.

"What do you go by?" he asked.

"I'm new at this," I informed him. "What do you usually call the convoy escorts?"

"We usually call them Peacekeepers."

"That works for me." I took the radio from his hand. "Call me Peacekeeper."

"Sounds good, we're going to operate on channel three this morning. I've got the radio all set up for you. I'll let you know when the trucks are ready to go."

"We'll be ready when you are." I shook his hand and walked toward the road's edge.

"Jungers," I shouted.

He glanced up at me and followed my instructions to position the gun truck on the road in preparation to lead the convoy through the camp and out the front gate.

We left Cedar and within three hours arrived without incident at the edge of Safwan. Radio traffic indicated the rock throwers were busy on the streets leading to the border. As we escorted the convoy through the outskirts of the city, I watched as the ICDC patrolled the roadside in an attempt to dissuade those wanting to steal from or damage the trucks.

With an unusually quick turnaround in the MCT lot, we found a push and proceeded north. Our good fortune would not continue for the return trip as it did going down.

Ping. "One-Six, this is One-Six Bravo. Over."

Ping. "This is One-Six. Over."

Ping. "Stop the convoy. We had a truck whose brakes locked up back here. Over."

Ping. "Roger. Did you catch that alpha? Over."

"This is One-Six Alpha. Roger. We're pulling the convoy over. Out."

As we waited along the highway for the truck to make repairs, groups of kids began appearing from the mud houses sparsely scattered throughout the area. Running toward the trucks in hopes of receiving snacks or bottled water, some stopped momentarily in their pursuit to assist younger siblings in maintaining the speed of the pack.

Not wanting them near the trucks, I reached into my backpack and pulled out a bag of candy that I purchased from the PX for such an occasion. Walking out into the sand on the shoulder of the highway, I lifted the bag of sweets high into the air.

"Candy!" I yelled, "Who wants candy?"

Little heads quickly turned and stared. Noticing the colorful bag, they left the trucks and raced over encircling me. Some reached for the candy while others displayed knives and counterfeit Iraqi currency that they attempted to sell. I shook my head at their offers for trade and began handing out the candy.

As I placed a small amount of the candy into each of the many hands, a younger boy reached up with a worn taped bayonet and shoved it at my chest. "Clink!" The metal blade echoed as it struck against the SAPI plates inserted within my armor vest. The hasty act surprised me.

"No. No." I sternly scolded the young boy as I pulled back.

He ducked away as the others slapped at his head in disapproval. With a foolish expression upon his face, he stood at the rear of the crowd and watched. He did not intend to hurt me. He was a curious little boy testing my armor with his knife. I reached into my bag and handed him some candy. He smiled and understood we remained friends.

Distributing the sweets to the kids must have been quite a sight. As I stood at the side of the road in the center of the crowd, a British escort slowed as it passed. Cameras protruded from the windows as they waved and laughed. Some of the truck drivers from our convoy as well as other passing security escorts snapped pictures of our small group.

I talked with the children as we waited for the drivers to finish their repairs. With some becoming bored and beginning to wander away and toward the trucks, I brought them back with the enticement of more candy. The process worked much better than yelling and swearing.

Over the following days, Intel reported the insurgents targeting the rear gun trucks escorting convoys. The SAW, mounted in their turrets, did not possess the intimidating strength of the .50 caliber heavy machine gun of the lead trucks. The LT decided to swap the weapons. Leptien brought his SAW to the alpha truck while Bloom moved his .50 cal. back to the bravo humvee.

After performing maintenance on the gun trucks at the motor pool during the team vehicle maintenance day, we received anthrax shots and then escorted the mail truck to Tallil. Waiting outside the

PX for departure to Cedar, we passed the time by watching the Japanese and Italians moving their trucks along the streets through the air base.

"I can't believe I have to be in the alpha truck," Leptien grumbled. "This sucks. We don't do anything up here. I want to be back in bravo where you can do stuff."

He became upset with moving to the lead gun truck ever since the lieutenant made the decision to switch weaponry. Kicking equipment around in the vehicle, he berated the lieutenant and us for his miserable situation. I fully understood why he did not want to ride in the alpha truck but taking it out on Jungers and me seemed a poor solution.

"The way I see it, Tony, this is your gun truck and we're just helping you out," I began explaining.

He hesitated in his fit of temper. "What do you mean by that?"

"With the LT switching the SAW and .50 cal., it sounds like that change is permanent. That means you're in this gun truck for the duration. Jungers over there is through helping out in a few days. When Hanson returns from leave in two weeks, I'll go back to the bravo truck."

Leptien sat and listened.

"The way I see it, Jungers and I are just helping you out for a few days. The least you could do is be a little more cordial to us."

"Yeah!" Jungers looked at Leptien and began laughing.

Leptien closed his mouth and did not say another word. Quickly realizing his mistake, his attitude improved substantially. After awhile, he returned to his old self and began treating us like part of his gun truck crew.

A few days later, we prepared to go back on the road again. With the gun trucks ready to leave, we waited in the early morning light at the MCT lot for a mission south.

"What's the holdup, LT?" one of the guys asked. "What are they waiting for?"

"There was an incident last night near the border. We're waiting for word to see if we are going to leave at all today."

In walking between the gun trucks, I spotted one of the interpreters sitting alone in the backseat of a humvee. Retrieved earlier in the morning from the gates of Tallil by another Road Hunter team, he sat patiently contemplating the long ride to Navistar and back.

I stepped over to his opened door. "Raad, how are you this morning?"

"I am good. I am waiting here to go."

He looked a little tired and hungry so I handed him an apple that I picked up from the dining facility earlier in the morning. Searching though my bag in the alpha gun truck, I found some peanut butter, crackers, and a bottle of water for him. As he ate, a few others joined our early morning conversation. We talked about various customs, gestures, religion, and politics.

"With your county forming a democracy, you should run for political office," I suggested. "You could become an elected official."

"No, I am a teacher. I like to teach," he insisted.

"But as an elected official, you could assist your country by forming new laws for the good of the people. They need thoughtful citizens like you to stand up and help guide the country."

"I help my country by teaching." He began laughing at my suggestions.

In talking with him, he answered many questions about the various things we have seen during the past several months.

"The convoys are canceled for today," the lieutenant informed us. "Take the gun trucks back to the tent area and wait until further notice."

With shouts of happiness, the teams started their vehicles and began leaving the lot. They would not need Raad's services today. The Road Hunter team that retrieved him would return him back to Tallil.

"Thank you for talking with me," Raad said as he shook my hand. "No one ever usually talks with me."

The military closed MSR Tampa to convoy traffic near the Kuwaiti border. During the night, a British patrol came under attack by insurgents twenty miles north of Safwan. In firing an RPG at the British, the insurgents missed their intended target and struck an oil pipeline running underneath the highway. Catching fire, the oil burned steadily throughout the night and into the early morning. The intense flames destroyed the paved highway halting all convoy activity.

The next morning we assembled the gun trucks and began leaving with a KBR convoy to Navistar. With a large portion of the road missing north of Safwan, we received an alternate route to escort the trucks to the border. Alternate supply route (ASR) Circle, a narrow pothole filled section of road, bypassed the damaged highway and led directly to the MSR Tampa exit at Safwan. The detour lengthened the journey by only a few miles but because of the poor condition of the road on ASR Circle, our travel time would greatly suffer.

With Severson appointed our new driver, we left Cedar's front gate with the convoy following behind. To maneuver the convoy through the new route, I requested a small map from the lieutenant. He felt it unnecessary and chose to direct us through the correct route with radio contact. As we traveled, information from the 201st Bulldog Teams leaving Navistar with convoys bound for Cedar began reporting ASR Circle filled with numerous hidden tire spikes and large pieces of debris.

"One-Six, this is One-Six Alpha. We are nearing the broken lamppost bridge. You have the map. Let me know where the Circle turnoff is located. Over."

Ping. "This is it. Turn off here and lead the convoy north until we arrive at Circle. Over."

"One-Six Alpha. Roger. Out."

We guided the convoy off Tampa and traveled down the sandy path a good five miles without finding another turnoff in sight.

Click. "Peacekeeper?"

"Yeah, this is Peacekeeper," I answered the hand-held fm radio.

Click. "I don't think this is the road. According to my map, we should have traveled down Tampa a few more miles."

"I was not given a map but I think you're right," I responded. "There doesn't seem to be anything up this road but sand. I'll contact the LT and we'll get turned around."

Click. "OK, we'll follow you, Peacekeeper."

I picked up the radio handset. "One-Six, this is One-Six Alpha. The KBR commander has informed me that we may have taken the wrong turnoff. I suggest we turn around and go back to Tampa. Over."

Ping. "Roger. Turn around up here somewhere and take us

back. Out."

We gradually turned the thirty-truck convoy over a desolate, unimproved path. A cloud of fine, white dust hovered in the air as each truck attempted the unsteady shoulders. Returning to Tampa, we continued traveling south once more.

Click. "I think this is our turnoff up here, Peacekeeper."

"OK, I'll let the LT know."

I picked up the handset. "One-Six, this is One-Six Alpha. The KBR commander has indicated that this next exit is the correct turn-off. Over."

Ping. "Negative. Keep going. Out."

I keyed the hand-held radio. "Cook, this is Peacekeeper. He doesn't think it's the correct exit. He wants to keep on going."

Click. "OK." He laughed. "We're following you."

Severson looked over the top of the radio and shook his head.

"Why don't you have the map, Lew?" he asked. "I don't think he knows where the hell he is going."

"He's the team leader," I explained, "and that's the way he wants to run things. As long as no one gets hurt, it's fine with me."

As we drove, we waited for the radio to ping with the correction.

Ping. "One-Six Alpha, this is One-Six. Turn the convoy around. That was our turnoff. Over."

"Roger," I answered, "Turning the convoy around. Out."

We pulled the convoy through a jagged set of bent guardrail posts separating the six-lane and proceeded to the exit. Once off Tampa, we easily located ASR Circle and turned for Safwan. We found the road littered with chunks of tires, pieces of scrap metal, and an assortment of garbage. Severson maintained the gun truck at a slow steady pace as we scanned the items for pieces large enough to cause damage to the convoy trucks and our humvees.

To our right we observed the black smoke drifting upward in the distance from the remnants of the oil pipeline destroyed by the insurgent attack. It would be many months before they repaired the damaged road.

"Tire spikes!" Leptien yelled from the turret.

Hidden underneath some of the debris in the road were large, metal spikes deliberately set to damage the truck tires. I quickly informed the KBR commander and the lieutenant of the hazard.

"You have a good eye, Tony," I yelled up the turret. "We didn't catch that one down here."

"Yeah, I barely caught it myself."

I watched through the side mirror as the trucks swerved one by one to avoid the road spikes. Our luck would not hold. One of the rear trucks ran over a spike, which destroyed its tire. The rotation of the wheel kicked the spike up and punctured the truck's fuel tank. We pulled the convoy over and waited while the truck drivers attempted repairs.

The kids gradually approached the convoy from the berm where they sat and watched. They were most likely the culprits who set the trap for the trucks in hopes of begging from the drivers once they stopped. Like the kids along Tampa, they were friendly and talkative as well.

With the truck's fuel completely drained onto the ground, a bobtail driver attached a tow bar and pulled the truck. We traveled a little farther down the road when another truck pulled over with brake problems. The driver quickly repaired the brake line and we continued to the border where we released the trucks.

That evening, I read the oil pipeline story in the *Stars and Stripes* newspaper. The damage caused by the attack resulted in the shutdown of oil shipments leaving the country. The story did not provide information as to when the oil flow would resume.

"Lew, I talked with the captain about the treatment I've been receiving from the LT," Boz said as he walked into the tent. "I told him I want off the team now. There's no reason for him to treat anyone that way."

The lieutenant tore into Boz today while we waited for a convoy at Navistar. Upset over a minor issue, he verbally disciplined him in front of the entire team. This was not the only incident upsetting Boz. During the past week, the LT has found fault in most everything Boz has done.

"What did the captain say?" I asked.

"He told me I had to stay on the team. He wasn't letting anyone off."

"That's what he always tells you. He's not going to change his mind. You know that."

"I'm sick and tired of the LT's crap. No one should have to put up with it so I told him that I'm not responsible. I'm not responsible if someone gets hurt."

"I agree with your reasons for wanting off the team but you didn't tell him that did you?"

"Yes, I did and it's the truth. I'm not going to be held responsible if someone gets hurt because of my driving. I've told them multiple times of my problems with falling asleep and not staying focused. If someone gets hurt I will not be held responsible."

CHAPTER 16

Hearts and Minds

"Welcome to TaHell" read the graffiti on a concrete barricade along the main road leading into Tallil. With a few short strokes of black spray paint, a soldier or airman altered the hand painted welcome sign and proclaimed their thoughts of the southern Iraqi air base.

After a grease and oil filled morning performing vehicle maintenance on the gun trucks, the team received the task of escorting the mail run to Tallil for delivery and pick up of the battalion's mail. It provided an opportunity to visit the post office and mail a package or stop at the finance building to replenish individual cash reserves. After completion of our personal business, we assembled at a designated time in the PX parking area for the return trip to Cedar.

With an assortment of small businesses, the PX area remained one of the busiest locations on the air base second only to the dining facility. A barber, uniform alterations, jeweler, film developer, and a gift shop were set up in crude makeshift trailers. A steady stream of coalition force soldiers moved in and out of the area. Noticing the gun trucks parked in the lot, some inquisitively stopped and asked to have their photograph taken as they stood next to the armed humvees.

Later that afternoon at Cedar, Top approached me to ask if I would have dinner at the dining facility later in the evening with a general who toured the camp.

"He's a Polish general so they're asking each unit to provide someone of Polish descent," Top explained. "Your name came up so here is an opportunity to have dinner with a general."

"Sure, Top, I'll do it. It might be interesting and maybe even fun."

I enjoyed talking with the Polish coalition forces. Only knowing a few words of Polish, the conversation quickly turned to English whenever possible. As with the Italians, Japanese, Mongolians, and the rest of the coalition forces, if they did not speak English, we conducted most of the conversations with a series of hand signs and charades. Patience and a sense of humor went a long way.

Arriving at the DFAC, I met a small group of soldiers who were there for the same reason. Not all were of Polish ancestry. They were pleased to read the qualifying last name sewn across my name tape. We sat at a table reserved and arranged especially for the occasion. With the general running late, we talked as we watched others walk by the table searching for a place to sit and eat their meals. Our table offered the only noticeable open space in the crowded dining hall. Many attempted seating themselves but the DFAC workers redirected them elsewhere.

The patches on our left shoulders indicated which units we were with but we found it interesting to ask where each originated from and what their duties were. We were a diverse group with representatives from many states and trained in a variety of military occupations. As with our unit, very few performed tasks they originally went to school for.

"Sergeant Lewandowski, what do they have you doing here?" one of the soldiers asked.

"I ride on a gun truck."

Some in the group stopped talking and glanced over at me. I felt as though I might have said something to offend them until one of them spoke up. "Wow, I really respect that. How do you do it?"

At first, I thought she was teasing but I quickly realized she and the others were very sincere. Since beginning convoy operations, not one of my peers has ever shared a concern or respect for what the others or I do on the road. I felt uncomfortable and did not know how to respond at first.

"I don't know." I shrugged my shoulders. "It's just a job. You don't really think about it. You just do it."

"*Atten-tion!*" a yell came from the back of the dining room as the door swung open.

All in the building instantly jumped to their feet as the general walked into the dining facility. We stood straight and tall as he and his entourage made their way to the table. Colonels, lieutenant colonels, majors, captains, sergeant majors, the remainder of the table quickly filled with brass and chevrons.

Looking out of the corner of my eye, I identified the red maple leaf of the Canadian flag sewn on the general's uniform. He was not a Polish general. He was a Canadian general of Polish descent. He was in fact Major General Walter Natynczyk the Deputy Commander of the U.S. Army's III Corps in Iraq, the second top ranking soldier in the county. To my knowledge, none of us had expected this.

He walked down the table and gracefully shook each one's hand.

"I see you have a name with the same background as mine." He laughed.

"Yes, sir," I replied with a smile.

As we dined, he shared his views on the direction of the war and the future of Iraq. With the major hostilities ended, we now acquired the task of winning the hearts and minds of the Iraqi people. We needed to win the peace. He seemed like a friendly, personable, and a genuinely caring person.

As we ate, a colonel sitting beside me spoke with our half of the dining table. "This is what the general loves to do. This is his element. This is where he shines. He enjoys being with the troops."

He definitely supported the general and just as friendly to us in his conversation.

My thoughts drifted to the Iraqis along the road and in the villages. The rough treatment they received every day from the U.S. and coalition forces certainly did not fit with the general's idea of winning the hearts and minds of the Iraqi people.

It felt inspiring to hear his pleasant thoughts on helping the people. Tempted to approach him with the details of the road, I hesitated in fear of losing my position as a gun truck commander. If they actually pursued the mistreatment, an investigation could possibly pull me from the road to answer questions. As with everything else, nothing would ever become of it and they could possibly pigeonhole me in the camp for the remainder of my tour. It would benefit no one, especially not the people along the road and the drivers in the convoys. As long as I performed convoy security, I contributed in making a difference, even if it only encompassed the scope of my gun truck.

In the course of the evening, the time flew and the dinner with the general ended. We chuckled as we left the dining facility and walked to the tents. The dinner with the Polish general proved an enjoyable surprise to us all.

A few days later, the team received a mission to provide security for a convoy on the return trip to Cedar. We departed the MCT lot in Navistar with a convoy of trucks trailing closely behind. As we approached the border, the coalition forces checkpoint stopped us. The previous day they searched all the trucks looking for Nepalese drivers. The country of Nepal ordered all Nepalese to leave Iraq after the insurgents executed twelve of its citizens in Baghdad without reason.

I thought of the friendly Nepalese worker I met at the dining facility while at Camp Virginia. As I sat in one of the white, plastic deck chairs and finished my meal, a smaller dark skinned man, wearing a white shirt and white paper hat, approached my table and stood quietly smiling at me.

Curious as to why he watched me as I ate my meal, I greeted him, "Hello. How are you?"

"Fine, sir," he slightly nodded his head as he answered. "Where are you from?" he asked.

"The United States." I wiped my mouth with a napkin and turned toward him. "Where are you from?"

"I am from Nepal. I am Nepalese," he proudly answered.

"Yes, I know where Nepal is located. Mount Everest, right?"

"Highest mountain in the whole world." He lifted his hand high into the air.

"Do you work here?" I asked.

"Yes, I work here seven days now. If I work two to three years, I will not work again, ever."

Excited about his new job and the comfortable life in Nepal he would live when finished, he continued chatting with me as I stood up and moved to the rear of the dining facility to discard my Styrofoam plate. Concerned he would be in trouble for taking time from his work to talk with me, I thought it best to wish him well and leave. I hoped he continued to work his job at Camp Virginia in Kuwait, and did not become one of those brutally murdered in Baghdad.

"Do you have the paperwork, Lew?" Leptien asked as the Dutch soldier stood waiting by the driver's window to view them.

I handed the papers to Leptien who in turn passed them through the humvee window to the guard. The paperwork consisted of copies of travel papers for the truck drivers in the convoy. Without the papers, the drivers could not cross the border.

The soldier looked through the papers. "These papers are not stamped. We cannot let you pass unless there is a red stamp on each paper."

"These are copies of the same papers the drivers travel with," I explained. "It's all right. Each driver has his own original with a stamp."

He sorted through the papers once more and then walked over to his American counterpart who stood observing from their plywood checkpoint booth.

We passed through this same point numerous times in the past with the exact same type of paperwork. On each occasion, they gave a quick look at the papers and asked how many vehicles were in the convoy. The whole process took less than thirty seconds.

I stepped out of the humvee and walked over to their booth. The specialist stood examining the paperwork. "We can't let you pass unless there is a red stamp on each page," he confirmed what the Dutch soldier previously stated.

I shook my head. "We have passed through this checkpoint every day without any problems. Now you're telling me the paperwork is wrong and you're not allowing us to pass."

"If the paperwork doesn't have a red stamp, they can't pass," he repeated.

"I think you need to call someone and get this straightened out," I explained. "Our trucks are blocking the road and no other convoys will pass through here until we leave. The MCT lot is starting to become congested and people will get angry if they can't get on the road soon."

The two checkpoint guards discussed the matter between themselves and eventually decided to make the call to the MCT lot for guidance.

We waited in the sun as sweat dripped from our faces and flies buzzed through the air. Some of the doors of the backed-up convoy trucks behind us opened as the drivers attempted to cool themselves with an almost nonexistent breeze. This represented another typical army screw up. Someone in the upper ranks became tired of sitting around doing nothing all day and decided to exercise their authority and make a decision. They did not coordinate the decision with others who would be involved so the information did not pass to those directly influenced by it.

A black SUV roared up to the border checkpoint and came to a sudden stop next to the booth with a cloud of sand and dust overtaking it. The door of the vehicle flew open and Dave, a civilian manager for the MCT, stepped out.

A big guy, Dave could have passed for a bear in civilian clothing and sunglasses. He walked up to the booth, grabbed the paperwork from the specialist, and threw it down on the plywood countertop. In his right hand, he displayed a red stamp and began pounding on the pages as he flipped each one with his left hand.

He hesitated in mid-strike and growled at the specialist, "Is this why you held this convoy up?"

The soldier's eyes widened. Opening his mouth, he pushed out a sound, "uh-huh."

When he finished stamping the last page, Dave handed the paperwork across the counter to me. He turned without saying a word and walked back to the SUV. At that moment, an army captain from the MCT drove up in a humvee. He made big strides toward the booth and quickly turned and followed at Dave's heels as he passed.

"Do you want to see the paperwork now?" I held out the documents for the specialist to examine.

With wide eyes, he whimpered, "No, you can go."

I walked back to the humvee and radioed the team, we were now moving. I did not blame the specialist for holding the convoy at the checkpoint. I respected his ability to hold firmly to his orders no matter how absurd.

The next day we left Cedar with a mixture of NTV, military, and KBR trucks. With the first push out, we would be the first down to the border and then the first to return. If all went well it would be a quick, smooth trip. Not for us though. That was not typically our luck. We may have received the first push out but there were only a few missions scheduled for the day. The remaining Road Hunter teams patrolled down to Navistar without convoys and passed around us. The day started off about average.

Hanson returned from R&R. Needing Hanson's assistance in the command vehicle, the LT extended my assignment as the commander of the alpha gun truck. Leptien remained on the SAW and Severson continued to drive.

There were no problems with the convoy as we left the front gate but a mile down the road, one of the military vehicles located directly behind the gun truck began having problems. Usually, military vehicles rarely caused problems during convoys. They were the best maintained on the road. With a series of established preventative maintenance checks, the mechanics repaired all problems before dispatching the vehicle from the motor pool.

With the convoy pulled to the side of the road, I walked back to investigate the trouble. "What's wrong with your humvee? Is it something you can repair?"

The driver leaned under the hood and checked through the engine. "I don't know. It overheated and then the engine locked up. There shouldn't be any problems with this humvee. They just installed a new engine yesterday and this is the first time we've taken it out."

Severson assisted the driver as they checked through the fluid levels.

"You've got to be kidding me," the driver shouted.

"That's it. That's your problem." Severson pointed out.

"What did you find?" I asked.

"There's no coolant in the engine." Severson shook his head. "The mechanic forgot to replace the coolant in the engine."

The problem belonged to their unit and did not concern us. The second humvee in their group attached a tow bar to the deadlined vehicle to pull it the remainder of the trip. Someone would lose rank over the mistake and possibly end up paying for a new engine.

Continuing with the mission, we began receiving a large amount of oncoming traffic—civilian vehicles moving directly at us in our lane. As the vehicles neared us, most of them moved onto the shoulder of the road next to the median strip in order to avoid a head-on collision. Some remained in our lane expecting us to move the column of trucks into another lane.

Oncoming traffic resulted from something or someone slowing or blocking the opposite side of the six-lane highway. Quite often, the problem involved a military convoy not allowing the drivers to pass around their trucks. Frustrated, the civilians crossed over the median strip into our lanes. They continued driving against the traffic until forced to return to their appropriate side of the highway.

I picked up the radio handset. "One-Six, this is One-Six Alpha. Over."

Ping. "This is One-Six. Over."

"Be advised, we have oncoming traffic. Over."

Ping. "Roger. Out."

Severson held the convoy steady in the left lane. It became quite nerve racking at times. The speed at which we traveled combined with the speed of the head-on traffic would make for a horrendous collision. On top of that, add the momentum of the thirty trucks on our tail. None of us would walk away from the impact.

The drivers flashed their headlights in an attempt to persuade us to move to the right and allow them to remain in the lane. We did not move. We owned the lane. Less than fifty meters from the front of the gun truck, the drivers realized we were not moving from the lane. They suddenly veered to the side and in passing, threw up an infuriated wave acknowledging our stubbornness in refusing to pacify them.

The turret gunner retained the final judgment in deciding which vehicle posed a threat. With every head-on car moving toward us, Leptien tensed in anticipation of the next move.

One of the younger guys drove for us when we suddenly received a line of oncoming traffic. He moved the steering wheel slightly as if to switch lanes.

"No, don't switch lanes," I instructed him. "Hold this lane. We have a whole convoy following behind us. We're not changing lanes."

Apprehensive eyes looked at the oncoming traffic and then back at me. "They're coming straight for us!" he yelled. "What if they don't move out of the way?"

"Let's hope they do, otherwise, it's not going to be a good day for them or us."

As the traffic approached, he clenched the steering wheel with both hands. "Aaaahhh!" he began screaming.

At that moment, the traffic swerved to our right narrowly missing us. He looked at me with a pale white face and asked, "How do you know they'll move over all of the time?"

I smiled. "You don't."

I did not appreciate the head-on traffic any more than the next guy did but we could not do much about it. It seemed similar to the game of chicken, played by two opposing cars driving on a back road or highway. They cruise toward each other at high speeds until one of the cars swerves out of the way. The person who swerved, lost the game and then labeled the chicken. The person who remained in the lane, received the title of the idiot.

We drove through Safwan and released the convoy at the border. After a long wait, we finally received another convoy ready to move north. I walked the truck line and woke the drivers. With their heads propped against the side windows, some fell asleep as they waited to leave. Leptien and Severson switched positions for the return trip. The paperwork did not display the red ink stamp but the checkpoint said nothing and casually waved us through.

On the Iraqi side of the border, one of the convoy trucks began having problems. It could not travel faster than thirty-five miles per hour. With the temperature at 118 degrees and rising, many of the trucks began developing problems in maintaining a good speed so we slowed the convoy considerably to accommodate them. A few miles from relay point twelve, the LT decided to remove the truck. We stopped the convoy along the left-hand lane and waited while the command vehicle, along with the rear gun truck, escorted the disabled truck to the relay point.

Positioned at the front of the convoy with the gun truck, we observed activity along both sides of the thirty-truck column. If a problem developed, it would easily be noticeable from there. I covered the passenger's side, Leptien the driver's side, and Severson observed both from the gun turret. We had difficulty monitoring the radio over the sound of the engine noise so we shut the vehicle off and listened to the team traffic.

The TCN driver seated in the truck directly behind us seemed particularly playful. He offered us a drag from his hookah pipe, which

he positioned between the front seats in his cab. By his carefree behavior, we did not have difficulty imagining what he may have been
smoking.

As the sun beat down on us, we drank water to stay hydrated
and made small talk to pass the time. Acting strangely, Leptien ran to
the truck located behind us and pressed his back up against its grill.
He slid along the front of the vehicle as if trying to sneak up on
someone standing on the opposite side. Both he and Severson
laughed at his antics. It may have been an attempt to take the edge
off with a little humor so I laughed along in hopes he would end his
fun and get back to work.

He walked over to the passenger door of the truck, reached
up for the handle, and opened it.

"Severson," he yelled, "take a picture of me in the truck with
the hajji."

"OK, just wait a bit." Severson pulled out his camera.

"No, you need to stay out of that truck," I informed Leptien.
"The fun is over. We need to get back to pulling security."

Leptien pulled himself up by the grab bar attached to the side
of the cab.

"Come on, one picture. It'll be funny."

"Get down from there and get away from that truck. You
need to provide security on the other side of the convoy. Now get
over there and do it."

Leptien slammed the truck door closed. He pointed at me
and began yelling as he walked over to the driver's side of the convoy
to check on traffic. "You always give out candy to the kids and we're
not supposed to. I just wanted to take a picture inside the truck and I
can't. It's OK for you to do things but not for me…"

He was not making sense at all, as he ranted on. I let him
blow off some steam. When he finished, things would be back to
normal. For some reason, he seemed wound up and wanted to screw
off in the worst way. We were the only gun truck providing security
for this convoy in the middle of the desert. We were an easy target.
At any time, insurgents could drive by and engage us while the rest of
the team remained too far off to assist. This was certainly not the
time to goof off.

"…He lets us do things. Why don't you?"

I let him continue talking. At the moment, as long as he watched his side of the convoy, it did not matter what he said to me. If it had been anyone else, I would have come down on them but it was Leptien. We were on the team since the beginning and we had seen a lot together. I owed him at least that much. Maybe it finally got to us. After all, in the past six months of convoy security operations, we performed well over two hundred convoy missions and numerous patrols while traveling close to thirty thousand miles of dangerous highway. Mile after mile of searching for IEDs and snipers has to take its toll somewhere.

I glanced toward the back of the convoy. An Iraqi civilian car approached from the rear. They slowed down as they passed next to me. All in the vehicle smiled and gave the thumbs up. I wondered if they were actually happier with their lives now that we were here. Were things any better than before the invasion? They may have been just going through the motions and hoping one day soon, we would disappear. I would like to think they were better off now, that this year, which I gave up in being with my family, made at least one person's life a little more satisfying.

"You crazy shit." Severson laughed.

It sounded as though everything was back to normal. I turned and looked up at the gun turret to see what Severson found so amusing. Holding his camera in front of his face, he pointed it across the median strip to the opposite side of the southbound lanes where Leptien lay on the ground, rolling back and forth through a pile of sand.

"Leptien!" I yelled as I stepped toward the median. "What the fuck are you doing? Get the fuck off the ground right now and get your fuckin' ass over here."

Leptien picked himself up off the ground and jumped to his feet. He seemed surprised, hurt, and angry all at the same time.

"What? What? Severson is taking…"

"I don't give a fuck what Severson is doing. Get your ass over here right now."

Running back to the humvee, Leptien yelled and cussed as he crossed the highway. "He lets us fuckin' do it. We're just having fun and taking pictures. It's not fuckin' hurting anything."

"There could have been a UXO (unexploded ordinance) or

IED buried in that sand." I explained. "You could have been blown to hell, killed, dead."

I shook my head and thought of his wife back home. How would I have explained him blowing himself to pieces while rolling through a pile of sand on the side of the road?

Leptien became defensive as he continued yelling. He felt mad, probably more from being hollered at than anything else. I tried calming him down.

He walked up to the front of the gun truck and looked across the hood at me. Reaching down, he pulled the magazine out of his M-16 rifle. He glared at me with hate in his eyes as he slammed the magazine down onto the hood of the humvee. I knew what he meant. He did not have to say a word.

It all came out, anger that had built over the past six months on convoys, fury at everyone and everything that ticked him off. He let it all out. If he needed to purge his system, it worked best for him if he took it out on me. Someone else would not have understood. They would have slapped him with a pile of counseling statements and possibly an article fifteen. It would not have been pretty.

He was too good of a soldier for that. I knew what he had gone through. Day after day of putting your life out there tempting someone to try and take it, not knowing if you would return at the end of each day.

"It looks like Lew's got a pair of stones." Severson laughed.

I looked up at Severson. "When we get back to camp, don't tell anyone what Leptien did out here. No one needs to know. There is no point in anyone getting into trouble. They don't come out here. They would never understand."

If the leadership found out about this incident, they would have sent him to the camp psychiatrist at the combat stress tent. Prozac would have been the answer. I did not want that for him. There were too many guys wandering around the camp on Prozac already. They were noticeable by their blank stares and lack of aggressiveness.

During a visit to the medic's tent, I questioned Doc Kenney about the Prozac use in the unit.

He looked at me and hesitated as if he should say anything about it at all. "Yeah, there are some." He paused. "Why?"

I held nothing against those on Prozac. If they needed help, it was great they found it. In a way, I felt sorry for them. They had done their part over here to the point of strangling their peace of mind to death. The time had come for them to return home. Their war ended.

The leadership viewed things differently though. Patch them up with Prozac and send them out again. They could take care of their problems when they returned home.

As my gunner, I needed Leptien on the edge. Things could happen in the blink of an eye. You needed to be quick to think and act when necessary. If you dulled your senses and lost that edge, you were more of a hindrance to the gun truck than a support. People could die.

Leptien eventually calmed down and pulled security. The screwing around came to a painful end.

When the command vehicle and rear gun truck returned from the relay point, we started the convoy moving and continued on to Cedar. With the exception of the engine's roar, the gun truck remained silent as we drove down the highway.

We neared Cedar when the radio sounded.

Ping. "One-Six, this is One-Six Bravo. We just broke an axle on the gun truck. Bloom was able to make repairs to keep us going. We should make it back to Cedar but it will be slow moving. Over."

Ping. "This is One-Six. Roger. Let me know if you have any more problems with it and we'll stop the convoy. Over."

Ping. "Roger. Out."

They fell behind but managed to hobble through the front gates of the camp and drove to the motor pool for repairs.

We unpacked the alpha gun truck and carried the equipment into the tent. A puppy met us at the doorway. The guys in the bravo gun truck discovered a pack of wild dogs living in a burrow just outside of Cedar. They stopped the humvee on the road allowing Bloom to run out into the field and snatch one of the pups.

"What are you going to name her?" I asked.

"I think I'll call her Dirty," Bloom answered as he searched through the tent for cleaning supplies.

"Dirty? Why is that?"

"Because she's filthy and full of bugs." He laughed.

He was right. They bathed and scrubbed on the dog for some time but could not get rid of all the bugs. Bloom cared for the dog in the tent for a few days before taking it to the motor pool. Dirty did not stay at the motor pool for long. The lieutenant colonel enforced a "no pet policy" that forbid anyone from taking on a pet of any type. They gave the puppy to some soldiers from another unit who were happy to raise her. The motor pool crew built a doghouse and tied a small stuffed animal to its doorway in protest of the policy. While there, the puppy provided some life to the tent, if not in heightened spirits, then at least in bugs and mites.

A few days later, as we waited for a push south, the lieutenant informed us of an upcoming change in convoy missions. "We received word that the 178th will be arriving within the next month to take over the convoy missions to Navistar."

"What will they have us doing once the 178th takes over our jobs?" one of the guys asked.

"After we train them in convoy operations, we will take some of the missions north to Scania."

The change in missions sounded like welcomed news to my ears. I became excited about taking the convoys to Scania. It provided a chance to travel farther north and see more of the country. The change also positioned us one step closer to going home.

CHAPTER 17

No One Gets off the Team

"We are at threat level Delta Red. All pushes north have been canceled until further notice," the LT informed us as we waited by the Cedar MCT lot.

The military discovered several vehicle borne improvised explosive devices (VBIEDs) in the Baghdad area provoking the KBR to shut down their supply trucks on MSR Tampa until security conditions improved. Intel showed a spread in the activity of civilian vehicles carrying the explosive charges that the insurgents created to detonate next to coalition forces, disrupting their checkpoints and convoys.

The convoy restriction did not apply to the TCN drivers and their trucks. Waiting patiently in their vehicles, the drivers watched us in anticipation of leaving soon.

"What the hell is threat level Delta Red?" Leptien asked.

"I don't know," I replied. "I've never heard of it before. It must be a term used by the KRB."

We received a mission to escort a small convoy of TCN trucks to the border. Hesitant in allowing us to depart, the battalion finally decided to let us leave and established a departure time of no earlier than 8 A.M..

As the team gathered around the gun trucks, I noticed Boz absent from the group, which was unlike him. Recognizing him sitting alone in the driver's seat of the command humvee, I walked over to talk.

As I approached the vehicle, I found him whimpering and wiping tears from his face.

"Boz, what's wrong?" I asked.

"Nothing." He dried the tears in his eyes.

"What's wrong? What's going on?"

239

"There are a lot of things that are wrong." He cleared his throat. "I've had enough of those two chewing on me every minute they can. I've hit the point where I can't take it anymore."

Two days ago, our team assisted another security escort with an extended fifty-nine vehicle convoy to Kuwait. After leaving the trucks at the border, we refueled and drove to Navistar to retrieve the next mission. As the bravo gun truck rounded a blind curve into the camp, they stopped suddenly in the middle of the road to pick up a humvee fuel cap lying half buried in the sand. Driving the command vehicle and following directly behind, Boz rounded the short curve and collided instantly with the rear of the stationary bravo gun truck. The command vehicle received extensive damage to the grill and radiator while only a slight indentation existed on the rear quarter panel of the bravo truck.

Riding along with Boz, the LT, Hanson, and the interpreter were fortunate in only receiving a few minor bruises along with sore knees from the impact with the inside of the humvee. They quickly blamed Boz as the reason for the accident occurring and threatened him with everything from a reduction in rank to paying for the damages out of his own pocket.

Since beginning convoy duty after arriving in Iraq, Boz has pleaded with the leadership to take him off the road. He continued citing his limited ability to perform as a driver but they ignored him. When driving, he experienced difficulty in staying awake during the three-hour trip and had often fallen asleep at the wheel. To relieve the road fatigue, he and Scotting alternated in the driver's position on the two segments of the journey.

With Scotting taking command of the bravo humvee, Boz had no choice but to drive both legs of the journey himself. Seeing this as a problem, the LT sought to switch Boz for Severson in the alpha gun truck but Severson refused to drive for the lieutenant. The humvee accident proved to the LT and the leadership that Boz should not be driving for convoy missions.

"It's eight, let's go!" a yell came from the group.

"Are you going to be all right?" I grabbed Boz's shoulder.

"Yeah, don't worry about me, Lew. I'll be fine."

As I watched the shattered man in his mid-forties pull himself together for the convoy mission, I realized they finally broke him.

Through a continuous barrage of berating and humiliation, they succeeded in smothering the life from his heart.

I found it difficult to understand why they would do this to him. They have known him personally in the guard unit and the community for many years. We were not like a regular army unit where most members stemmed from various parts of the country. Once we returned home after the deployment, many would again see one another as they walked the streets of the small towns or traveled the highways throughout the state. In time, Boz may forgive them for what they did to him there but it would be understandably difficult for him ever to completely forget.

We staged the convoy and began moving toward Cedar's front gate when the radio sounded.

Ping. "Road Hunter One-Six Alpha, this is One-Six. Stop the convoy. The Delta Red has been lifted and a few more trucks want to join the convoy. Over."

I grabbed the radio handset. "This is One-Six Alpha. Stopping the convoy. Roger. Out."

During the trip to the border, the civilian traffic seemed practically nonexistent but a large number of Iraqi police and National Guard patrolled the highway. An uneasy feeling came over me whenever we passed a civilian vehicle. The Intel description for a possible VBIED stated to look for a lone occupant in a vehicle wearing nice clothes in preparation to meet Allah. It did not provide much to go by. Any one of the vehicles moving next to us potentially carried explosives. A detonation would have been our only clue.

We arrived at Navistar without incident and immediately received a return push north. As we traveled down the highway, I listened to the KBR drivers talking with each other over the hand-held radio as they discussed a problem truck moving within the convoy.

Click. "He doesn't seem to want to keep up with the other trucks," the bobtail driver spoke.

Click. "Indicate to him that he needs to step on it and stay with the group. I got a feeling he's playing lame so he won't have to go north," said the convoy commander.

Click. "It could be. He seemed nervous about coming along."

Click. "Keep an eye on him and don't let him turn around. Are you catching any of this, Peacekeeper?"

I picked up the hand-held radio. "This is Peacekeeper. Roger. Don't worry about him turning around. If he happens to stop, the boys will motivate him to continue on. There's no going back now."

Click. "Thanks, Peacekeeper. Awhile back, we had one that pulled out of the convoy on the way to Cedar. He turned around and joined a convoy heading for Kuwait."

Click. "He decided he didn't want to go with?" the bobtail driver asked.

Click. "Yeah, he got scared and turned around. They had a plane ticket waiting for him when he returned."

We escorted the convoy into Cedar and pulled the gun truck into the fuel point ahead of the convoy to refuel. Watching through the window of their air-conditioned shack, the air force fuel handlers rushed out and hurried to fire up the generator providing power for the pumps. They walked over to the gun truck with their clipboard in hand for a signature on the fuel.

Very talkative, the two young airmen in their late teens stood and chatted as I filled the humvee.

"I can't wait to get out of this hellhole and back to civilization," one of the airmen said.

"You guys sound like you're ready to go home," I said as I applied a steady grip on the oversized fuel nozzle.

"Damn right we're ready. It won't be long now and we'll be drinking beer and partying."

"How long have you two been here?" I asked.

"One week. Ain't that right?"

"Yeah," the other airman answered, "that's one week longer than anyone should have to be here."

"One week?" I asked. "When are you leaving?"

"We're leaving in less than three months. How long have you been here, sarge?" they asked.

I replaced the fuel nozzle on its post. "Close to nine months."

Their chatter stopped and both stood silently staring at me. I reached down to the airman's side and took the clipboard from his hand.

"We'll be here most likely another four months." I signed the fuel sheet and returned it with a smile. "Thanks for the fuel, guys."

The two young airmen were having a difficult time adjusting to the idea they would be here another three months. After they settle in for a few weeks, they may eventually adapt to the reality of their tour and accept it. It must be tougher on the younger ones knowing their friends are back home living large while they sweat it out in the Middle East. They must feel like they are missing out on life.

The next day we were off the road as scheduled. After performing vehicle maintenance on the gun truck, we loaded the vehicles and staged them by the tents awaiting the drive to the TOC. Once there, we would hold for the mail truck and leave for our turn on the daily mail run to Tallil.

I noticed Boz waiting in the turret of the command vehicle. Normally he sat in the driver's seat. "Boz, what are you doing in the turret?"

He looked at me with a somber expression. "I was told that I was going to be the gunner from now on."

"But that's not even a real turret. It's just a hole you guys cut through the top of the fiberglass shell. It's not safe. You could get hurt standing in there."

"I'm just doing what I was told." He slid his M-16 down inside the humvee.

"Are you OK with that?" I asked. "Let me see if I can talk with someone about this before you hurt yourself."

"No, Lew, I don't mind. At least I won't have to listen to them two bitch at me the whole trip."

I stopped the lieutenant as he walked toward the humvee. "LT, is that wise to have Boz ride in the turret? It's not safe."

He quickly angered. "I don't want to hear any more about it. I'm tired of the bitching. The commander said he stays on the team so that's where he's going to be."

Ping. "Road Hunter One-Six, this is Pride Base. Over." The radio sounded with a call from the battalion headquarters.

The LT tossed his helmet into the humvee and reached for the radio handset. "This is One-Six. Over."

Ping. "We just received word that the gates of Tallil are closed. They're investigating a possible VBIED. The mail run has been canceled for today. Over."

"One-Six. Roger. Out."

"Looks like we're done for the day." The LT retrieved his helmet and walked back to his tent.

Without the mail run to Tallil, we received the remainder of the afternoon off. We returned the vehicles to the motor pool and retired to the coolness of the air-conditioned tents to relax. Some of the guys played video games, watched DVDs, and slept. We talked about home, the unit, and the Road Hunter teams.

"Why don't they just let Boz off the team instead of treating him that way?" Severson asked.

"They won't let him off because no one wants to do convoys," Scotting replied. "If they let him off, then they would have to let others off as well. Who are they going to find to replace them?"

"Boz can't get off. I can't get off. No one can get off the team. At least if it were possible to switch teams. The LT is dangerous. This is the worst team in the unit and no one can get off."

"I know. It's been like this from the beginning. I tried talking to the commander about it but it's like Lew said, no one wants to go on the road so who are they going to find to replace him."

There were others in the leadership who held the rank to command the team. Truthfully, I knew of only one person whom I would have actually trusted on the road and he was not an option. Not because he did not want to do convoys, I think he would have jumped at the chance, but the leadership maintained other plans for him that involved their administrative paperwork.

The LT has been our team leader since the beginning. We came to know him as well as any one of us and we could anticipate his actions and reactions in various situations whether good or bad. At this point, a new leader would not be beneficial to the team. The choices provided would be of the same or worse qualities and the learning experience would start all over again.

"Lew, why don't you want off?" Severson asked. "You're the only one who wants to stay on the team."

"I don't mind the road," I replied. "I want to be out where I can actually do something that makes a difference. To me, if I wasn't on the road, it would be like dressing for the big game and ending up sitting on the bench. As long as you are here, you might as well get as much game time as possible."

"Yeah, but we've spent enough time on the road. Let the others get out there. While the guys on the road have been working their asses off, the others back here have been sitting around the camp doing nothing."

"That's OK with me. Let them do nothing if that's what they want. This will all be over soon. One day we will get on that airplane and never come back here again. There will be no do-overs. Once it's done, it's done. We will each have to live with what we did or did not do over here."

Severson shook his head. "Meanwhile, we get stuck doing all the grunt work."

"There is nothing wrong with that. You've earned your money. When you get home and someone asks you what you did in Iraq, the only thing you will need to tell them is that you were on a gun truck. It speaks for itself."

In an attempt to pull some of the other guys out of the camp, I tried persuading them to ride along with us during the convoy missions. The convoys would give them a chance to meet the people along the road and experience the happenings in the country. A chance to say they were actually out there. Who knows, some may even have preferred it to what they presently did and chose to join a team. They always gave the same reply.

"You're Road Hunter One-Six, right?"

"Yeah."

"Hell no, I'm not going with you guys. Shit always happens to you guys."

A few days later, we were back on the road with a mission to escort the advance party of our replacements to Navistar. The morning sunlight began reaching over the eastern horizon. It was early. The DFAC opened its doors but we did not even have enough time for a quick, takeout, hard-boiled egg.

"Are you the field artillery guys?" a flirtatious voice asked through the window of the gun truck.

We stared at the young female captain in disbelief. Could she be serious? Were we the field artillery guys? By the sound of her voice, she attempted to manipulate us into assisting her with her bags.

She belonged to the advance party from the 56th Infantry

Brigade out of Texas who would be replacing us in about four months. Their officers and senior NCOs toured our convoy operations over the past ten days. They would use this information to prepare their troops who presently trained in Texas for deployment to Iraq. Hopefully, they would arrive sooner if possible.

We were one of four teams escorting the advance party back to Kuwait for their return trip to the States. Radio problems in the gun truck caused a delay in our departure from the tent area. We were on our way to the TOC to meet up with the other gun trucks. Each gun truck would accommodate two extra riders on the chauffeur mission to the border.

Driving through the tent area, we noticed the captain, carrying a full ruck and waving her arm to get our attention.

"We better stop and pick her up," I told Severson. "She's one of the advance party members. She's running behind schedule just like us."

Severson looked at me. "It's an officer, she needs the exercise, let her walk."

"Yeah, Lew, it's an officer," Leptien joined in. "Do you actually think one of them would stop to pick one of us up?"

I understood where they were coming from but letting her walk would prove nothing. "We better stop and pick her up. She's weighted down with quite a few bags. Besides, if we don't stop and pick her up, we'll be stuck waiting with all the other officers at the TOC for her to arrive."

"We wouldn't want that," Severson said as he slammed on the brakes.

"Are you the field artillery guys?" she asked in an endearing manner.

We stared at her in silence as the humvee engine rattled. Her tone of voice may have provided her a free bar drink back home but it certainly did not work here, at least not on us. Severson pulled his foot off the brake as if to drive off and leave her.

I quickly jumped out of the humvee to avoid any problems and bit my tongue as I replied, "Yes, ma'am, we are the field artillery guys."

I took her ruck off her back and placed it underneath the hatch in the rear of the gun truck. We made some quick adjustments and found room for her to sit on one of the rear seats. I helped her latch the humvee door and we were on our way.

A hundred meters up the path, another soldier stumbled with twice as many bags.

"Oh, there she is." The captain pointed to the major desperately struggling along. "Can we give her a ride too?"

What else were we going to do? Severson let out a sigh as he reluctantly stopped the humvee. Once again, I jumped out and helped with the bags. We created more room and were off again.

We arrived at the TOC, unloaded their gear, and waited for the convoy briefing on the mission to Navistar. No one said a word about our tardiness with others also late in arriving.

After a detailed convoy briefing, we loaded the gun trucks. Our riders were two officers, a major and a lieutenant colonel. They had definitely gone on a shopping spree while in theater. Their bags contained many desert camouflage items purchased from the PX, things they would not easily find back in the States. We lined up the humvees and left camp. The gun trucks traveled in four groups of three humvees each. Barring any problems along the way, it would make for a quick ride down.

I tried making small talk with our riders but they were not interested. They did not seem to care who we were so I did not attempt to get their names. The major quickly fell asleep a few miles out of Cedar and the lieutenant colonel closed his eyes behind a propped book he placed in front of his face.

Midway to Navistar, the group of humvees pulled over to the side of the road providing an opportunity to stretch our legs and relieve ourselves. Scanning the area around the humvees, I spotted the top of an Iraqi army helmet protruding from the mud in the ditch next to the road.

With the LT standing by my side pulling security, I pointed to the helmet and said, "I'll give you a dollar if you go down and kick that helmet over."

"Yeah, not today," he replied as we both laughed.

There were many war souvenirs scattered around the country but the rule stated very clearly, "if you didn't drop it, don't pick it up." Anything worth picking up could be a booby trap. This resembled a textbook example of a souvenir to leave alone and walk away from.

We continued pulling security on the road's edge as traffic passed. The lieutenant colonel finished his business and walked around to our side of the humvee. He looked out at the sand berm where the half-buried helmet in the ditch caught his eye.

"Hey!" he squealed with excitement as he began taking quick strides toward it.

"Sir!" I shouted, "I wouldn't do that if I were you."

He stopped dead in his tracks and glared at me. Who was I to tell a lieutenant colonel what to do? I was just a road grunt, a taxi driver shuttling him to his next destination.

He looked at the helmet and then back. "Why?" he sternly asked.

"It may be booby trapped," I explained. "There could be an IED attached. If you didn't drop it, don't pick it up, sir."

I pointed to a set of tire tracks next to the helmet. "Someone has recently been here. I can't say for sure the helmet is booby trapped but I certainly wouldn't touch it."

He really wanted the helmet in the worst way. It would have made a nice conversation piece to take back home with him. He studied the helmet, thinking of ways in which he could somehow retrieve it. He did not want to leave the souvenir behind.

He would have provided his soldiers a greater service by taking a picture of it. A real example of what soldiers were not supposed to touch. He could share with them his own personal account of the day he almost blew himself to pieces in Iraq. That information could possibly save some lives in his unit.

We loaded back into the humvees and continued on to Navistar. Both started nodding off again. I thought as long as they were in Iraq, I did not want them to miss the sites along the road. Every so often, I woke them, indicating points of interest, information that might help them during their future deployment. They were not interested so I let them sleep.

We arrived at Navistar and sent them on their way. The next time we would see them, they would be arriving with their brigade to relieve us so we could return home. It will be a good day when we see them again.

The next day we were on our usual convoy mission run to the

border when the trucks pulled over on ASR Circle to repair a break-down. We stood in the sun at the front of the convoy scanning the berm and returning waves to the kids in the distance.

"It's a film crew." Standing on the driver's side of the vehicle, Severson pointed his cigarette down to the rear of the convoy. "There is a film crew coming down the line."

"Oh yeah?" Leptien hung out of the turret and leaned over the roof of the humvee to get a better look. "It must be KBR. I'll bet they are making another training film."

In the past, we ran into the KBR film crew when we were picking up a convoy mission at the MCT lot in Navistar. They produced training films to educate new truck drivers as to what to expect when driving convoys throughout Iraq.

As the film crew and their security escort slowly passed, a soldier hung off the side of the truck shouting greetings to us in an attempt to coax us to look into the camera's lens and wave.

I could not believe my eyes when they passed. It was him. The last person I ever expected to see again.

"Do you see that, Lew?" Leptien said as he stared at the soldier.

"Yeah, and I don't believe it."

"See what?" Severson asked. "What are you guys talking about?"

"That's him." Leptien pointed. "That's the captain who was going to shoot us at the border."

Severson knew of the incident and quickly looked back toward the film crew to get a look at the captain. "No shit? That's him? What's he doing here?"

What's he doing here? That was a good question. It appeared the higher you were in rank, the more likely leadership looked the other way when you made a huge mistake. Threatening fellow soldiers with loaded weapons was a major violation. They should have thrown the book at him or at least sent him back to the States for psychiatric treatment but the system did not work that way here.

During a small outdoor church service at Camp Virginia in Kuwait, one of our captains became upset when he noticed some of the guys were not practicing proper muzzle awareness. At that time, juggling the weapons throughout the day seemed new to us and we all did our best to keep the weapons pointed toward the ground and not directly at one another.

As the service went on, we sat and rose from nylon cots according to the chaplain's direction. With the weapons slung over our shoulders and draped down our backs, a barrel would occasionally point in the direction of another soldier. Not that anyone was in immediate danger. We were in a camp and in Kuwait. The weapons were not loaded.

The service ended and Communion about to begin when the captain rushed from the rear and stood in front of the group. He cleared an M-16 and pulled it up to his shoulder in a firing position.

"How does it feel? How does it feel?" he yelled as he shoved the rifle barrel toward us. "How does it feel to have a rifle pointing at you?"

No one said a word as we stared at him down the barrel of the weapon.

"It scares the fuck out of me," he answered his question.

A long period of silence followed, at that time he then realized his mistake. He dropped the weapon to his side and returned to his seat without saying another word. The chaplain, just as surprised as we were of the incident, continued with Communion as though nothing out of the ordinary occurred.

The rules were different if you were not an officer. If you were merely an enlisted soldier, penalties applied.

As one of the Road Hunter teams prepared for a convoy mission to the border, an incident occurred involving an enlisted man. Continually harassed by a fellow soldier, he finally broke under the pressure. While the team prepared to leave the camp, he locked and loaded his M-16 and pointed it at the soldier who tormented him.

This did not sit well with the leadership. They sent him to Baghdad for a court-martial hearing. From there, he spent some time behind bars in Germany.

As we watched the disturbed captain pass by with a smile on his face and a laugh in his voice, the question remained unanswered. What was he doing here?

His violation involved the use of gun trucks and heavy machine guns in the threatening of a dozen soldiers' lives. For him, his situation did not worsen. He apparently now occupied a much better job than before. As a fellow sergeant once told me years ago, "mess up and move up".

CHAPTER 18

The Road of Good and Evil

Abrahiem stepped out of the white, older compact automobile that sat quietly idling near the Tallil gates. Tightly clutching a briefcase close to his chest, he acted slightly nervous as he rushed over to the command vehicle, entered, and slammed the heavy armored door closed behind him. We were there to retrieve him to be our interpreter for the day on the escort run to Kuwait. Before we left with the convoy mission to the border, we received orders instructing us to escort Abrahiem to Cedar where they expected him at the TOC.

The concerned Iraqi schoolteacher prepared to make a valuable delivery. Within the briefcase rested millions in Iraqi dinar for some in the unit who became involved in currency speculation. The exchange rate for the Iraqi dinar now stood at roughly 1,500 dinar for every U.S. dollar. Lured by the temptation of easy money, some were betting on striking it rich down the road from their tour in Iraq.

After the delivery, we drove to Navistar escorting a convoy of empty semi trucks destined for storage facilities in Kuwait to reload. After leaving the trucks at the border, we raced the humvees to the MCT lot to pick up another mission and depart.

Created by the dry heat, a dirt devil meandered an unpredictable path through the truck lot pulling loose sand and trash into the air. Covering my face with my hand, I held my breath and squinted as the miniature tornado quickly passed near us.

"Watch the radios," I instructed the guys in the gun truck. "I'll get the ice for the return trip."

Standing by the trailer to retrieve a bag of ice for their journey north into Iraq, a long, staggered line of drivers waited their turn to enter. Finding only a few pallets of ice remaining in the front of the refrigerated trailer, I stepped into the truck to grab two bags. As the sole of my boot hit the floor, I nearly lost my balance as I skated toward the front of the trailer across a slick coating of slush.

Pulling the bags from the top of the pile, I turned and noticed one of the drivers attempting to enter the truck.

"Stay there," I advised him. "The floor is icy. You might fall and hurt yourself."

Placing a bag of ice on the floor, I gently shoved it over to him. "There you go."

Picking up the ice, he thankfully nodded as he stepped away from the open door. Once again, a small line of drivers formed outside the trailer. I began pulling ice from the pallets and sliding it a-cross the floor to those in need. Each driver expressed his sincere gratitude many times.

"Sir, sir, you must come out of there right now," a man with a heavy Indian accent demanded from the doorway. "It is too cold in there. You must come out right now."

I paused in my new job and laughed. "Where I come from back in the States, it is this cold for many months of the year."

He shook his head in disbelief. "You do not come from a very good place."

As we returned through Safwan, the cigarette vendors lined the road with their small two-wheeled carts. Waving cartons of cigarettes above their heads, they occasionally ran toward the moving trucks to make a quick sale.

To discourage them from approaching the convoy, some of the gunners began pelting them with small "AA" batteries as the peddlers stood waiting along the roadsides.

In seeing the humvees approach, the vendors darted away while keeping a cautious eye on the gunners with the expectation of the small projectiles rapidly flying their way. Bruised and sore from the impact caused by the batteries, the vendors were quick to return a yell or curse. With the unnecessary roughness, it would not be long before they would be retaliating with flinging objects of their own.

We returned to Cedar and completed the mission just before sunset. The trucks followed our humvee into the staging area and waited behind us in their designated holding lines for release.

I stepped out of the gun truck with the convoy paperwork in hand and presented it to the MCT personnel housed in a small, air-conditioned shack. After providing a quick report on the number and types of vehicles we arrived with, I left to return to the gun truck and end the day on the road.

As I walked back to the humvee, I noticed a small group of locals yelling with great excitement. They pointed to the ground next to them as they quickly backed away from a small snake slithering a-cross the sand and rocks.

Attempting to avoid the flurry of activity, the snake quickly scuttled underneath one of their vehicles to hide. Not seeing a snake in awhile, I moved over to take a closer look. Most of the locals stood a slight distance off with some hopping onto the hoods of the vehicles to get away. Unsure where the snake may have disappeared to, the driver of the SUV started his vehicle and slowly backed away revealing it once again.

I bent down to examine the small creature. Dark in color and eight to ten inches in length, the snake instinctively became motion-less at my presence.

"That's a cool looking snake," I told the group of locals who looked on, nervously smiling and nodding.

With the attraction now faded, I turned and walked toward the humvee when one of the men began yelling, "No! No! No!"

Wearing open-toed sandals on their feet, a few of the men made stomping motions with their legs. They wanted me to kill the snake.

"Such a little snake," I laughed to myself. "I will take care of this menace for them." Moving toward the snake, it suddenly coiled in anticipation of its fate. Lifting my boot into the air, I stomped down to crush the snake against the rocks.

The snake quickly jumped to one side and arched up next to my heel. At that moment, I realized I had no business being any-where near that snake. This was not a common garter snake from the plains of the Dakotas back home. Whatever it was, it sure had the locals frightened.

Too close to back away, I stood reluctantly committed to the task. I quickly raised my boot and stomped once more, this time just barely catching the snake as it jumped. Split open against the rocks, the snake now lay defeated. With its tail slightly quivering, it slowly turned and then became still.

A loud cheer roared from the contented group. With hands

thrust into the air, they waved while displaying the thumbs up. I smiled, waved, and bowed my head. "They were now safe," I chuckled to myself. As I left for the humvee, they rushed to examine the defeated remains of the small terror.

That evening, I spoke with Sergeant Jason Everson regarding the snake incident. With a tremendous amount of knowledge and experience handling poisonous snakes during his summer job back home, he naturally became our resident expert. Without seeing the snake, he could not positively identify it but from what I explained, he speculated it could have been an adder or viper, an extremely poisonous snake. He suggested I stay away from the snakes from now on. I could not agree with him more.

With Scotting leaving for home to use his R&R, the LT made additional changes in positions on the team. Staff Sergeant Mike Wiley joined us for the next two weeks taking the command position in the alpha gun truck. I moved back to my original position as commander of the bravo gun truck with Wright as its driver and Specialist Tony Roerig manning the .50 caliber machine gun.

With adjustments in the unit's inventory of humvees, the motor pool dispatched a gun truck to us that did not provide the standard up-armor kit. Instead, it retained its homemade, 3/8th inch steel armor plating, cut to size and bolted to the fiberglass doors. It did not offer the best in protection but certainly provided more than having nothing at all.

Our convoy moved along very smoothly with a mission to the border. As we pulled rear security, Wright began randomly switching lanes. In a rhythmic sequence, he drove in the middle lane for a short period and then pulled into the right lane and back again. Looking at him in disapproval of his antics, he acknowledged with a satisfying deviant smile.

"Just keep the humvee in the middle lane," I instructed him.

Carefully watching the line of trucks in the convoy, I did not pay much attention to him. In my occasional glance into the side mirror, I noticed an Iraqi driver trailing directly behind us. There were times when they were not sure if they should pass so they cautiously followed at the rear. I reached my arm out of the window and waved him around. Wright suddenly cranked the steering wheel, pulling the humvee into the right-hand lane and cutting the Iraqi driver off as he attempted to pass.

"Quick, move back to the center lane, there is a vehicle pass-ing," I informed him thinking he may not have seen the civilian car.

"I don't want him to pass." Wright laughed. "He can stay be-hind me until I am ready to let him by."

I realized then, the driver had attempted many passes with each effort maliciously blocked.

"You pull this humvee into the middle lane and let him pass now!" I yelled.

Wright hesitated and then grudgingly swung into the center lane. I waved for the driver to pass. He cautiously drove his car around us and once by, quickly sped away.

"Don't you ever pull that crap again. You have no business treating these people that way."

He seemed to shrug it off as if it seemed like no big deal at all.

Turning off Tampa, the convoy found ASR Circle and con-tinued south. The narrow and difficult to travel road continued to be our alternate route to Navistar. Lining both sides of the road, the kids, finished with school for the day, walked together in small groups on their way home. They waved and gave the thumbs up hop-ing one of the trucks would throw a few snacks out the window to them.

A tanker from the convoy suddenly pulled over to the right side of the road with those following him quickly passing around and continuing down the highway. As Wright stopped the humvee be-hind the truck, I contacted the LT.

"One-Six, this is One-Six Bravo. Over."

Ping. "This is One-Six. Over."

"One of the trucks stopped back here. I'll let you know what I find. Over."

Ping. "Roger. Out."

With the convoy waiting up the road, I stepped out of the humvee to check on the driver. Seated in the cab of his truck, he wiped a stream of blood from his left forearm with a white rag. Questioning him as to what may have happened, he indicated one of the kids threw a rock at his truck and broke the side window with the shattering glass cutting his arm. Not able to exactly identify which kid may have thrown the rock, he knew it happened during the last mile we traveled.

I contacted the LT and filled him in on the situation. A minute later, the command vehicle came roaring up and stopped next to the tanker. The LT stepped out of the humvee and assessed the damage.

"I know which one of those little bastards he's talking about," one of the guys said.

"If you know which one it is, let's go pay them a visit," the LT ordered. "I think its time we taught them a lesson."

They jumped into their humvee and quickly left in search of the mischievous kid who had broken the window.

A separate group of kids curiously approached the gun truck. As they talked and laughed, we distributed a small amount of hard candy we found in the humvee.

Out of our sight, the LT, in the command vehicle, handled the rock thrower his own way. Driving toward a group of small kids, they pulled the humvee off the road and began pursuit. The kids darted and ran through a small tomato field to escape the roaring humvee at their heels. Tearing the vehicle through the turned earth and green vegetation, dark soil and sand flew through the air as a farmer ran from his mud house to decipher the confusion. Narrowly missing a small child who had fallen in front of the humvee, they cranked the steering wheel pulling the vehicle back onto the paved road.

Deciding the Iraqis sufficiently learned a lesson, the command vehicle returned to the convoy. As they laughed and described the details as to what exactly they had taught, I could not believe my ears. Disgusted, I shook my head and walked away. Why do some of these people want us to leave their country? Why would anyone in his or her right mind want to join the insurgency? This was complete madness.

The LT gave the order to continue and the trucks began moving. As Wright shifted the gun truck into gear and proceeded behind the convoy, a shower of small rocks rained down upon the humvee. Looking through my side mirror I watched as the kids darted for their homes.

After releasing the trucks and clearing our weapons at the

border, we drove the gun truck to the fuel point to fill the tank. As I began refueling, a blue van raced to our position and locked its brakes up next to us scattering a wave of rocks along the ground. When the dust finally cleared, a captain approached us from the vehicle.

"Who did it? Who had the discharge?" he demanded to know.

I held my tongue and continued refueling the humvee. There were soldiers dying from wounds they received in firefights and from roadside bomb explosions throughout the country while this man had nothing better to do than watch for people firing into the clearing barrels.

"I want to know which one of you fired your weapon back there," he continued accusing us.

"It wasn't us, sir," Roerig finally spoke up. "It might have been another humvee."

"Yeah, it wasn't us, sir," Wright joined in. "To tell you the truth, I don't think I even heard a shot go off."

I looked up with a stoic glare at the captain as he watched me finish refueling the gun truck. He understood. Leave us alone and go play your foolish games somewhere else.

"OK, yeah," he said, "I don't think it was any of you guys. It might have been someone else."

Upset that someone may have gotten away with firing a round, he stood kicking the rocks to the side as he studied the traffic routes in contemplating where they may have disappeared. If it happened at all, they were now far away and impossible to charge.

Before our arrival in theater, the military decided to consider the firing of a weapon into a clearing barrel during the clearing process a negligent discharge. Not everyone agreed with this. After all, a clearing barrel's sole purpose involved making sure weapons were clear of any ammunition.

By placing this in the category of a negligent discharge, anyone doing so would be subject to receiving an article fifteen, punishable by whatever the commanding officer decided. Actually, it gave some of those who previously had done nothing while over here, a job. Paperwork and punishment required supervision.

This captain was not the only one with a fabricated job. A

few months ago, another officer positioned himself at this same location with a radar gun. With a posted speed limit of five miles per hour, he stayed busy detaining and threatening the escorts as they passed though on their way to receive convoys to take north.

People like these were bottlenecks to the process. The system would have run much better if they packed up their office chairs and returned home. The military would actually accomplish more over here if they replaced these people with privates, specialists, buck sergeants, and lieutenants. We needed soldiers over here who could actually do the work, not someone collecting a paycheck to do nothing.

Over the next ten days, we assisted in training convoy escort teams to take over the missions to the border. The First Battalion of the 178th Field Artillery, a National Guard unit out of South Carolina, arrived to assume control over the southbound convoys. They began accompanying us in the humvees to get the feel for the road. Once comfortable with the operations, we would turn the missions over to them.

No one actually knew what we would then be doing but all signs pointed to assisting with the missions escorting trucks to Scania, a convoy support center located north of Diwaniyah and roughly sixty miles south of Baghdad.

As we were about to hand over control, the 1/178th received a side mission. A unit out of Tallil refused an escort mission to Baghdad claiming inadequate armor, poor fuel quality, and an increase in the amount of IEDs. Not knowing the exact details to their situation, I did not hold it against them for not wanting to take the mission. Convoys moving down the highway were similar to mechanical ducks rotating through a shooting gallery. You crossed your fingers and hoped you were not in the line of fire.

The camps up north required the fuel and the supplies so someone needed to escort the trucks. Somehow, they chose the 1/178th. After completing the Baghdad mission, they returned to take control of the southbound convoys.

Carrying my gear over my shoulder, I walked the line of humvees searching for my ride. After riding along and observing us, we would now accompany them.

Previously, during their training with us, two 1/178th soldiers rode along in the backseat of the gun truck and asked questions as we drove to Navistar. On the return leg to Cedar, I allowed them to switch positions with our crew placing one in the driver's seat and the other in the gun turret. Although the unit stated the riders were only to observe, I felt it more beneficial if they actually performed the work. After all, some of our guys, without convoy experience, drove and rode the gunner positions at a moments notice.

Allowing the soldiers of the 1/178th to actively participate seemed to work well. The soldiers were always excited to get behind the wheel or man the gun. The training went smoothly with the exception of one ride-along.

"It's a three hour trip to Cedar. Are you capable of driving that long without stopping?" I asked Specialist Williams as he sat in the driver's seat of the bravo gun truck.

He held up a CD player with ear buds. "No problem, sergeant, as long as I can listen to my music, I'll be fine."

"No, I can't let you do that. Right now, I need you to pay attention to your driving. When your unit assumes control of the convoy missions then you guys can do whatever you like."

"Oh, please, sergeant, you've got to let me listen to my music."

I shook my head. "No, actually our guys didn't start listening to music until after they were on the road for a few weeks and felt comfortable with the missions."

He looked disappointed as he placed his CD player back inside his bag and pulled his sunglasses to his face.

His first day on convoy missions, Williams felt excited to drive the gun truck. Participating in a second consecutive day on the road, Sergeant Cribb manned the .50 caliber machine gun in the turret.

As we traveled on MSR Tampa with a column of trucks bound for Cedar, we came upon a slow moving marine convoy heading our direction as they occupied the middle lane. I instructed Williams to move from the middle to the left lane and drive behind our convoy until we passed the military vehicles.

Our convoy came to a sudden stop but the gun truck continued its quick pace without slowing as we charged toward the rear end of the last convoy truck.

"Ho! Ho! Stop! Stop!" I yelled as I braced my hands against the windshield.

Williams quickly jumped on the brake pedal stopping us two humvee lengths from the last truck.

"Are you all right?" I asked him.

"Yeah, I'm all right. I'm sorry. I'm really sorry."

I looked at Roerig and Wright occupying the backseats. Both indicated they were fine. I grabbed Cribb's leg and he gave me the thumbs up signal.

"That's all right. These things happen," I reassured Williams. "Stay alert."

"OK, I'm sorry, sergeant. I'm really sorry."

I picked up the radio handset. "Road Hunter One-Six Alpha, this is One-Six Bravo. The convoy stopped back here. Are you still moving? Over."

Ping. "This is One-Six Alpha. Yeah, we're still moving. We're still passing this marine convoy. They're a mess and spread out for miles. They must be new. Over."

"With the marines in the center lane, I can't see around the convoy to tell what's happening up there. Over."

Ping. "Do you want us to slow down or stop? Over."

Without indication, the convoy began to move forward as unexpectedly as it had stopped.

"Negative. Our convoy is now moving. Maintain your speed. I'm sure we will catch up shortly. Over."

Ping. "Let us know if you have any problems. Over."

"Roger. This is One-Six Bravo. Out."

Williams stomped on the accelerator and we picked up speed traveling close to seventy miles per hour following directly behind our convoy. As before, the convoy again stopped without warning while we continued at cruising speed barreling toward it.

"Stop! Stop! Stop!" I yelled again.

This time we came to a halt one humvee length behind the convoy.

"I'm sorry, sergeant. I'm really sorry."

"Are you falling asleep?" I asked Williams.

"No, I'm not sleeping. Really I'm not."

"You need to stay alert or you're going to kill us. Do you

understand?"

"Yes, sergeant, I'm sorry. Maybe I should let someone else drive."

Roerig nodded uneasily from the backseat. Two close calls were more than we needed to experience in one day. Common sense told me to exchange Williams from behind the wheel but replacing him would teach him nothing.

"No, you drive," I insisted. "You need to learn to stay alert."

As I picked up the radio handset to contact the team, the convoy began proceeding forward.

"We must be yo-yoing," I explained to Williams. "The lead truck in our convoy is maintaining a steady speed but those following are slowing and accelerating to the point where the convoy comes to a complete stop back here."

"What should I do?" he asked.

"If this military convoy wasn't blocking the center lane, we could drive up and straighten the drivers out. There is nothing we can do now but stay alert and enjoy the carnival ride."

We followed along at high speeds to maintain contact with the convoy. It occasionally slowed and then picked up speed. As we trailed our column of trucks, Williams began to understand the mechanics involved.

The convoy came to sudden halt. Once again, we stormed toward the back of the last truck.

"Stop!" I yelled at the top of my lungs.

Williams jumped on the brake pedal with both feet and with screeching wheels, we came to a stop less than five feet from the rear trailer's bumper.

He hesitated as he stared through his sunglasses at the trailer stopped directly in front of us. A fraction of a second later and we would have been eating the rear of the cargo trailer.

"I'm sorry, sergeant. I'm sorry."

"You're falling asleep," I accused him once more.

"No, no, I'm not."

"Take those sunglasses off so I can see your eyes."

"No, please sergeant. I need my glasses."

"Take them off now or I'll take them off for you. You're going to get someone killed if you don't pay attention to what you are doing out here."

"OK, OK." He pulled the sunglasses from his face, folded the frames, and placed them next to the radio.

Our convoy attempted to move ahead of the military convoy but their lead vehicle accelerated and slowed to maintain their position in front of us. It looked obvious, with the number of large gaps in their convoy, they had no idea what they were doing. With the safety of both convoys in question, the lieutenant decided to stop our convoy and allow the marines to move ahead of us.

With the marine convoy well in front of us, Williams experienced no further problems with the gun truck maintaining a safe distance from the convoy. The riders learned important lessons that day.

Today, I searched for Yellow Jacket Four-Two, the call sign of my ride-along. Sergeant Holloway, the commander of the gun truck, introduced me to the gunner and his driver. Many of their unit's members have ridden along with us during the past few days. Now, they took control and occupied the drivers' seats. I would ride with as an observer in their bravo gun truck and would assist if a problem occurred on the road.

The LT rode along accompanying their command vehicle as well as Hanson in the lead gun truck. We talked as we waited for the MCT people to assign us a push. The lieutenant and another soldier from the 1/178th laughed as they discussed a convoy mission from the previous day.

"The hajjis do it every time," the LT said as he shook his head.

"Yeah, the hajjis were moving pretty slow when they started to change that tire," the soldier recounted. "I was really surprised on how fast they picked up pace when an M-16 is shoved in their face. He and his buddies sure started to hop then."

"You've got to keep the hajjis motivated," the LT explained. "Don't let them get away with anything."

As the lieutenant shared hajji stories, Holloway looked as though he did not quite know what to think about all of this. I remembered that feeling from when I first began convoy missions.

"Come on. Follow me." I nodded toward the drivers. "I have some people for you to meet."

Less than fifty meters from the escort team humvees, the convoy trucks stood parked in long rows waiting for the signal to leave. Making last minute adjustments to their trucks, the drivers, in noticing us approach, began gathering at the front of the vehicles to welcome us.

I reached out my hand and began shaking theirs. "Hi, how are you this morning?"

Looking surprised that the escorts would talk with them, they smiled with excitement and greeted us in English as well as other languages.

"This is Sergeant Holloway." I patted him on the shoulder. "He's going to be taking good care of you on your trip to Kuwait today."

They nodded and shook his hand.

"Where are you from?" I inquired as they encircled us. Sri Lanka, Pakistan, India, the list went on. As always, they were from a variety of countries throughout the world.

"Yes, I know where that is located," I said, which brightened their faces, "you're a long way from home."

"How long have you been driving convoys?" I asked. Some only a few weeks while others close to a year.

Holloway observed the drivers as they truly were—friendly and definitely not a threat. As we talked with them, all shared something personal or convoy related with us.

Thanking them for their time, we allowed them to continue with their preparations as we walked back to the gun trucks to wait for the convoy briefing.

"The drivers are not hajjis in the demeaning sense others might make them out to be," I explained to Holloway. "As you can see, they are people. People just like you and me. They are here to earn money to send back home to support their families. They are not the enemy."

I pointed to the escort group gathered with the LT. "You have some soldiers in your unit similar to ours."

Holloway glanced toward the soldiers who laughed and told stories next to the humvees.

"I have found that every unit has them. It doesn't bother them to intimidate and frighten the drivers and then joke about it later."

He shook his head as he listened.

"You need to understand, with the high stress experienced on the road, there is a disorder out there, a psychological sickness. You'll see it. There will be occasions when your guys will lose their heads. They'll start taking it out on the drivers or even the Iraqi people along the roadsides. Why? Because they can, because the leadership turns a blind eye toward it."

I stopped midway to the gun trucks and turned toward him.

"It is important there is a balance out there. Someone, who in the face of all insanity, can distinguish between what is right and what is wrong. To pull others back to reality when the adrenaline blows through their veins and they do crazy things they would have never thought of doing back home. There needs to be someone there for the drivers and the people along the road, to help them out of a situation with a fellow soldier. You'll find it's not a popular stance to take but it is definitely necessary."

"I understand, sergeant," he said as we began walking back to the gun trucks, "I could tell that you had that way about you. I'll do my best."

After shifting the responsibility of the southbound missions to the escort teams of the 1/178th, we retired the original Road Hunter teams as the leadership debated on what they would do with us next. On the agenda remained a move for the unit from Camp Cedar II to Tallil Air Base. Except for an occasional mail run escort, we sat and waited to pass the time.

The day after the escort missions ended, I began a period of withdrawal. Feelings of extreme anxiety gripped me as I coped with the loss of the road. After nine months of continuous, intense stress, it all came to an abrupt end. My heart repeatedly raced in expectation of eminent danger. In talking with other team members, some shared the same powerful sensations. I could not take the restlessness any longer so I increased the distance of my runs within the camp.

I ran and I ran, fourteen miles in the beating sun and dry desert heat. Around and around the camp perimeter I pursued my fears, pushing my body to its limits in an attempt to destroy the pain. I ran until I knew I completely extinguished the relentless demon that burned within me.

How would I make it through the next three months without the adrenaline rush of the gun truck chasing down the highway? My only hope lay in Scania. Once we moved to Tallil, the chance still existed to assist with the convoy escort missions north to Scania. I would bide my time and pray for a mission to come my way, soon.

CHAPTER 19

Missions North

In the twenty-first century B.C., Ur-Nammu, King of Ur, slowly climbed the numerous steps of the majestic multi-tiered tower. An entourage of torchbearers followed closely behind singing songs of praise to the great moon god, Nanna. The musical tones of the priestesses and priests resonated off the brick walls of the courtyard below and amplified high into the darkening late evening sky above.

He paused at the top of the first level as the priests slowly encircled the ledge presenting the sacred offerings of fruits and grains. The priests bowed and prayed as the king, followed by a high priestess and four holy men, continued the journey up the steps of the tower.

Reaching the second tier, the high priestess removed the king's headdress, robe, and gold adornments, leaving him bare to his god as he first existed when he entered this life. The four priests took their positions of sanctity at their respective corners of the level while the high priestess kneeled at the steps.

After ascending the final rise of steps to the top of the tower, the king bowed and prayed. The tower's peak represented the halfway point between heaven and earth, the point at which men conversed with gods.

The ceremony recognized the end of the thirty-day period, the sanctified night when the gods of the earth and of the sky consulted with Nanna, chief of all gods, creator of all things. To the men of the earth, it offered a unique opportunity for a mere mortal to seek holy guidance by asking an essential question or making a vital request.

He rose up from his knees and gazed out over his flourishing kingdom. Farmers returned from the green fields to their homes and herders settled their flocks for the night. Cook fires lighted the maze of streets as children hurried off to bed. To the north, the boat filled Euphrates River sparkled under the bright glow of the full moon and provided the waters of life to the people of his city.

He raised his hands to the sky and called out, "Nanna, it is I, Ur-Nammu—King of Ur, King of Sumer, King of Akkad. Speak with me."

With a sudden gust of wind gently brushing his face, he knew he stood in the presence of gods.

On this day, he brought a special request. He would not ask for an abundance of crops and animals. He would not ask of the outcomes of future battles. He gazed up into the sky while stretching his hands into the air and demanded, "Show me the future of my people."

He slowly closed his eyes and waited. Neither hearing nor feeling a response, he continued, "I have brought this land together. It flourishes like no other kingdom in history. Trade is established and peace is abundant. My people are content with the law and know they live better than their ancestors would have ever dreamed possible. I have brought civilization to the world. I ask once more. Show me their future."

Silence remained as another gust of wind softly touched his skin. With the question asked, a long wait for a reply began. The horizon absorbed the last of the daylight and the stars began their slow journey across the dark sky. As the night grew cooler, the king wondered if the gods had forgotten him. During periods of doubt, his patience suddenly sparked at the random appearances of quick arcs of light streaking across the sky, signifying the holy counsel remained in session. As he continued his long wait, drowsiness swept over him and carried him off into a deep sleep.

Ur-Nammu awakened to the sound of thunder approaching from the west. Daylight filled the sky. At first, he became upset with himself at his lack of discipline but quickly realized this to be the work of the gods. He rose to his feet and raised a trembling hand to shade his eyes from the bright hot sun. A large dragonfly appeared on the horizon. With the sound of thunder, it increased in size as it quickly moved toward him at an unimaginable speed. In its wake, the creature slowly transformed the fields from a lush green to dark red and finally a blacken ash.

He fell to his knees in tears and screamed, "How? How did this happen?"

The razor sharp edge of a glistening sword gently tapped his shoulder. He glanced up and before him stood a dark shiny serpent with brilliant multicolored rings encircling its body. The serpent smiled through long white fangs and a forked tongue as it raised the sword high into the air in a motion to sever the king's head.

A great eagle suddenly appeared leading a variety of fierce creatures. The taloned bird and its many companions bled from numerous open wounds covering their bodies. The eagle wielded a large wooden spear knocking the sword from its path. The animals fought off the serpent in a vicious battle until all dissolved into a fine crystalline dust and vanished with the wind.

The sky darkened as the deafening insect pressed closer. With tears on his cheeks, the king stumbled back to his feet to face the monster. The thunder grew louder as the hot wind blew sand into his face from the barren earth below.

An entity of white light suddenly materialized before the king and calmly declared, "Do not weep, Ur-Nammu, your people will persevere."

The being vanished as quickly as it appeared.

Pushed by its strong winds, the king fell onto his back as the massive beast, producing an awful shrieking noise, grazed the top of the tower.

"They're Italian," Moss shouted. "Those are Italian choppers from the air base."

Standing at the top of the Temple of Ur, we looked out over the surrounding area and observed a group of helicopters skimming across the sand. It felt good to be away from the confines of the camp on this beautiful, sunshiny day.

"They sure are active today," Moss continued. "They must be performing some type of flight maneuvers."

Scotting, Severson, and I persuaded Moss to transport us to the temple with his gun truck. It took little convincing, he felt as eager as we did to see the ancient ziggurat. We told no one we were leaving. Someone in authority would have decided against it only to find later that it would have been fine. With the temple located on the edge of Tallil Air Base, we did not travel far to get there.

After moving to Tallil two weeks ago, we settled into our new home on the air base hoping it would be the final move during the remaining three months of our tour. The trailers, or living containers as the base called them, offered a definite improvement over the eight-man tents we endured at Cedar.

I was fortunate to room with Specialist Dave Schuttloffel, an intellect who enjoyed a stimulating conversation on politics and world events. We worked opposite shifts, he at the TOC during the night and I at the motor pool during the day. This allowed each of us the opportunity for a little privacy, a valuable benefit difficult to come by.

With the convoy escort missions to Navistar handed to the 178th, we had little to do. A few convoy missions north to Scania trickled our way, but for the most part, many of the guys remained unemployed.

With a new slot as the unit's 92 Alpha, I was one of the fortunate who possessed a meaningful job to help pass the time. The leadership required those without employment to report to the motor pool every morning to look for work. After wandering around for an hour or two, they returned to their living containers to read books, play video games, or watch movies on their DVD players.

As we left the DFAC one evening, I noticed the sergeant major stopped ahead of us along the path.

"Sergeant Lewandowski, have you been getting enough rest?" he asked with a smile.

"Enough rest?" I curiously responded.

"Yeah, you're probably spending most of your time catching up on rest."

I finally understood what he meant by his question. Not knowing of my job at the motor pool, he thought I was one of those occupationally confined to their living containers with nothing to do.

"I'm the units new 92 Alpha at the motor pool," I explained. "I'm training on dispatching vehicles and managing the replacement parts. I stay pretty busy. I'm getting enough rest but like everyone else, I suppose I could use a little more."

His expression quickly changed. "Oh, I didn't know that. So, you're staying busy?"

"Yeah, I need to stay busy, otherwise, I would go nuts. If

there were no tasks to do, I would probably make work for myself. I would plant grass and maintain it, just to stay occupied."

The sergeant major slowly nodded his head. I sensed it was not what he expected to hear. Without saying another word, he turned and walked away.

Although I worked at the motor pool, like the other security escorts, I received no immunity to convoy duty. The missions took priority. We usually received orders of a mission at the last moment. After acquiring the information, the team leaders searched the living containers awakening their members to ready the gun trucks.

Knock. Knock. Knock. The door of my living container slowly opened. "Lew, are you in there?"

It was Sergeant First Class Les Kolden. When he knocked on the door well before sunrise, it usually meant one thing—convoy mission.

"Yeah, I'm up. Come on in." I sat up and grabbed my pants.

"We have a mission to Scania this morning. The 201st has some extra convoys that need escorts. Sorry about the short notice but I just found out, myself."

"That's all right." I pulled my bootlaces tight. "What time are we leaving?"

"We're in no rush but the sooner we get going, the sooner we'll be back."

"Are Miller and Roerig with me today?"

"Yeah, I'll let them know. I'm heading that way right now."

"OK, thanks, Les. I'll shave, and then I'm ready to go."

The drivers picked up the gun trucks from the motor pool and parked them next to the containers for easier access in loading. I carried my equipment to the gun truck and made radio contact with the TOC.

Specialist Eric Peters popped his head through the turret ring of the command vehicle. "Hey, Lew," he shouted. "Are you coming along today too?" Peters worked with me in the motor pool. A bright, energetic, young soldier, he spoke proudly of his Sioux Indian heritage.

"Of course, I can't let you enjoy all the fun by yourself."

"Fun? Ha. Don't you know that it's gonna suck today?"

"Suck? It never sucks, does it?"

"Yeah, it's gonna suck, Lew. It's gonna suck because I'm coming along."

"Oh, you're not that bad. Are you?"

"No, I'm not bad. It's the mission that's bad. They never send me out on the good missions, only the bad ones."

He mounted his SAW on the humvee's pintle. "Whenever a bad mission comes up and no one else wants to go, they always say, 'send the Indian, send Peters.' This morning, someone looked at this mission and said, 'send the Indian.'"

"If that is why you're coming along, then tell me why I'm here?"

"I don't know, Lew, maybe you're part Indian too."

Specialist Dana Stockland cranked opened the latch on the command humvee driver's door. "I can't believe we're going today. I thought we were supposed to be through with this crap."

"What's wrong, Piggy?" Peters asked. "You don't look too happy."

Stockland threw his gear across the seat. "I can't believe we're going today. OK, all right, we're going to take a vote. Who's all in favor of staying? Come on. Who's in favor?"

The guys on the team gave a roaring response to stay.

"See. See. Now, who's all in favor of hauling our sorry asses all the way up to Scania and back?"

"I am!" I played along.

"Me too!" Kolden shouted as he walked up to the humvees.

"That's two to seven." Stockland smiled. "Looks like we're staying."

"No, sorry, but Lew and I outnumber all of your votes added together because we're older." Kolden laughed. "We're going."

We left Tallil and arrived at Cedar to pick up a push to Scania. The drivers worked steadily preparing their trucks for the trip north. Many wrapped woolen blankets around themselves to stay warm in the cool morning air as they stood in groups drawing puffs of smoke from their large hookah pipes.

Thirty TCN trucks readied and counted off for the convoy mission. The new fifteen trucks per convoy safety rule pertained only to the KBR convoys and not the TCNs. We knew the convoy would be a challenge when a truck hauling pallets of plywood experienced difficulties in leaving the yard. Five miles north of the Euphrates River, the truck broke down.

The driver did not have any luck at all in repairing his vehicle. It looked as though we would have to leave it along the road and continue on.

"Lew, you stay here with the truck," Kolden instructed. "I'm going to head back to the Euphrates and see if I can't get the Italians to watch the truck until the recovery team picks it up. I'm afraid if we leave this plywood unprotected, it would be gone in no time."

"Oh yeah," I agreed. "You can bet there would be some serious remodeling in the area if we left this plywood unattended for more than five minutes."

The command vehicle took off leaving me alone with the truck and driver. Our two gun trucks remained with the convoy, a few miles up the road. With no recent insurgent activity reported in the area, there should not be any serious security problems. I stayed alert and kept the traffic flowing just in case. Some of the passing vehicles rolled slowly by the truck with its occupants eagerly eying the load of plywood. Upon discovering my presence, they politely waved and continued driving.

The driver ran himself ragged trying to fix his truck. He jumped down to the ground, ran to the passenger side of the truck, and repositioned a vacuum cap on the engine that would not stay seated. He climbed back into the cab and started the engine. The engine ran momentarily then quit when the cap fell loose.

I walked around his truck and examined the shipment of plywood. Not loaded properly, most of the material appeared damaged beyond use. The idea seemed to be in getting supplies from one place to another without concern as to what condition they actually arrived.

I spotted the command vehicle approaching a few miles down the road trailed by an Iraqi National Guard (ING) pickup. Nervous about his truck, the driver continued his unsuccessful routine. His hands trembled as he feverishly worked the vacuum hose and cap. Noticing the vehicles approaching, his eyes began to tear up. He did not want to leave the truck. He may have abandoned a truck in the past and feared the consequences of doing so again.

"Wrap some wire around the hose and attach it to the block," I explained. "It's an easy fix."

Not understanding English, he stood there shaking his head. We were not to touch the trucks but this looked too simple. I pulled out my Leatherman multi-tool and cut a small piece of wire from his flatbed trailer. Pushing him aside, I firmly wired the vacuum cap into place. It would stay seated now. The driver shrieked with joy and practically pulled my arm off as he shook my hand in appreciation.

As the command humvee pulled up and stopped, the plywood loaded truck leaped forward and raced for the convoy.

Kolden stepped out of the humvee. "He got it going? That's good. Now we won't need the ING. I couldn't get the Italians. They weren't able to spare anyone at the moment."

I joined my gun truck and we continued with the convoy to Scania. Ten minutes later the command vehicle overheated and pulled to the side of the road. Green engine coolant spread across the highway as the vehicle rolled to a stop.

We pulled the gun truck in behind the disabled humvee as the convoy pulled over a mile down the road. Roerig and Peters examined the engine and determined it "deadlined"—not drivable.

We would need to contact the TOC to get a replacement humvee in order to continue. Our distance from Tallil placed us out of radio range so Kolden pulled out the satellite phone and dialed the number of the battalion TOC telephone.

"You've got to be kidding me." He pulled the phone away from his ear and stared at it.

"What happened?" I asked.

"I don't believe this. It says, 'out of time.' Someone used up all the satellite phone minutes."

"That's just great," Stockland spoke up. "One of the officers at the TOC used up all of the satellite minutes having phone sex with his wife, now we're stuck out in the middle of nowhere with a trashed humvee and not able to call for help. That's just great."

Kolden tossed the phone into the humvee. "No, we're OK. I can still send a text message to the TOC over the radio. It just upsets me though. This is the reason we have these satellite phones."

"It's still not too late to turn around and go back," Stockland continued. "I say we vote on whether we should turn around or keep going. This is a democracy, we should vote."

"Voting isn't going to make any difference, Piggy," Peters interrupted. "Lew and Kolden hold the most votes, besides, this isn't a democracy, this is the army."

We towed the command vehicle to the rear of the convoy where it would wait until a replacement arrived with an escort team from Tallil. Kolden pulled the front gun truck to the rear and we placed our humvee toward the front center of the convoy to provide security. The .50 caliber heavy machine gun mounted in the turret would better intimidate those having thoughts of bothering us.

The highway was under construction by Iraqi contractors. The column of trucks stopped at the end of a narrow lane of newly laid bituminous pavement. Wooden engineering stakes and smoothly bladed gravel covered the remainder of the road and shoulders.

It would be a long wait. The people living along the roadside began congregating around the convoy and the gun truck. Specialist Don Miller and Roerig talked with the kids while passing out snacks and water.

Ping. "One Six Bravo, this is One Six. Over."

Standing in the turret, Roerig reached down and grabbed the handset off the radio.

"Lew, they said that a convoy is coming our way. I can see it from here. It should be passing us shortly."

"OK, thanks. Move these people back and pull the humvee to the edge of the road. With this construction, they are going to need all the room they can get to maneuver around us."

It looked like a 201st Bulldog team escorting a convoy of supply trucks to Scania. They encountered a late morning start.

Everyone quickly cleared from the highway as the convoy gradually slowed to make its pass. The Bulldog convoy contained numerous open spaces and spread itself out for many miles. By the time the last half of the convoy passed, the remaining trucks cruised close to seventy miles per hour in an effort to catch up.

Crack! A truck from the passing convoy sideswiped the corner of a bottled water flatbed parked next to us. We stopped on a dip in the highway, a spot where the newly laid pavement ended and the gravel began. The passing trucks were dangerously close to ours and swayed during their drop from the pavement.

With the accidental collision, bottles of water flew high into the air and bounced off the passing trucks. The plastic bottles rained down covering the road. Water splashed and sprayed as the bottles burst under the crushing tires of the moving trucks. We restrained those back who frantically tried retrieving the water, and let them collect it once the convoy finished its pass.

The roadside people cheerfully danced with their hands filled full of water bottles. I examined the flatbed with the truck drivers. No damage occurred to the vehicle. The passing truck merely hooked the water pallets protruding from its side.

A small, white pickup rolled to a stop next to the scattered plastic bottles. Four passengers dressed in white, soiled thawb robes quickly emerged.

Two began picking up water from the road while the driver rushed to the front of the pickup and raised its hood.

One approached me and began begging, "Please, mista. Please, mista."

He eagerly pointed to the vehicle wanting me to believe they suffered engine trouble. Fine, they were like the others along the road in that they were interested in getting as many bottles of water as they could possibly carry.

I nodded and smiled which instantly pleased him.

Looking up the line, I noticed a driver getting out of his truck. As his foot hit the ground, he turned and reached up grabbing the small hand of one of the roadside beggars who stepped from his cab. He smiled as he helped the young man down. This caught me by surprise. I recognized the driver as one who made small talk in broken English with me earlier. The beggar was one of the teens from along the road, an acne faced boy who seemed a little slow to understand.

"What was he doing in your truck? What was he doing in your truck?" I yelled at the driver as I pointed at the boy.

The driver's face turned sheepish with embarrassment. He hung his head and did not say a word as the boy walked off into the crowd. I spotted a small plastic sack filled with food in the boy's hand. It suddenly dawned on me.

"Were you having sex with that boy?"

The man continued hanging his head and remained silent. I possessed no proof. I did not catch him in the act and if questioned, the boy would not say a word in fear of losing the food.

"Did you have sex with that boy?" I demanded to know.

He said nothing.

How many other kids had this man harmed along the road? He looked very comfortable in his actions, as if he had done this many times before.

It was our duty to protect the drivers during the mission but it was also our duty to protect the Iraqis from harm. I knew he did something terribly wrong to the young boy but I could not prove it.

I pointed my finger at him and angrily ordered. "Get back into your truck. I don't want to see your face out on the road again. Do you understand me?"

The driver stepped up into his cab and closed the door behind him.

How many of the other drivers were molesting kids along the road? I was always concerned with protecting the drivers. It never occurred to me the drivers were abusing the kids. We were usually not stopped this long and surrounded by this many civilians near the trucks. What about the ROM back at Cedar? When it existed, many of the local kids crept in during the night to steal from and sell to the drivers. How many of them did the drivers sexually abuse?

I heard the heavy clunk of the gun truck window closing. As I turned to look, I saw a small group surrounding the humvee with Miller looking concerned as he sat in the driver's seat. "Now what?" I thought to myself.

I walked over to the humvee and yelled up to Roerig who bent down inside the vehicle and talked with Miller, "Tony, what's up?"

He sat up, pulling his head from within the turret.

"What's going on?" I asked. "Why are the windows closed on the humvee?"

He raised his hands and shook his head.

I pushed my way through the small crowd. "Koft. Koft," I shouted as I moved some of the Iraqis away from the vehicle.

I opened my passenger side door. "Miller, what happened? What's going on? Why aren't you out here pulling security?"

He looked overwhelmed. "These kids are driving me nuts. They won't leave me alone," he began to explain. "I gave them some food and they just wanted more. Roerig and I practically cleaned out the humvee and gave them everything we had. They still wanted more. They're crazy, Lew. I sat back in the humvee to get away from them but they started shoving their arms through the windows. They're driving me nuts."

I looked around the inside of the humvee. Not a sunflower seed or MRE snack remained.

"Hey, man, you made some friends. There is nothing wrong with that. We do need to keep them away from the gun truck though. I need you out here pulling security. This is very real. You need to be ready if something should happen to go wrong."

"Sorry, Lew, but these kids just drove me nuts."

"No, there is no need to be sorry. You learned a good lesson. It's OK to give out food and water but you need to stay in control of the situation. I'll move these people away from the humvee so you can get out."

I talked with some of the kids and positioned them away from the gun truck. Miller stepped out, looked around, and closed the door behind him. "How'd you do that?" he asked.

I laughed. "Keep them away from the gun truck. Be friendly but firm. Don't give them anything. OK?"

Miller nodded his head.

"Tony, keep an eye on those trucks. Remember, we're on our own up here. Stay alert."

"You got it, Lew."

I walked back to the stalled, white pickup truck. Its occupants stood nowhere near it. After clearing the bottled water from the road, the four of them began begging from the drivers.

The time had come for them to leave. They were an obstacle on the road and someone could get hurt.

"*Hey!*" I yelled.

Everyone instantly froze. I sternly pointed to the four in question and then back to their pickup indicating they now needed to move the vehicle.

One ran up to me displaying a sad expression. "Mista. Mista. Please. Please," he begged as he shook his folded hands in my face. He looked at his vehicle with the hood still raised as though he wanted me to feel sorry for him.

"Move it, now. Go. Leave." I pointed down the road toward

the rear of the convoy. He continued begging in an attempt to allow them to stay.

My patience had run out. They were a danger to us, to the convoy, and to those standing along the roadway. I pulled my M-16 up and placed it across the front of my chest in a show of force. "*Now!*" I yelled.

The man's eyes widened. His three companions sprinted to the pickup. They opened the doors as they scolded one another and began pushing the stalled vehicle down the highway.

They stopped a little less than ten meters from where they began and started begging again from the drivers.

I became upset. "Roerig! Miller!" I shouted. Both their heads turned toward me.

"I want you to take that humvee and help those guys along."

They looked at the white pickup.

I took my right fist and smacked it into the palm of my left hand making a loud crack. "Push them. Ram them back to the end of the convoy."

Miller looked confused. "Push them with the humvee?" he asked.

I smacked my fist into the palm of my hand one more time. "Ram that son of a bitch back to the end of the convoy. I don't care if you end up wrecking that little pickup. Don't stop no matter what they say. Don't stop until you get them there. Do you understand?"

Miller jumped into the humvee and with a cloud of dust, he swung it around moving behind the pickup. The four men, understanding very well what I just indicated, jumped into their vehicle. A puff of smoke shot from the tail pipe as they took off with the gun truck on their rear.

The crowd roared with cheers and then burst into laughter. The drivers patted me on my back. The kids pointed at the pickup and laughed as they smacked their little fists into their hands.

Five minutes later, the gun truck returned.

"Lew, we didn't have to push them." Miller smiled. "They made it on their own."

"Good job, guys."

"Kolden wants us in the rear," he informed me. "The recovery team showed up with a replacement humvee. We're going to leave in a bit."

During the three-hour wait, some of the drivers fell asleep on top of their steering wheels in the trucks. We drove up and down the line sounding the humvee horn to awaken them and begin moving.

All the trucks in the convoy started rolling with the exception of the last truck. It stood motionless, about fifty meters behind us.

"There's one left," Roerig yelled. "He's not moving at all."

I looked in the side mirror. "Yeah, he's not moving. Back up and we'll find out what's going on."

Miller shifted the transmission into reverse and stepped on the accelerator. Looking through his side mirror, he quickly lost track of the vehicle as we approached it.

"I can't see him anymore," he said as he turned his head from side to side attempting to look through both mirrors. "Tell me when we're getting close."

We moved along at a fast speed and began nearing the truck.

"Ho! Ho! Ho!" I yelled.

"Stop! Stop!" Roerig screamed as he pounded on the top of the humvee with his hands.

Crunch!! We hit the front driver's side of the truck with the rear passenger side of the humvee.

The driver jumped from his seat. Black smoke shot from the trucks exhaust pipes as he leaped ahead desperately trying to catch the convoy.

"Is everyone OK?" I asked.

Both indicated they were unhurt.

"I'm sorry. I'm sorry," Miller apologized profusely.

"We better check for damage before we go." I stepped out of the gun truck.

Roerig and I examined the rear of the humvee. A few noticeable gouges and scratches marred the finish, otherwise, there was no real damage.

Miller worried as to what the impact may have caused. "What does it look like?"

"It's pretty bad," Roerig said with a straight face. "The whole back quarter is pushed in and the taillights are missing."

"No, please tell me you're kidding."

We burst into laughter. Miller shifted the transmission into drive and we left to catch the convoy.

I yelled over to Miller, "I've never seen that before."

"Seen what?"

"I've never seen anyone become so angry at a driver who was sleeping that he would ram his humvee into his truck just to wake him up." I laughed.

"I swear. I didn't know he was that close."

"Miller," Roerig joined in, "I think you better go see the combat stress docs when we get back. You've got some serious anger issues."

We laughed about the incident during the remainder of the trip. I thought of how the poor driver must have thought we were really upset with him.

When we arrived at Scania, I searched for the driver who abused the boy on the road but I could not locate him. With the long delay on the road, it became too late to take a convoy so we patrolled MSR Tampa back to Tallil. It would be well after dark before we arrived.

Late that evening, Kolden knocked on my living container door. "Lew, just a heads up, you're down for the Black Watch mission."

"The British Army Black Watch?" I sat up in my chair.

"Yeah, they're still up by Fallujah and we are going up there to provide security for their return to Basra."

"Thanks, I'll be ready."

This was my chance to journey farther north. I was excited about the mission. Not only would we be traveling near Fallujah, but we would also be providing security for the famous Black Watch.

CHAPTER 20

The Black Watch

Sand and dust slowly settled on the flat-brown painted surface of the British Warrior Fighting Vehicle as braking road wheels ended the ratcheting grind of its multilinked track. Scottish soldiers from the Royal Highland Regiment jumped from the open hatches and slapped their arms and legs, brushing the fine sediment away from their clothing. Scanning the area, they visually located two additional Warriors taking up protective positions on each side.

"We're establishing a checkpoint at location Zulu. All clear at the moment. Over," the commander verified radio contact with his superiors at the Black Watch headquarters located within the boundaries of Dogwood, a small barren camp constructed in the desolate sands south of Fallujah.

Ping. "Roger. Out."

The commander removed his headset and stepped from the vehicle, quickly dropping to the ground. "Relieve yourselves if you must but stay ready."

Reaching into his pocket, the gunner pulled out a package of cigarettes covered in Arabic lettering removing one and placing it between his lips. He took a quick inventory of the remaining pack while blowing a puff of smoke into the air.

"One for me?" the driver leaned toward him and asked.

Lightly tossing the package through the air he replied, "just one, they've got to last me a few more days." He hesitated with curiosity. "Where're yours? You out?"

"Oh no, I'm not out. I left them back in the bunker. They've got to last me a few more days ya know."

"You prick. Give em back." The two playfully wrestled for the cigarettes.

"Knock it off, the two of you," the commander shouted.

285

"We've only got four days left here. Keep it together. We don't want no foolish mistakes."

Positioned along the roadside ahead of the tracked vehicles, large signs indicated a checkpoint was now in place. The Arabic writing across the newly painted boards signified all civilian traffic must stop at the sign and exit their vehicles or risk the use of deadly force.

The driver finished his smoke and leaned toward the gunner. "When we get back to Shaibah, the first thing I'm doing is taking you to the pub."

"The pub? You know I don't drink."

"Exactly, no sense in wasting your two drink tickets. I'll help you put em to good use."

The commander laughed quietly at the amusing plan. "In less than two weeks we'll be back on Scottish soil," he reminded them. "Just in time for Christmas as Blair promised."

"Back for Christmas?" the driver replied. "That's what we thought a month ago when our six-month tour was up. As special recognition for a job well done, they extended our duty and sent us here, merry bloody Christmas."

The gunner spit the windblown sand from his mouth. "Now, tell me again why we are here?"

The commander climbed back onto the Warrior. "We stopped the insurgents from entering and exiting Fallujah during the American assault. We cut off their rat runs."

"But this is the American zone, why would they send us?"

"Politics," the driver broke in.

"Politics? How's that?"

"It's simple," he continued, "Bush was up for re-election in the States and the assault on Fallujah strengthened his bid. Having Blair send the famous Black Watch to assist, demonstrated to the Americans that the coalition forces were behind him."

The gunner blew a slow steady stream of smoke into the air. "I would have to say that was bloody cheeky of him to do that."

"Its politics, that's all."

"Tell that to the five poor lads who won't be returning with us, and their grieving families they left back home."

"Look alive," the commander shouted. "We've got company."

A civilian vehicle approached with its occupants following the commands of the soldiers. They exited their vehicle. They held still for a body search. They patiently waited while the soldiers searched their car and then they finally went on their way without incident.

The gunner lit another cigarette. "I'm dreading the trip back to Shaibah if it's anything like the convoy up. Everyone knew of our mission to Dogwood. The politicians, the media, and the insurgents, they all knew. It was a bloody circus with invitations. Come to Dogwood and give the Black Watch a go-around. See how tough they really are. We took it up the bum with that one."

"It's different this time," the commander replied. "It's a total media blackout."

"What about the security back to Shaibah? Have they decided that?"

"Yeah, they requested to have the same American chaps escort us back to Shaibah who brought us up here."

Another vehicle drew near their checkpoint.

"Here comes another one." The soldiers prepared to search the vehicle as it stopped in a cloud of dust next to the sign.

"What are they?" I stood in the motor pool at Tallil looking at a bundle of steel plates alongside Roerig and Specialist Travis Heasley.

"They're gun shields, for the turret." Roerig lifted one of the heavy plates from the stack to examine it. "They protect the gunner from shrapnel and small arms fire."

I shook my head. "After ten months of convoy duty, we finally get gun shields. That's unbelievable."

"They're nice aren't they?" Staff Sergeant Ed Selzler, one of the motor pool supervisors, commented as he arrived to check on our progress in preparing the gun trucks for the Black Watch escort mission.

"They'll look even nicer on my turret." Roerig smiled.

"Yeah, I'll bet they would but they're not for you. You can't have them." Ed pulled a cigarette from his package, placed it on his lips, and lit it.

"What do you mean? Why?"

"You're considered low priority." Ed laughed. "Isn't that messed up?"

"If we can't have them, who's getting them?" I asked.

"The colonel's team and one of the batteries."

"Why does the battery need them?" Roerig replaced the shield section back onto the stack.

"They're stationed up at forward operating base (FOB) Duke, by Karbala. Word from above says they get the gun shields."

"Yeah, but they're doing ammo site security," one of the gunners spoke up. "They don't need them. We're the ones doing convoy escort. We're the ones on the road every day. We should have the protection."

"Hey, that's the way the colonel wants it," Ed explained. "If you don't agree with it then go talk with him."

"Yeah, I see he's taking care of his boys too. They don't need them either."

"It's messed up isn't it?" Ed shook his head.

"I'll say."

Ed looked through the stack of gun shields studying their numbers. The possibility existed they would not need all of them at Duke. "If you want a gun shield, then go ask Mr. Flint," he told Roerig. "Being the battalion maintenance technician, he has a say in it. Maybe they can spare a few."

Roerig, Heasley, and some of the other gunners walked over to the maintenance office to visit with Chief Warrant Officer 2 Tom Flint about the gun shields. They quickly returned with good news.

After assembling the frames, we separated the steel plates and began positioning them onto the turrets.

Holding the shield into place, Roerig attempted to insert a bolt. "Shit! They don't fit."

"No, you're kidding," I stepped away from the humvee to get a better look.

"Look. None of the bolt holes match up with the frames."

"Shit!"

Ed moved over from assisting another gun truck crew. He attempted unsuccessfully to match the shield holes with the frame. "They're probably designed for the turrets in the newer armored humvees. It's a whole different setup altogether."

"If they don't fit our gun trucks, they're not going to fit on any of the battery's humvees either." Roerig pointed out.

Ed took a long drag from his cigarette and rubbed his forehead with his thumb. "Go get the drills out, boys. They may not fit now, but I got a strong feeling that in about an hour, they'll fit like a glove."

The next day, the Road Hunter teams, along with some of the Bulldog escorts, patrolled to the Kuwaiti border to retrieve the trucks used as transportation for the Black Watch mission. A mixture of eighty-five flatbeds and military transports waited for escort to Camp Cedar where they would continue the next day to FOB Duke, and finally arrive at Camp Dogwood the following day.

Upon arrival at the border, we patiently waited for the trucks to complete their final checks and coordinate their staging positions. With the extra time available, I walked over to the Navistar PX to pick up a quick snack.

New uniforms roamed the PX, soldiers just in from the real world. They talked, laughed, and made jokes with one another as we stood in line to check out.

I thought of how we once acted like them back when we initially arrived. It seemed so long ago. Now, the talking and laughing was almost nonexistent when we stood in lines to wait. Pick up what you need and leave. It became the norm. After ten months of missions, there was not much for us to laugh and joke about anymore anyway.

I looked at their bright, fresh clothes and then down at my faded desert uniform and worn-out tan suede boots. Their light colored skin displayed a slight red burn compared with the sun baked and wind dried appearance of my face and hands.

They looked at one another with friendly eyes as they talked. At that point, I suddenly realized how I had become accustomed to constantly staring off into the distance. Not really looking at anything. Not really wanting to. Just waiting, waiting for something to happen and then react.

I felt uncomfortable standing with the new soldiers, a feeling as though I did not belong. I needed to return to my own kind, those of us who survived on the other side of the border. It saddened me to think of what I had become. I changed, adapted to my environment. I was not proud of it but it was necessary for my survival, both physically and mentally.

New to the country, it was not too late for them. As they jokingly talked, I wanted to break into their conversation and warn them of the line a few miles north of there. A life changing line marked by razor wire and ten-foot deep trenches. If they chose to cross it, they would never be the same. They would lose themselves in the insanity of a war. They would quickly tarnish their innocence. Their thoughts of right and wrong would become clouded causing them to do un-forgettable things.

"Sergeant Lewandowski," a familiar voice called from the aisle. It was Jackson, a soldier from the 1/178th, who rode along with us on a convoy training mission when their unit first arrived in theater a few months ago.

"Sergeant Lewandowski, how are you doing?" He extended his hand as he walked up to me.

"Well, Specialist Jackson, it's good to see you again. Are you still on convoy missions?"

"Yeah, we're still running trucks up and down Tampa."

"That's good. You looked comfortable doing it, like you enjoyed it."

"I thought you guys were ready to leave. What do they have you doing?" he asked.

"Convoy missions." I smiled. "They tell us we're through with the road but we keep getting missions, mostly to Scania now. I imagine we will stay at it until we actually do leave."

"Do you remember Sergeant Montgomery?" he asked.

"Yeah, highway patrolman, excellent driver."

"His vehicle was hit with an IED."

"Is he OK?"

"He has some shrapnel wounds but he should be all right."

"When did this happen?" I asked.

"It happened on our first mission when we escorted a group of trucks up to Baghdad."

"That was your team who picked up that mission to Baghdad?"

"Yeah."

"That was a tough one to take for a first mission."

"Yeah, I know. Our commander told them we would take it so they gave it to us," he explained.

I shook my head. "That sounds about right."

"Well, I just stopped in to pick up a few things. We're going to take off shortly."

"Yeah, I know the drill. Take care. I'll be praying for Sergeant Montgomery and his family."

"Thank you. Take care, Sergeant Lewandowski." We shook hands and he disappeared down one of the aisles.

I sensed a sudden change in the cheerful atmosphere provided by the group standing in line directly behind me. The laughter and talking now ceased. Two lines of new soldiers and the cashiers stood silently staring at me. They regrettably overheard my conversation with Jackson.

Looking at the cashier, I placed my items onto the counter for purchase. "I'm sorry, I'm holding things up."

"That's OK, that's OK," the cashier spoke in broken English.

I handed her a few bills and then reached out to receive my AAFES plastic token change. In turning to leave, I hesitated and glanced back. All continued to stare with somber expressions. Not an eye blinked as I walked to the door and left.

The conversation they reluctantly overheard rendered a sobering reminder as to why we were there and what was actually happening.

The next morning my watch alarm woke me at 1:30 A.M. to begin the Black Watch mission north to Dogwood. The escort teams assembled in the 201st motor pool to finalize the planned route before retrieving the flatbeds at Cedar and then continuing on to Duke.

Our team, originally positioned to lead the convoy, received orders at the last minute to switch to extra security. We were to follow the convoy serials and provide additional security in the event an incident occurred.

As we drove into the early morning hours, we followed a string of red taillights snaking its way through the darkness. By first light, we passed through Diwaniyah and continued on to Najaf. In the colorful light of the rising sun, green fields and thick groves, watered by the miles of irrigation ditches stretching from the Euphrates, began to appear. The abundance of color provided a substantial difference in terrain than we were accustomed too.

While moving through the cities, we scanned the streets looking for possible IEDs and VBIEDs as the traffic waited at intersections and along the roadsides for us to pass. The sidewalks began filling with people on their way to work and school. Hundreds of cars, pickups, and trucks waited in line at closed fuel stations as donkey carts scampered by, hauling passengers and small loads. Iraqi police and uniformed security personnel carried AK-47s as they checked identification papers and performed vehicle searches of the civilians along the highway.

On the outskirts of Najaf, one of the military transports pulled over with a flat tire on its trailer. The larger portion of the convoy continued on to Duke while we provided security for the smaller detachment parked along the road for repair.

Najaf, located one hundred miles south of Baghdad, was one of the holy cities of the Shiite and considered their center of political power in Iraq. The city was also home to the world's largest Muslim cemetery, which contained the tombs of several prophets. During convoy missions, we often observed painted wooden coffins strapped to the roofs of cars as families traveled hundreds of miles to the city's cemetery for burial of their dead.

Uncomfortably quiet now, Najaf was a location marked with recent violence. Three months ago, the cemetery was host to a Shiite uprising. Coalition forces defeated the Mahdi army within its boundaries killing thousands of Shiite during the battle.

As we pulled security along the paved road, I scanned the green fields observing the local Iraqi farm workers cut and bundle their crops by hand. A short distance from the road a group of women, each wearing the customary black silk abaya which covered them from head to toe, sat upon the ground while briefly resting in their work.

As they watched us from the field, one raised her arm and began waving. I returned the gesture, which brought the entire group of women waving their arms high into the air. I chuckled as they then began teasing me with calls and laughs to come join them.

"Lew, make sure these guys stay alert back there," Kolden reminded me as he returned to the command vehicle from assisting with the truck breakdown.

Looking over at the guys, I found them talking together in a small group next to the humvees. Like me, they became distracted from their duties.

"I got it, Les," I assured him as I moved over to break them up.

"You guys are standing too close together," I informed them. "If you bunch up, you could draw fire, besides, if a mortar round lands next to you and everyone gets hit, there won't be anyone left to help pick up all the pieces." I smiled.

They laughed as they slowly moved to their respective positions to protect the trucks.

Two and a half hours later, the trucks began rolling again. After many failed attempts to replace the flat tire on the transport trailer, the drivers finally decided to load the trailer onto another and make repairs upon arrival at Duke.

As we traveled north of Najaf, the vegetation quickly disappeared revealing the dry, brown landscape similar to the terrain in the south. A bluff appeared on the horizon and as we neared it, the convoy slowed and eventually stopped. The incline of the road reaching to the bluff proved too great for the trucks to maneuver at a high speed. They slowly climbed the steep road, one at a time, until all of the trucks successfully ascended to the top.

Upon arrival at Duke, we found an empty tent to stay the night and left for Dogwood early the next morning. On our route, we passed near Karbala, another Shiite city. Like Najaf, they had also been marked with recent insurgent activity.

Turning off the paved road, we traveled down an endless sandy path, which eventually led us straight to Dogwood. As we neared the camp, stops became more frequent with numerous IEDs located and removed. During one such stop, the British discovered a series of explosives staggered along the road's edge, all of which the insurgents daisy chained to one another. The insurgents used this tactic in disabling large segments of passing convoys with all explosives detonating at once.

In the darkness, we entered the camp, found a location to park the gun trucks, and prepared to spend the night. Arranging the armored humvees in a circular formation, we assembled the cots in its protected inner area. As we searched the star filled sky in attempts to name various constellations, a slight orange glow projected onto its dark canopy in the directions of the eastern and northern horizons in the respective locations of Baghdad and Fallujah.

During the night, I awakened to the sound of artillery fire as the British propelled illumination rounds into the sky. The brightly glowing flares hovered high above the ground providing light in defining unknown objects in the surrounding desert terrain.

Sitting on my cot, I peered at the flares through the small opening of my sleeping bag as each burned for approximately two minutes and extinguished itself before touching the ground. As the area darkened, a loud boom sounded, followed by another ball of light floating in the sky. Looking around the circle of cots, all the guys slept quietly as the deafening sound beat upon the ground beside us.

"The field artillery guys." I laughed to myself. "Yeah, I guess we are the field artillery guys. Who else would take comfort in this noise?"

My eyes opened the next day to the predawn light discovering an extremely cool December morning. After debating whether to leave the warmth of my sleeping bag, I finally dressed and began the day waiting for the sun to rise higher in anticipation of its warming rays.

The following days would be long ones. The remaining tasks of the mission included waiting for the trucks to load and then provide security back to Duke and then down to Shaibah Logistics Base, near Basra, a journey of approximately 370 miles.

As the guys occupied themselves playing football, poker, and occasionally wrestled, Kolden and I explored the small camp and discovered more about the Black Watch.

Originally formed to keep the peace in the Scottish Highlands during the early part of the 1700s, the Black Watch consisted of a Scottish division of the British Army. Their name stemmed from the dark tartan cloth they wore and from their responsibility to watch the Highlands.

Rich with famous battles, their history included participation in the protection of the American colonies and eventually fighting against them in the American Revolution. They fought in the Napoleonic Wars, World Wars I and II, Korea, Desert Storm, and now Iraq.

With many of the troops hurrying in preparation to leave, we managed to talk with a few who performed small work details. One of which was a soldier assigned to burn a trailer loaded with boxes full of food rations.

"Take all you want," he insisted as he pulled out and displayed a half dozen British ration boxes.

"Are they safe to eat?" I asked.

"Yes, they're safe. We just have no room for them to transport back."

Kolden and I secured a few for souvenirs. If nothing else, at least the Nestles chocolate bars they contained were enjoyable. That evening, the same soldier along with a companion, visited the gun trucks looking for spare MREs. They destroyed the rations too soon and were now in need of food.

Later, we cocooned within our sleeping bags and once again watched the illumination rounds light the night sky before we all fell asleep.

The escort teams rose at 2:30 A.M. and motivated by the cool night air, quickly folded their cots and packed the gun trucks for departure to Duke.

One of the British officers approached me as the trucks staged to leave the camp. "Sergeant, are you the last gun truck in the movement?"

"Yes, sir, we'll be pulling security as we follow the end of the convoy."

"Good. Would you stop at each Warrior along the route and make sure they know this? They are instructed to fall in behind you. There shouldn't be any problems but we want to make sure we do not leave anyone behind."

"Yes, we can do that. Would you like us to drive through the camp to make sure everyone is out?"

"No, that won't be necessary. Others are taking charge of that."

"OK, we'll make sure the Warriors are rolling behind us as we pass."

"Very good. Thank you, sergeant."

We waited in the warmth of the humvee listening to the radio traffic choreograph the operation and watching each truck leave the camp following along in single file.

After waving one last humvee around the gun truck and out

the gate, I stood at the rear of the vehicle and slowly scanned the va-cated camp. Covered in a blanket of cold silence, the slight highlights of the remaining few buildings and berm softly reflected the glow of the starlight shining from above.

During their arrival over a month ago, the British assumed control of the camp with a proper change of command ceremony. The departing American commanders formally exchanged flags, ban-ners, and salutes. With our hasty departure into the night, they may have opted for a smaller change of command observance conducted at a higher level.

It seemed a shame to leave the camp empty where at one time brave men shed blood in its defense. The camp would not be still for long. The marines would be there sometime over the coming days and secure the camp, pumping life back into its existence.

"Lew, they're calling on the radio. We have to get going," Roerig shouted down from the turret.

Opening the humvee door, I picked up the radio handset and contacted Kolden, "all vehicles have left the camp, and we have ex-ited the gates of Dogwood. Over."

Ping. "Roger. Out."

"Are we ready, Lew?" Heasley asked over the top of the radio.

I sat down and closed the humvee door. "Yeah, let's get out of here."

Heasley shifted the transmission into gear and we departed to catch the long trail of taillights meandering into the darkness.

As we moved down the dusty, narrow road, one by one the Warriors fell in behind us. With the sun slowly rising over the des-olate landscape, we identified numerous tracked fighting vehicles paralleling our flanks in the distance. The trucks continued a routine of slowing to a crawl, stopping, and then proceeding forward as the exceptionally long convoy pushed its way through the sand. During each stop, we stepped out of the gun truck and scanned the horizon for possible insurgent activity.

The convoy passed over the soft, sandy road and eventually met with a narrow, paved highway. The intersection was the des-ignated loading point for the Warriors onto the flatbeds. The pro-cess was not without difficulty. Once loaded, the trucks sank to their axles in the sand caused by the massive weight of the tracked vehicles. Attaching chains to the sunken trucks, the fighting vehicles towed the semis out of the sand and onto the highway.

As we waited for the Warriors to load, we stood next to the humvees in the midmorning sunlight attempting to warm ourselves in its powerful rays. The Black Watch soldiers waited patiently in their vehicles parked directly behind us. Knowing they also may not have eaten, I offered them breakfast.

"Are you hungry? Did you guys eat this morning?" I asked.

"No, we haven't eaten since yesterday. All the rations were gone."

"I can give you some MREs. How many do you need?"

The soldier talked with the others concealed within the Warrior's shell. "How many can you spare?"

"I think we can accommodate all you would need."

The soldier removed his headset and jumped from the vehicle. He swiftly followed me to the gun truck where I opened the back hatch and crawled up inside. Sifting through the gear, I found an opened case of MREs and pulled it to the top of the pile.

"I'll take three if you got em," he said as he produced an Arabic labeled package of cigarettes with one extended from the rest. "Smoke?"

"No thanks, they make me cough." I laughed.

"Yes, these are nasty tasting. I can't wait to get back and smoke some real ones."

Sorting through the variety of brown, sealed bags, I found it difficult to determine which meals they would like although I did not think it would have mattered. "Here," I said as I handed him the box, "why don't you take them all. Hand some of these to the guys in the vehicles behind you. I imagine they are just as hungry as you are. We can pick up more at Duke."

He thanked us for our generosity and rushed back with the unexpected morning breakfast to share with the others. As they looked through the open box of MREs, appreciative waves returned from the Scots standing on their Warriors indicating their approval.

With all the Warriors loaded onto the flatbeds, we began the long drive to Duke. The sparse civilian traffic dwindled to practically nonexistent at times. As we drove through the morning hours, we continued monitor the convoy and the distant surroundings.

Upon arrival at Duke, the cameras of the BBC at the camp's main approach met the British. The television network readily recorded the return of the Black Watch from Dogwood. The long convoy slowed to a crawl as the trucks gradually entered the camp. By the time our gun truck arrived at the intersection, the camera crew was through with their taping of the event.

"Hey! What about us?" Roerig and Heasley yelled from the humvee as we passed.

The camera crew smiled and waved as they continued packing their equipment.

"It looks like we're not going to make the news in the U.K. tonight," I laughed with them.

The next morning, the convoy left for Shaibah Logistics Base located in the southeastern portion of the country on the final leg of the mission. Positioned roughly ten miles southwest of Basra, the British considered the base their premier camp in theater. They boasted of fast food establishments and a pub, an environment the exact opposite from the conditions they have endured the past month at Dogwood.

With expectations of arriving after dark, the trip would consume most of the day. We returned through the same towns and cities that we passed on the venture north, Najaf, Diwaniyah and the smaller villages. Scanning the roadsides and berm, we continued focusing on possible IEDs and VBIEDS.

Twenty miles from the Euphrates we came upon a small group of green, woodland camouflage painted humvees positioned in a perfect box formation parked directly on the highway. During training at Fort Sill, the instructors taught us how to stage a box formation in providing a defensive perimeter to shield us from attacks. As far as I knew, no one had ever actually used it in theater. The clean, bright colors of the humvees gave us a clue as to why the vehicles now formed where they sat.

Positioned around the wheels and hidden from view, soldiers readied to fire. The small unit's leader decided to perform training which would have been wiser to complete in the confines and safety of a camp.

Slowing the gun truck and opening his door, Heasley leaned

out and spoke with the soldiers lying prone on the pavement, "I like your box formation. It looks real nice. You guys did a good job."

The sarcasm drove home an important point. Performing this type of training out here was an absurd and dangerous move. The way they were starting out, the unit would no doubt have an extremely long year in Iraq.

Nearing Camp Cedar, the trucks began slowing in anticipation of refueling and taking a break from the drive. While waiting in the camp, we stopped at the DFAC and picked up some take-out meals. There was no reason to eat MREs with the availability of hot food.

As we ate our meals out of white Styrofoam boxes on the hoods of the gun trucks, we talked about our experiences of the past few days.

A young British soldier approached us from the convoy. "I've got a rat patch and chevron board for trade."

"A rat patch? Let me take a look at what you have," one of the guys said as he picked up the items from the soldier's hand to examine.

Worn on the sleeve of their uniforms, the British received the rat patch in performing a tour of duty in the desert. Originating during World War II, their Seventh Armored Division adopted the patch during their experiences while pushing through Northern Africa. Changed slightly from the original design, it now featured a black jerboa, or desert rat, centered on a tan square patch.

"What are you looking for in trade?" I inquired.

He hesitated and then smiled. "I'll take a pair of your Wiley-X sunglasses for both of them."

During my time here, I have been fortunate in knowing soldiers from a variety of countries. At times, we even traded patches or pieces of personal equipment as a reminder of our meeting. The trades were usually even, without the need to gouge for more than the item was actually worth. The rat patch looked nice but the price seemed steep.

"Wiley-X sunglasses? Wow, what else do you have to give?"

He looked confused at my suggestion. "But that's a rat patch. I thought you chaps were crazy about this sort of thing."

"Yes, I know it's a rat patch. We can buy one off the Internet for a few bucks," I explained. "The Wiley-Xs are worth close to $100. Now, what else do you have to throw in to even out the trade?"

"This is it. A rat patch and a chevron board for Wiley-Xs," he insisted.

The guys laughed at his attempt to deal and returned the items.

"No, no, here, let me take a look at that," one of the guys spoke up as he walked toward the gun truck. We left them to barter as we prepared the humvee for the remainder of the journey.

The convoy eventually arrived at Shaibah as the sun fell below the horizon. Even in the dark, the camp looked very accommodating. At the dining facility, the presence of a self-serve food line and a decorated Christmas tree surprised us. With the Christmas holiday just three weeks off, it comforted us to gaze at the tree's colorful adornments and sparkling lights.

As the team members settled in for the evening, the Brits informed us of a mortar attack with a round detonating at the edge of the camp. A strange looking canister recovered at the site prompted a suggestion to keep our protective masks within reach during the night.

Expecting to remain at Shaibah an additional day to allow the trucks to unload, good news greeted us the next morning with information we would be leaving that day. Working through the night preparing the trucks, the drivers were ready to leave for Kuwait. After releasing the convoy of empty trucks at the border, we would return to Cedar to end the mission.

"Lew, if you don't mind, on our way back to Cedar, lets take a little detour," Kolden suggested as we loaded the gun trucks with our gear.

"I'm always up for something new. What did you have in mind?"

"There's a British memorial located not too far from here. On our way back, let's stop and check it out."

The Basra Memorial stood in honor to those who died while fighting a virtually forgotten campaign. During World War I, the British sent a force to protect their oil interests in the German friendly Turkish Ottoman Empire. From 1914 to 1921, some 40,500 members of the Commonwealth forces lost their lives in the

Mesopotamian operations.

Originally constructed north of Basra sometime after the war, Saddam ordered the monument removed in 1997 and reassembled in its present location, a desolate piece of sand hidden in the middle of the open desert.

From the road, I viewed this structure in the distance many times in passing. With an interpreter accompanying us, I once inquired as to its nature.

"Old factory, made bricks for building, no longer in operation," the interpreter indifferently explained.

As the gun trucks rolled to a dusty stop at the face of the worn and beaten memorial, I stepped out of the humvee and stood looking in wonder at the magnificent structure. Over 260 feet in length, its light sandstone construction supported a fifty-foot tall obelisk at its center.

Carved into numerous black slate tablets set in and under multiple connecting archways, the tens of thousands of names listed the young men who lost their lives while performing their duty to the empire.

Kneeling down, I picked up a small piece of the broken slate and read some of the partial names that remained. Names long forgotten in a family tree on a branch that suddenly ended. I hoped somewhere there stood a young student telling of how one of her relatives, an uncle perhaps, fought bravely against the Turks during the "Great War."

"Mista. Mista. Please. Please," pleading words made familiar requests from behind us.

In watching the arrival of the gun trucks, the local kids rushed to the monument to beg for snacks and water. Not understanding English, they could not read the inscriptions chiseled deep into the stone walls. They did not know of the hallowed ground on which they walked.

I gently replaced the dark slate fragment alongside the adjoining pieces and respectfully stepped away. Less than ninety years have passed since the end of the "war to end all wars" and the British were back once more. How many more times would we be returning?

By studying the events of the past, we strive to prevent repeating history's mistakes. Hopefully, as generations pass, another forgotten campaign will not fall between the cracks of history with countless names also fading away.

CHAPTER 21

And They Lived…

"Here's another friend of mine, ladies and gentlemen. He's a musical genius. Paul Shaffer."

"Thank you, David. Good afternoon, everybody. It's Christmas Eve pretty baby. The snow ain't falling on the ground, however, Santa Claus is coming to town. Let's get this party started. Here's David Letterman."

"He's a musical genius, ladies and gentlemen…"

As I stood at the edge of the crowd watching the show in the cool afternoon air, thoughts of being home for Christmas drifted through my mind. I could have been there. Why didn't I go?

With the R&R slots established by lottery at the beginning of the leave cycle last spring, some in the unit traded their leave in negotiating a better date that suited their needs to travel home. Others, like me, traded their slot for a later date to help those wishing to take earlier leave. With many of the younger guys located toward the end of the list, I decided to trade with them providing a chance for them to get home and see their families.

After multiple trades, the end of the list finally arrived. There was no one left who needed an earlier slot. My turn to take leave had arrived. At the beginning of the cycle, the leadership informed us not everyone would get to go home for R&R. The system worked smoother than anticipated with all allowed to take their leave.

Home for Christmas, that was every soldier's dream and every family's greatest wish. In the process of trading my leave over the past year, it surprisingly came up for the holidays. Spending time with my family and holding Donna in my arms, what a Christmas present that would be.

Like an old Christmas movie, I would return home surprising everyone for the holidays. Unaware of my arrival, my unsuspecting

303

mother would shriek with joy as she rushed to hug me. Shaking my dad's hand, I would pull him close for a big squeeze.

Peaking my head around the corner, my little boy and girl would catch a surprising glimpse of their dad and squeal with delight. They would rush to my side with an abundance of hugs and kisses to share.

Wrapping my arms around my Donna, I would gently lift her up off the floor, kiss her sweet lips, and not ever want to let her go. Oh, those beautiful, magical, sweet lips, which made every kiss, feel as though it was the first.

Norman Rockwell could not have portrayed a more genuine warmer feeling of reunion. As the classic Christmas song goes, "I'll be home for Christmas, if only in my dreams". For me, it would not have been just a dream. It would have been a dream come true.

I could have been there. Why didn't I go? I passed my R&R slot for the last time. Another soldier from a different unit would now take my seat on that great airplane as it left the country. He or she would be the person surprising their family on Christmas. For me, it would have to remain a soldier's dream.

The reasons for staying varied. I knew I was just a common soldier, a small cog in the mighty machine. It ran smoothly before I arrived and would continue to run without problems after I left, however, what if something happened while I was away? How could I have ever forgiven myself for not being there when the guys needed me the most?

The effect on my family also concerned me. From what those who previously left for R&R had stated, leaving the second time seemed much tougher on their families than when they left the first time. I could see the sorrow in their tired faces as they returned. It was not something I wanted to put my family through again, especially not over the holidays, besides, if I would have left on R&R, by the time I returned to Iraq, a few short weeks later, I could be turning around and leaving for home once more. The process of bouncing back and forth would only amount to an unnecessary rollercoaster ride of emotions.

There was no sense in analyzing it any longer. With the decision already made, it was too late to change now.

After the holidays, we began preparing for our redeployment

back to the States as the 56th Infantry Brigade out of Texas arrived to replace us. In taking control of the missions, they developed their own ideas regarding convoy security operations. Before leaving on their first missions, they removed the homemade armor doors from some of the humvees and discarded them into the drainage ditch near the motor pool. Apparently, they appreciated the breeze more than the protection.

As I assisted a small group of the new soldiers in becoming familiar with the motor pool, one of them straggled behind as the others continued walking on.

"Sergeant, can I talk with you?" he hesitantly asked.

"Yeah, what do you need?" I replied as I slowed my pace.

He moved in closer and lowered his voice. "How did you do it?" He slowly shook his head. "I mean, I don't think I'm going to make it."

A concerning look in his eyes peered though a tired, sun-burned face. There existed no magic or secret to share with him. I had no way of guaranteeing he would make it. He needed re-assurance, if not to carry him through his deployment, then at least to hold him together until his next period of self-doubt.

"Just take it one day at a time. That's all you can do," I re-assured him.

He continued shaking his head. "Between the time in Kuwait and the time we've been here, it's only been a month. I don't know if I can last a whole year."

"See, you've already been in theater for one month," I explained. "It's behind you now. That's a month you'll never have to do again. Just keep that in mind. At the end of every day, think of it as a day behind you. At the end of every month, its one month behind you. It won't be long and your unit will begin rotating people for R&R. It's closer than you think."

He began smiling at my attempts in expressing optimism.

"You're going to need something to take your mind off of your present situation," I continued. "How about a hobby? Do you journal?"

"I suppose I could pick up a hobby of some kind, something to keep me busy."

"Now you're talking." I patted him on the shoulder. "Read,

collect, draw, anything to keep your mind occupied."

"Yeah, I'll do that. Everyone should have a hobby. This would be a good time to start one."

"How about your chaplain? Is he a good guy?"

"Yeah," he scratched the side of his head, "he seems to be OK."

"Start talking with him now," I suggested. "Don't wait until you're in over your head with problems. They're like anyone else. They like to shoot the bull once in awhile too."

After our discussion, he seemed to have a better grip on himself. Knowing there was something he could do to alleviate his worries might have offered him temporary relief. Now, it was up to him whether he made it or not.

As has been since we began convoy security operations, when gathered, the guys continued to recount their incidents on the road. With less time on escort missions, some stories were not as fresh and related to happenings last summer.

As Reif retold a convoy escort story, one where his team leader became enraged at a rock thrower and wrecked the young boy's bike while trashing his hajji stand, some of the guys listened with a slight regret set deep within their eyes. Our tour was almost over and they have witnessed very little if nothing while there. For some, their experience was comparable to visiting an amusement park and refusing to try any of the rides or taste the carnival cuisine. When they arrived at the beginning of their tour, it was as if they entered the carnival, quickly located the park exit, and sat there waiting to go home.

If they had it to do all over again, would they have gone on the road? It's hard to say, they would still face the fear of not returning at the end of the day. From the second we left the front gates of the camp in the morning and until we returned later in evening, our lives meant nothing. We did not exist as human beings but only as pawns moving equipment down the highway. That was just the way it was. If an incident occurred that destroyed or damaged the pawn, replace it.

With reenlistment numbers dwindling, those like me, whose enlistment ended while deployed and now held on a "stop-loss" status, felt the push to stay in the guard. Some, upset with the leadership, became outspoken as to their plans of leaving the unit once we returned. One sergeant told of how his gear would be packed and ready to turn in on the day we arrived back at home station. It surprised me when he presented a sudden change of heart.

"Yeah, it was a tough decision," he explained, "but there were fifteen thousand little reasons telling me why I should reenlist."

The leadership smiled as a $15,000 bonus for a six-year reenlistment pulled many back to the ranks. In a low income state such as ours, their current thoughts of paying down their debt superseded the future amount of time they would take away from their families. With the need for college benefits and extra income as reasons why some originally joined, the tax-free money easily lured them back.

At the end of January, we finally left Iraq convoying our vehicles and equipment back to Kuwait for shipment home. The leadership sent some of us to Doha for a short period of time to clean the battalion's vehicles before placing them on a ship for return to the States. It was a wet, sloppy, muddy job.

To assist in the cleaning, the military arranged a series of wash racks that allowed access to the vehicles' undercarriages. Using high-pressure water hoses, we removed all the sand and mud from the vehicles that had built up over the past year's usage.

On the final day of washing, the battalion executive officer, along with a master sergeant, visited the wash racks inspecting the operations.

After a long shift of washing trucks, exhausted, one of the guys fell asleep while sitting on the concrete curb at the road's edge. Covered in mud and dripping wet with his arms crossed over his knees, he laid his head upon his limbs and slept.

The executive officer, a major, walked over to the soldier, stood next to him, and reached his arm out toward him as the sergeant held his camera ready to snap a picture.

"Look at that, Lew," one of the guys said as he shook his head.

Things had not changed all year for those two. They were tourists and this was just another photo opportunity at the expense of the men.

Having all I could stand, I began laughing aloud. Startled, a look of embarrassment came over them as the sergeant quickly dropped the camera to his side and the major stepped away from the soldier.

"Good job, Lew," the soldier said as we watched the two leave the tired man's side.

In continuing their inspection, they meandered toward us.

"Sir, I think it would be an excellent gesture if you provided pizza for the guys," I suggested to the major. "It wouldn't run you any more than fifty bucks, after all, these guys have been working their rear ends off around the clock down here for days getting these vehicles ready to go for you."

He hesitated and looked at me as if I were kidding. "Yeah," he laughed, "Pizza? Right."

The guy's hard work was spectacular enough to capture in his photo album but not worth the fifty bucks to buy a few pizzas. I handed him an opportunity to give back to his troops and he laughingly refused.

With the vehicles cleaned and waiting at port for their transport back to home station, our two and a half week wait in Kuwait came to an end.

As the wind blew through the cloth flaps of the vacated tents in Camp Virginia, we stood patiently outside with our gear, waiting for a bus to arrive and begin the end of our journey home. Excited about finally leaving, we made small talk as we gathered in the cool midday sun. Suddenly, the crowd burst into jeers and laughter.

"Look at the fuckin' hajjis in the dumpster! They're dumpster diving. Look at them fuckers, just look at them," some of the guys began yelling.

The dumpsters, located outside of the tents, overflowed with discarded refuse. Clothes, nylon folding chairs, DVD players, televisions, and anything not small enough to pack in a bag or carry onto the airplane sat piled high. Our unit was the last in the brigade to leave the theater. The trash bins stood full with our garbage and that of a 201st unit that left earlier.

The camp workers discovered the bins of treasure on their daily maintenance rounds. Excited with the find, they retrieved many of the usable items as the crowd stood shouting and cursing at them.

A soldier reached down and picked up a handful of jagged-edged, oversized rocks. He excitedly bounced one in the palm of his hand. "Fuckin' hajjis, I hate them bastards." He cocked his arm back in readying to throw.

"Isn't it sad," I spoke up.

He hesitated and looked at me as he lowered his arm.

"Isn't it sad how these people are so poor, they have to travel thousands of miles to find work to support their families back home," I continued. "On top of that, they aren't even paid enough in wages to provide for themselves when they are here. They have to resort to diving into a dumpster in order to find a few comforts for their tents."

I half-smiled at the soldier with the rock in his hand.

He looked toward those digging through the dumpster, bounced the rock a few more times in his hand, and allowed it fall to the ground as the others continued taunting the workers.

While upon the eve of our departure, some continued to detest the hajjis. Our garbage was not even good enough to permit them to rummage through. The actions of many in the group surprised me, especially the soldier prepared to bombard the workers with rocks. He was one of the medics.

After a long plane ride back to the States, we out-processed through the system at Fort Sill, Oklahoma. Once there, we filled the days with waiting in lines to complete massive amounts of paperwork. They advised those claiming minor ailments to wait until they returned home and approach the Veteran's Administration to handle it. Those needing immediate attention saw the medical personnel.

During an after action review conducted by the Fort Sill training personnel, advisors questioned us as to new ideas or changes in current practices that would assist new troops destined for Iraq. Previously, while on break, Chaplain Wilson and I discussed a possible ethics class in the treatment of civilians. We felt deploying troops would greatly benefit as evidenced by our negative attitudes in handling the truck drivers, workers, and the people along the road.

The lieutenant colonel quickly squashed the idea stating the nature of our work and the tempo at which we deployed would not allow for it. While back in the States, they continued to ignore the problem. Concerned that if they acknowledged it and recommended a solution, eventually, someone may question their previous decisions in closing their eyes to the abuse.

Having forgone R&R to remain in Iraq, I had not been home in over fourteen months. I felt eager to see my children, my family, and my fiancé. As I stepped from the airplane and onto the pavement, tremendous feelings of excitement and joy rushed through my mind as their familiar faces greeted me. I now have a minute feeling of what entering heaven must be like.

With a grand sense of accomplishing anything in which I would set my mind to, I embraced life like never before. I set out in an attempt to keep all those promises I made to myself during the long hours of endless convoy missions. Promises of a better life for my family. Promises of my future with Donna. Promises not to waste one precious moment of this glorious existence on earth.

As it often does to those with ambitious dreams, life blindsided us by its ruthless satire and knocked us flat on our face. Within six months of arriving home from my tour in Iraq, the doctors diagnosed Donna with malignant melanoma. A few days short of a year since she welcomed me on the tarmac at the local airport, she left this world for the next. Where thousands of miles once separated our bodies, a single dimension now held our souls apart.

My journals rested quietly for over a year. Tied together in a bundle of sealed envelopes, each sat separately marked with the black and red ink stamps noting various APOs in Iraq. With little trust in the unit's leadership, I mailed the writings to my home address every two to three weeks assuring my family would know of my experiences if I were to have met with an unfortunate end. Now, I hesitated in opening them in fear of stirring the strong emotions from the unpleasant memories of the past.

I did not reenlist in the guard unit where I attended drills for many years. The time away was tough on my family and especially my children. Thinking I would leave them once again, they slightly hesitated in bonding upon my return. To this day, my children become spooked when they see me in a fresh short haircut.

While out in the public, I occasionally run into some of the guys from the unit. We silently acknowledge one another from across a room or make small talk in passing. Our discussions rarely include the war but center on day-to-day life in general. The meetings provide more of an unspoken assurance to each other that "Yes, I am holding it together."

Of the convoy teams that I was a part of, I look back at myself not as being a supervising sergeant but more as an overbearing big brother providing guidance to a small group of goodhearted and at times mischievous siblings. The numerous occasions where I made a slight suggestion to some in steering them in the right direction may have led to a more favorable outcome than what could have been.

On occasion, I find myself recalling the warmth of the dry desert wind as its gusts pushed the fine grains of sand over the many rows of berm and across a desolate highway. As my thoughts race down that long, uncertain road in the confines of a roaring gun truck with my driver and gunner, I quickly pull myself back to the present and calm my mind while the effect of the adrenaline pumping through my veins slowly fades. At times, in the silent darkness of my bedroom, my eyes will suddenly open to the distinct echoes of a phantom radio pinging for my response as it pulls me from a deep sleep.

My thoughts do not always dwell on the gun trucks and the convoy escort missions we performed. The smiling faces and friendly handshakes of the truck drivers and people I met along the road provide a comfort to my soul. Recollections of the cheerful sounds of the children offer a refreshing relief. In silencing the world within my mind, I can still faintly hear their beautiful voices singing a pleasant song next to the dusty road.

For the most part, I continue living with a great appreciation for life as I did before the deployment to Iraq. At times, I find it difficult to believe I was actually there. With television news as a constant reminder, I will occasionally enter into a conversation about the war. Some, in finding I served in the conflict, will often ask, "So, what did you do over there?"

I briefly hesitate in giving an answer as countless memories ripple through my mind and then I solemnly reply, "I was on a gun truck."

List of Acronyms

AAFES	(a-fees)	Army and Air Force Exchange Service
AAR	(a-a-r)	after action review
APO	(a-p-o)	Army Post Office
ASR	(a-s-r)	alternate supply route
C2	(c-2)	command and control
CSC	(c-s-c)	convoy support center
DCU	(d-c-u)	desert camouflage uniform
DFAC	(d-fak)	dining facility
EOD	(e-o-d)	explosive ordnance disposal
ETS	(e-t-s)	estimated time of separation
GPS	(g-p-s)	global positioning system
ICDC	(i-c-d-c)	Iraqi Civil Defense Corps
IED	(i-e-d)	improvised explosive device
ING	(i-n-g)	Iraqi National Guard
IP	(i-p)	Iraqi police
JAG	(jag)	Judge Advocate General
KBR	(k-b-r)	Kellogg, Brown and Root
MCT	(m-c-t)	movement control team
MEDEVAC	(med-evack)	medical evacuation
MP	(m-p)	military police
MRE	(m-r-e)	meal, ready to eat
MSR	(m-s-r)	main supply route
MWR	(m-w-r)	morale, welfare, and recreation
NCO	(n-c-o)	noncommissioned officer
NTV	(n-t-v)	non-tactical vehicle
OIF	(o-i-f)	Operation Iraqi Freedom
PX	(p-x)	Post Exchange
R&R	(r and r)	rest and recuperation
ROM	(rom)	refuel on the move

RPG	(r-p-g) - rocket propelled grenade
SAPI	(sappy) - small arms protective insert
SAW	(saw) - squad automatic weapon
SOG	(s-o-g) - sergeant of the guard
SOP	(s-o-p) - standard operating procedure
SP	(s-p) - separation point
TCN	(t-c-n) - third country national
TOC	(tock) - tactical operations center
UXO	(u-x-o) - unexploded ordnance
VBIED	(v-bid) - vehicle-borne improvised explosive device

16794JLV00001B/96/P
23 December 2009
LaVergne, TN USA